Personal Identity in the Modern World

Personal Identity in the Modern World

A Society of Strangers

Lawrence M. Friedman

ROWMAN & LITTLEFIELD
Lanham • Boulder • New York • London

Published by Rowman & Littlefield
An imprint of The Rowman & Littlefield Publishing Group, Inc.
4501 Forbes Boulevard, Suite 200, Lanham, Maryland 20706
www.rowman.com

86-90 Paul Street, London EC2A 4NE, United Kingdom

British Library Cataloguing in Publication Information Available

Library of Congress Cataloging-in-Publication Data

Names: Friedman, Lawrence M. (Lawrence Meir), 1930– author.
Title: Personal identity in the modern world: a society of strangers / Lawrence M. Friedman.
Description: Lanham: Rowman & Littlefield, [2022] | Includes bibliographical references and index. | Summary: "In a society of strangers, there develops what can be called crimes of mobility—forms of criminality rare in traditional societies: bigamy, the confidence game, and blackmail, for example. What they have in common is a kind of fraudulent role-playing, which the new society makes possible"—Provided by publisher.
Identifiers: LCCN 2022001251 (print) | LCCN 2022001252 (ebook) | ISBN 9781538166840 (cloth) | ISBN 9781538166857 (epub) | ISBN 9781538166864 (paper)
Subjects: LCSH: Swindlers and swindling. | Fraud. | Commercial crimes.
Classification: LCC HV6691 .F75 2022 (print) | LCC HV6691 (ebook) | DDC 364.16/3—dc23/eng/20220118
LC record available at https://lccn.loc.gov/2022001251
LC ebook record available at https://lccn.loc.gov/2022001252

To Leah, Jane, Amy, Sarah, David, Lucy, and Irene

Contents

Acknowledgments

I've benefited from many friends and scholars over the years; and I am grateful to all of them. I want to single out a few who have been of particular value: very notably, my colleague Robert W. Gordon; I would mention, too, Stuart Banner among others.

I would also like to express gratitude to my friend and colleague, Rogelio Perez-Perdomo, who believed in this project, and encouraged it in so many ways. My research assistant, Omar Patricio Vasquez Duque was also enormously helpful to me, especially with regard to the bibliography and related issues.

I have to express special gratitude to my friend and collaborator, Joanna L. Grossman; Joanna and I have worked together for many years, and I have profited enormously from our joint efforts. Her influence is apparent on page after page of this book. Thank you, Joanna!

Special thanks too to my wife, Leah, who proof-read every page of the manuscript and saved me from many errors—as she has done all through my life in all sorts of ways.

I also want to thank the staff of the Stanford Law Library, and its director, Beth Williams, for all of the help they have given me, on this and all of my other projects. They made it possible to go ahead with the work, despite lockdowns and shutdowns, and all the other recent obstacles. There could not be a more helpful bunch.

Introduction

A saying, attributed to the ancient Greek philosopher Heraclitus, has it that you cannot step into the same river twice, which apparently means that everything changes, nothing remains the same—not the person, not the river. Basically, I think, Heraclitus got it right. Social change is a law of nature. Of course, there are rivers that flow fast, and rivers that flow much more slowly. Each society, each culture, and each historical period has its own special river. The river in this book is mostly (though not entirely) the United States, and to a lesser extent, England. In either case, it is about modern times, roughly from 1800 to the present.

We can ask what the term "modern" really means and what makes modern society (the society of today) what it is. In what way are we different from our ancestors? Obviously, there is no single answer. In this book, I am not going to try to answer this question. Rather, I take "modern" merely to mean the customs, habits, and ways of life of rich, developed societies, and how they have changed since the beginning of the industrial revolution; and my special emphasis, as I said, is on the United States and England, two major English-speaking countries. Rich developed countries have many things in common: their populations exploded in the nineteenth century; they developed rapidly, in terms of technology, politics, economics, and social structure; they became the richest countries (at least the richest ones not swimming in oil); and, the ones that profited most from the revolution in applied science and engineering. The process of modernization began in the West in European countries, and in the settler countries outside Europe: the United States, Canada, Australia, and New Zealand. But by now such terms as "modern," "industrial," and "developed" also fit countries in other parts of the world—very notably Japan, Singapore, Israel, South Korea, Taiwan. The elite in developing countries, including China and India, share in much of the culture of modernity. Each country, of course, has its own history, its own special features, each one a tributary of a single, vast river.

In modern societies people confront the issue of *personal identity* with the questions, Who am I really and who are these other people? In some ways, this is not a new issue. Perhaps even a thoughtful caveman might have asked who am I really? But the form and content of both question and answer have surely changed over the years, because the structure and nature of society has changed, in dramatic and profound ways.

This book, I should make clear, is an extended essay on the concept of *personal* identity. This is not to deny the importance of group identity—both past and present. Nothing seems more significant today than group identity: racial identity, gender identity, ethnic identity. The answer to the questions "Who am I" and "who are you?" can take a double form, or to put it another way, "two contradictory impulses: identity as the unique individuality of a person (as in 'identity' card), or identity as a common denominator that places an individual within a group (as in 'identity politics')."[1] This book deals with the first form of identity: not race, religion, or gender, but that notion of identity, which is unique to a particular individual.

There is, as there should be, a big, bustling literature on group identity. The period this book covers was a period in which (in Eugen Weber's phrase) peasants became Frenchmen;[2] in which a women's movement struggled for recognition; in which Zionism emerged and became an element in Jewish identity; in which the Church of Jesus Christ of Latter-day Saints burst on to the American scene; in which slavery and its abolition tore the United States in two, and issues of race and gender continue to dominate the political agenda. The two forms of identity (of course) are both important, and they interact. If you ask someone, "Who are you really?" you may get a personal, or a group answer, or both, though of course this depends on who you ask. And if one asks, "Who is that *other* person really, that person I see on the street?" there is more likely to be a group answer (it's a woman, it's an African American, it's a nun) as well as a more personal, individual answer. But in any event, in these pages we deal with *personal* identity, which is, of course, significant in its own right.

The main theme is this: in the modern world—or to be more precise, in the nineteenth century and beyond—*personal identity* became more problematic, more confused, mixed up, and blurred in a fairly new way; or at the very least, in heightened forms of the old ways. How this happened and why—and what the consequences have been—is the main subject of this book. That is, we will discuss changes in peoples' own sense of identity, in the identity they conveyed or chose to convey, and in their feelings about the identity of the people around them.

Personal identity became problematic in particular ways in the Victorian age, as later chapters will explore. Since nothing in society stands totally still, the issue of personal identity changed, evolved, and developed over time. In the twentieth century, particularly in the latter half of that century, it was transformed: both the inner sense of identity and the way the outside world impinged on this sense of identity. Modernity—big city life, very notably—and social and geographic mobility carved out new forms of identity, new forms of personality. In particular, the context gave people *choices* they had rarely had before, choices about personal identity. The twentieth century magnified this feeling of freedom of choice. Very notably today (that is, in the twenty-first century), people feel that they have the ability to *choose* aspects of personal identity in ways that seem new and dramatic. Identity, in short, is not fixed and stable: the river keeps flowing and very swiftly at times.

Personal identity is a feeling, an inner feeling, about the nature of the self. It is also what is projected to other people. It is both a subjective feeling and an objective role—the part I play in the drama of life. Other people also have an identity, which they project onto me. Hence, personal identity has three quite separate meanings. Each meaning became, in the modern world, problematic in new ways and each continues to be problematic. Many people, in many different ways, are "passing." Historically, this referred to the strained definition of "Black" in the United States; a light-skinned person, with some African heritage, could sometimes choose to "pass" for White; could choose, in other words, to project an identity that conflicted with the *social* definition of their identity. It also perhaps conflicted with their own sense of who they "really" were. But this was only one form of "passing," that is, one way of projecting an image that conflicts with the sense of identity "inside." A spy passes as a loyal citizen. An embezzler passes for an honest worker. In a broader sense, all of us are "passing." We project one image and feel another. We read the messages broadcast by other people and we broadcast messages ourselves.

Each person has, in a way, many "identities"—identities that they can act on or not, can project or not, and the outside world can respond or not to any such projection. Many people have a strong religious identity. Faith is, very often, a form of group identity. But it translates freely into personal identity. Faith can be a deep, subjective feeling. It can also be projected to the outside world by wearing a cross, skullcap, or headscarf, for example. Expressions of faith can be a role played out in public or suppressed. All of us are in contact with other people and these people project or suppress aspects of their identity. Some of these may be "false." A smile might hide boiling anger or raging lust. Much role-playing is harmless or conventional. Some is not. A "conman" is a crook at heart who cheats his victims by projecting a false image. The mere existence of these criminals has consequences—for victims, potential victims, and society.

What "modernity" consists of, and what brought it about, are questions that have no simple answers—and I will not pretend to provide any. A few points about the world from, say, 1800 to the present, in the developed countries at any rate, are fairly obvious. Technology and science have utterly remade the social order. They have left a deep impress on the way people live, how they behave, and how they think. Even so simple a device as the modern clock or so ubiquitous a device as the camera have been transformative, not to mention modern medicine, or the computer, or jet airplanes. None of these are merely tools. They remake the culture and structure of society. They may be, at least in part, what lies behind the deeply ingrained *individualism*, the sense (if not the reality) of freedom of choice, which is so critical an aspect of the modern personality.

But first a word about the Victorian crisis of personal identity, which the first chapters of this book explore. At one time, most people lived in small villages, or in the countryside. Social roles in the village were relatively fixed. People were born, lived, and died in the village, as their parents had done. Most people never ventured into the bigger world. They rarely encountered a world of strangers. They perhaps felt they knew, not only who they were, but who other people were—the people they saw and dealt with, day in and day out. Of course, reality was (as always) messier and more complex. Village life was never entirely static. Outside forces produced changes: wars, plagues, political upheavals. Nor did everyone always cling like barnacles to their home villages. Geography made a difference. Coastal people were less provincial and isolated than inland people. Sailors and adventurers left home for distant places. Men went off to fight as soldiers or mercenaries far from home. There were also well-recognized trade routes, which merchants traveled to buy and sell and trade goods. Pilgrimages and fairs brought together people from different places. There were important cities and city-states: Florence, for example, and Milan and Venice, in what is now Italy. In the seventeenth century, there were also important cities in what is now the Netherlands. Every country had its urban centers. Still, for most people, in most countries, the picture of static village life essentially rings true. There were also extreme cases of isolation—a tribal community in the middle of the Amazon jungle, indigenous communities in Africa, in Siberia, in the high mountains of Asia—places with little or no contact with the outside world.

Yet the differences between then and now are clearly enormous. Most of the world's population lives in cities. In London, or Tokyo, or Sao Paulo, and in other urban centers, people constantly meet, confront, and interact with strangers. You never know exactly who they are, only what they seem to be. And they, in turn, can never know exactly who *you* are. Not much is left of what made village life what it was. Even in the tiniest village where strangers rarely penetrate, television, the movies, and the internet are a constant, and intrusive, feature. Strangers are beamed and streamed into the home.

The fluid new world was at its most fluid from (say) 1800 on. Lines between groups and classes were, or became, muddy and indistinct. This was truer in cities than in towns, and most true in big cities. What we describe here for the nineteenth century was already visible in London in the eighteenth century—London was already a great city, a huge and anonymous mass of people, already a place in which people could "don and doff identities with impunity."[3]

London was, of course, exceptional. But in the course of the nineteenth century, more and more people moved to the cities. Thus, it became harder to read the signs and signals other people sent out and harder for them to read the signals you yourself were sending out. It became harder to pigeonhole people, to be clear what they were up to. Personal identity became more problematic, first of all, and most obviously, problematic for the *viewer.* That is, the conditions of society made it hard to understand, to classify, to react to people one met or saw or had dealings with. Secondly, it became easier for people to assume new identities, to molt old ones and take on disguises, new forms of being and acting, like a new suit of clothing off the rack. This had always been, to a limited degree, possible, that is, cases of dubious identity. For example, the famous case of Martin Guerre, a peasant in sixteenth-century France. Guerre left his wife, child, and village. Years went by before a man appeared who claimed to be Martin Guerre. He was eventually exposed as an impostor.[4] There were cases of pretenders who assumed the identity of a dead king or claimed to be a dead king's heir, or took on the persona of a noble. In the Middle Ages, for example, a certain Dietrich Holzschuh passed himself off as the emperor, Frederick II of Hohenstaufen. There were other cases of impostors and spectacular frauds long before modern times.[5] A "False Dimitri" in sixteenth-century Russia claimed to be the dead son of a czar, and actually briefly held power. But these were exceptional cases, mostly of people who moved, or claimed to move, in the highest circles. What was difficult and rare, in the old world, became easy and common in the new world.

In short, in the big city, in big societies, it was easier for a person to send conflicting or false signals to other people; easier to pretend, simulate, or change identity; easier to put on and take off masks. Sometimes it was done deliberately. We mentioned one obvious case of historic importance in American society: "passing" for White—for a light-skinned man and woman, socially defined as Black, such a move within a profoundly racist society, was understandable. Also deliberate were less justifiable moves: the schemes of the bigamist, the con man, the fraud, men and women pretending to be something they were not in order to squeeze money out of victims. The anonymity of city life can also shake confidence in the identity of others. We feel we can trust people in a small, inner circle. But strangers in the big city—that is a different story. We can read clues from their behavior, what they wear, how they talk, but it is possible to be totally wrong.

Mobility is the key to the problem of personal identity. People leave their villages for the city or leave one city for another or one neighborhood for another or one country for another. Not everybody, of course, was mobile in this sense, not even in nineteenth-century America, an unusually mobile society. Mobility was most pronounced for free White men. Those who were enslaved—who were owned by other people—had no control over where they lived. They could be sold "down the river" against their will. Master and mistress were in control of their slaves' lives and many slaves, like villagers in the old, old world, were born, lived, and died within a tiny circle of movement. Mobility for women, too, was sharply restricted. Of course, some women did break free. There were women in business; women on the wagon trains headed to the West; women who settled on the frontier, in log cabins, or who were active in groups and organizations. But they were exceptions. It was mostly men who made the critical decisions. Women, too, had less sexual freedom than men. Mobility had a deep impact on women but in ways that were secondary, and more subtle, compared to the mobility of men.

Mobility was more than a matter of physical space. It was also a matter of social space. The lines between classes, between strata of society, were blurred in this period—more so than in the past. The United States had no king, no queen, no nobles; it thought of itself as a classless society. This was, of course, an illusion, but it was an important illusion. And, in fact, more than in the old country, more than in rigidly class-bound societies, there was a certain amount of movement between the classes—movement up and down the rungs of the social ladder. In the Middle Ages there were no "self-made men," or extremely few. In the nineteenth century this was no longer the case.

How mobility and personal identity intersect will be spelled out in subsequent chapters. Blurred identity, fluid identity, had both positive and negative consequences. It added to uncertainty. It led to a situation in which people could, and did, suppress or hide an inner or "true" identity. People could "pass," and not only racially. Some forms of suppressed identity were, in a sense, involuntary—they were imposed by society. Society rested, it was felt, on certain moral and structural pillars. In a restless, striving world, these pillars had to be maintained, strengthened, preserved. In Victorian society, there was a sharp divide between public behavior and private life. On the surface, propriety and correct behavior were critical. But there was also a hidden, underground world of attitudes, beliefs, and behaviors. This sharp divide was notoriously true for sexual behavior and sexual identity. Victorian society demanded—not always successfully—repression of what was, to many people, a vital aspect of their true identity.

In the contemporary world, the world of the late twentieth century, and the beginning of the twenty-first, the rules of the identity game have changed, in some ways quite radically. In many regards, society is more open, more permissive, in the developed world than it was in the past. Victorian morality is only a memory. People can express their identity in new ways. Many forms of sexual behavior once repressed (or supposed to be repressed) are now open, or at least legitimate. The role of women and minorities in society has been redefined. Some fundamentals have remained. This is still a world of strangers, even more so than in the nineteenth century. Personal identity is still problematic, though sometimes in new and different ways.

Even more problematic is group identity: it is center stage in modern politics and modern culture. Today, too, *genetic* identity is important to people—it colors both their sense of personal *and* group identity. Of course, modern genetics was unknown to Abraham Lincoln, Queen Victoria, Simon Bolivar, or the emperor of Japan. Nobody could send a dash of saliva to a laboratory and discover a connection to the tribe of Genghis Khan or the Neanderthals. Modern technology makes possible our links to the past. Before the camera, ordinary people could not know what great-great-grandmother looked like. All that changed in modern times.

The modern world and modern life—and modern science and technology—expand the menu of choices. This makes the sense of personal identity more fluid than ever. People who are middle class and above have a new kind of mobility—cultural mobility. People feel free to eat sushi, for example, even if they are not Japanese, or to eat fried chicken in Tokyo. They feel free to reject a religion inherited from Mom and Dad and become a Buddhist. Free to molt identities and take on new ones. So, paradoxically, despite the rainbow of choices, human cultures are oddly convergent, as we will see. People in Berlin or Caracas can eat tacos or pad thai and wear blue jeans; young people in Seoul can do the same. Convergence, too, is part of the story we are going to tell.

Chapter 1

Up and Down the Ladder

The last two centuries were times of enormous social change. In Europe, and in other parts of the world, the population exploded in unprecedented ways. The world's population was about seven hundred million in 1750. By the beginning of the nineteenth century, it had reached one billion and by 1900 it stood at 1.6 billion. The cause of this tremendous population growth is, apparently, obscure. Was it because of the humble potato, a gift from the Western Hemisphere, which fed people cheaply and efficiently? Was it better sanitation? Was it because fewer infants died? Whatever the cause, this explosion in population had huge consequences. People poured into the big cities, leaving the countryside behind. In 1800, London had already reached a population of one million and by the end of the century it reached six million.

During the colonial period, in what later became the United States, there was nothing on the scale of London. But growth was steady. Small, precarious settlements gradually turned into towns and then into cities. White settlers from the British Isles, and from Germany, fed population growth. Black slaves were imported from Africa by the thousands, especially into the southern states. In the nineteenth century, immigration to the United States accelerated. Millions of Europeans packed their bags, left their homes, crowded onto ships, and sailed off for the New World from the British Isles, Scandinavia, Germany, and then later from eastern and southern Europe. This stream of immigrants made places like Boston and New York into bustling urban centers with diverse populations that were different in scale and culture from the Puritan villages of the seventeenth century. In the nineteenth century, an agricultural society gradually turned into an industrial society. The nation urbanized and suburbanized. Cities grew like mushrooms. In 1800, Chicago did not even exist; Los Angeles was a tiny village; the largest city in the United States was New York with some sixty thousand residents. New York City reached a population of one million by 1880 and three million by 1900. Chicago had one million inhabitants by 1890. In other countries the nineteenth century was the century of the city. Paris, Amsterdam, and Berlin grew exponentially. Urbanization accelerated in the twentieth century. Mega cities like Tokyo and Mexico City dominated their countries and sucked in masses of people.

Life in the big city differed from life in a small village, where everyone knew everybody else. In a village, newcomers stood out in a crowd. In London or New York many people knew their neighbors and coworkers, but everyone else was at best a slight acquaintance, more usually an utter stranger. City streets were full of people coming and going, hardly taking note of each other. Some of these people had been born and raised in the city, others had just recently arrived. There was no easy way to tell these groups apart and no way to know what these strangers were really like.

The nineteenth century was a time of restlessness and movement, a time of cultural and social mobility. Lines between the classes blurred, and by the end of the century, in some countries at least, cracks appeared in inherited systems of autocracy. The political system became more democratic, at least for free White men. England was much more class bound than the United States, but that was changing. Economic opportunity was more open than before. It was possible—difficult, but not impossible—for a laborer or a farmer to end up rich. To be sure, the ladder of success was slippery. Those who started on the lowest rung had a difficult time. But still, the ladder was there.

Within the United States, upward mobility was more noticeable than in England (and the rest of Europe). People in the United States were also geographically mobile. Many of them were like rolling stones, moving from east to west, north to south, from village to town, from town to city. The United States is a country of immigrants and the descendants of immigrants, except for the Native peoples and the slaves kidnapped in Africa and sold into bondage. Many immigrants were not afraid to wander, which is evident after they arrived in the United States. In 1850, according to the census, only two-thirds of Americans still lived in the state they were born in; 11 percent were born outside the United States; and 21.3 percent had moved from one state to another.[1] In the middle of the nineteenth century, between one census period and another (a ten-year period), about 30 percent of the residents of any particular city shifted from one address or place to another.[2] This movement continued in later decades as well. Americans continually changed homes, towns, and regions—even, as we will see, changed identities.

At independence, most people lived in towns and villages close to the Atlantic coast. Some, however, were already pushing west, even before the Revolution. Westward migration continued in the nineteenth century. The movement seemed inexorable. Nothing was allowed to stand in the way of westward expansion: not the Native peoples who were ruthlessly shoved aside when they impeded the flow of White settlers; not the vast, thinly populated regions owned by Mexico, which were seized after the brief Mexican

War of the 1840s. By the middle of the nineteenth century, the United States had expanded from coast to coast. In 1867, it bought Alaska from the Russians. By 1900, it had swallowed and absorbed the island kingdom of Hawaii. In 1893, Frederick Jackson Turner published his famous essay "The Significance of the Frontier in American History."[3] He argued that the frontier had been a decisive influence on American character and personality: it made the country more democratic, more impatient of old rules and customs, freer, more innovative. It also acted as a kind of economic and social "safety valve." Turner was a product of his times. His essay was written when the wave of settlement had reached the Pacific coast. The frontier was officially dead and buried. His essay was both a celebration and an autopsy. What it celebrated was the relentless drive to expand, move, and change.

Americans had indeed pushed the frontier further and further back. Men and women went west to farm new land and claim forests and prairies for themselves. After gold was discovered in California in 1848, wagon trains headed west, crossing the forbidding landscape of the "Great American Desert." Others traveled to California by sea around the bottom of South America, or by boat to Central America, then over the narrow wasp-waist of jungle to the Pacific Ocean, and from there by boat to California. Young men tried their hand at politics or business in new, raw towns. The frontier was no country for old men (or old women, for that matter). It was a young man's frontier, a place to start or start over, a place to get rich. Of course, for many wanderers the dream turned into a nightmare. A few men found gold in the West. A few made money by selling supplies or by speculating and conniving, but many did not find gold, instead, they found disease, poverty, misery, and lonely death in cities full of strangers.[4] Still, nothing could kill the dream; certainly not reality. Nor did the closing of the frontier (literally and figuratively) kill the dream.

There were also urban frontiers. In the twentieth century, the frantic growth of cities and metropolitan areas showed no signs of abatement: new cities like Houston, Phoenix, and Miami, along with the older ones. Later in the century, young entrepreneurs (mostly men) flocked to Silicon Valley in California, dreaming of great wealth in the high-tech world. Nothing deterred the thousands who swarmed to Hollywood looking for stardom and New York looking for fame and fortune on Broadway, or who hoped to elbow their way into the art scene. The probability of failure does not stop young, hopeful people; nor, for that matter, does it deter the foreigners, who cross the borders legally or illegally, or Asian students who take advanced degrees at American universities. The frontier may be dead, but mobility is alive and thriving, certainly in a geographical sense and in the social and cultural sense as well.

Mobility, in all its meanings, is not the easiest variable to pin down or measure. Precise figures are elusive. Migrants can be counted. There are estimates of economic mobility, but there is no easy way to get a grip on restlessness, on the thought processes of thousands who move around, who change jobs and places, who go from town to town and from house to house. People move about in order to better themselves, to seek out opportunities, but also simply to change life course, to find satisfaction, to end an old phase of life and start a new one.

Restlessness occurred at all levels of the social scale. At the lower end were the tramps and hobos, the footloose and rootless. Thieves and con men were looking, too, for a better life—at the expense of their victims. Clearly, many American men (and some women) were a restless bunch, living in a restless society. This was certainly true in other societies as well, such as the Italians who flocked to Argentina, the peasants who came to Mexico City from their villages, immigrants who settled in Canada, Australia, New Zealand, and the country folk who filled the streets of London. Inner migration—from villages to cities, from farmland to urban slums—was just as important as migration from country to country.

Then, too, mobility means something more than simply changing your house, your street, your town, your state. Mobility means movement in *social* space: movement up and down in terms of rank and status. In the modern world—the world we live in—your rank, your status, your social position are not totally fixed at birth, compared to past societies. In the old days, a noble was born, lived, and died a noble; a commoner lived and died a commoner. Since the beginning of the Industrial Revolution, in Europe and North America, rank and status has become (relatively speaking) more fluid and flexible. The United States, already something of an outlier, had no kings and queens and made no distinction between nobles and commoners. The Declaration of Independence announced that all men were "created equal." This was, at the time, a revolutionary statement. To be sure, it was not to be taken literally, and from today's standpoint the statement seems almost hypocritical. There were millions of Black slaves in America. The free Black population suffered from gross discrimination. Equality never applied to women and certainly not to members of the Native tribes or the Chinese who came to work on the Western railroads.

Even White men were not *created* equal, except in some vague theological sense. They were certainly not equal once they came out of the womb. The United States had its own set of status markers. There were the rich and the poor. The educated and the uneducated. Men who worked with their hands and men who worked with their minds. Nonetheless, for most of the modern period, there has been more "equality" in the United States than in England or on the continent of Europe, let alone in China or Africa.

Victorian England was proud of its constitutional system, its government, its legal system. But it was far less "equal" than the United States. The king (or queen, during the long reign of Victoria) stood at the social apex of society. Below were the nobles of the realm, below them the commoners. Nobles sat in the House of Lords. The other branch was the House of Commons, but its members were hardly common people. They were almost invariably members of a small elite, the landed gentry, who owned almost all of the land, and who ran society.

Geographic mobility was much more of a reality. The population was growing rapidly. People were leaving behind their villages and farms and, as we said, moving to the cities: to London or to the growing industrial towns. Victorian society "was heavily structured"; few people in England managed to bridge the chasm between manual laborers and white-collar workers or between tenant farmers and landowners. Still, change was happening—however slowly. At least some newcomers to city life shifted into more genteel work and joined a growing middle class.[5] At least some successful merchants entered the ranks of the upper class—and might even gain entrée into the nobility.

Class structure in America was significantly different. Here, especially in the North and Midwest, millions of ordinary families owned farms, or small lots in town. There were, generally speaking, no large estates with rent-paying farmers as tenants. The vast holdings of "patroons" in Upstate New York were something of an exception; so, too, of the big men of the South, who owned plantations worked by gangs of slaves. In the early period of the republic, only White males who owned property or paid taxes had the right to vote in many jurisdictions. Kentucky abolished the property requirement as early as 1792. By the middle of the nineteenth century, all states had pretty much done away with it. In a few states the taxpaying requirement survived, but for the rest, adult White men had the right to vote without restriction.[6] This was true in few other countries at the time, and certainly not in England where the franchise was severely restricted. In the so-called rotten boroughs, before the 1832 Reform Act, a handful of electors had the right to choose a member to represent them in Parliament. Of course, leaders of American society were, in their own way, patrician—think of George Washington or Thomas Jefferson—but in the North and Midwest in particular, some office holders, especially in state and local government, came from more humble backgrounds, including the proverbial log cabin.

Equality (in the American sense) was more than a matter of money and position, it was also a matter of culture, a way of acting or behaving—even of speaking. This is the case in most societies. In George Bernard Shaw's famous play *Pygmalion* (written in 1912), Professor Higgins, an English expert on speech habits and accents, makes a bet that he can turn Eliza, a cockney-speaking flower vendor, into a lady of fashion simply by teaching her how to imitate the speech patterns of the upper class. In this, he is entirely successful. Professor Higgins demonstrated, in other words, that behavior (especially ways of speaking) could indicate class. It could therefore affect life chances in general. That Professor Higgins could pass this girl off as a member of the rarefied elite was a sign that society was changing, and that identity was more fluid than in the past. Eliza was trained to be able to "pass." Personal identity was malleable—it could be worked, fashioned, and changed. Personal identity could, in fact, be taught.

In England, ways of talking and acting were markers of class and influenced the course of life. This was true too in the United States, though perhaps to a somewhat lesser degree. American manners had a strong egalitarian flavor, a cultural trait that struck foreign visitors. The servants in America were "help" not servants and the "help" refused to behave in a servile way.[7] Visitors, like Frances Trollope, an English novelist who published books about her experiences, were generally people of high status. Who else could afford this sort of travel? They were, nonetheless, surprised (and impressed or sometimes shocked) by American manners—or lack of manners. Genteel travelers found Americans rather crude and vulgar. Their manners were far below European standards. Men chewed tobacco, and at the theater in Washington, Mrs. Trollope reported, spitting was "incessant."[8] Her son Anthony visited the United States in the 1860s. He agreed with his mother's views about the country. Americans were rude—they had no sense of propriety. They lacked respect for authority. He was "pelted with the braggadocio of equality." A traveler, he said, would soon find that the "corns of his Old-World conservatism will be trampled on hourly by the purposely vicious herd of uncouth democracy."[9] By British upper-class standards, Americans were indeed pushy and ill-bred.

Americans were if anything proud of this trait—proud of their democratic ways (such as they were), their sense of equality of condition. Of course, Americans were not naïve—they knew that people were not really equal in wealth, character, or ability. But they also firmly believed that in America people had openings and chances that were closed off in the Old World. No one (at least no White male) was frozen at birth into a social slot from which there was no escape. Society was a series of poles and ladders, and men climbed up or slid down, by virtue of their skill, drive, ambition and—of course—the luck of the draw.[10] A man could be born in a log cabin and end up in the White House. "Any man's son," wrote Mrs. Trollope, "may become the equal of any other man's son." This was a "spur to exertion," which was in general a good thing, but it was also, she thought, "a spur to that coarse familiarity, untempered by any shadow of respect, which is assumed by the grossest and the lowest in their intercourse with the highest and most refined."[11]

No doubt Mrs. Trollope exaggerated. But in fact, there was no small, dominant elite, with centuries of land and power in their very blood. America was the land of the self-made man (the self-made woman had not yet been invented). To be sure, in life there were winners and losers and every stage in between. There were men in the North who made great fortunes in banking or commerce. And a kind of landed gentry dominated large areas of the South; men who owned gangs of slaves, lived in great houses, and controlled vast acreage. The first presidents, except for John Adams, came from this class—wealthy slave owners from Virginia—Washington, Jefferson, Madison, and Monroe—Andrew Jackson, too, was a slave owner. In fact, very few men made the leap from log cabin to mansion; only a very few were born in poverty and ended up with millions. It was never easy to cross from low to high station in life. Still, compared to traditional societies—and to most European societies—the ladder of success was a reality.

Alexis de Tocqueville's classic *Democracy in America* was published in two volumes in 1835 and 1840, respectively. To a modern reader, the title almost seems ironic: Wasn't this a society with millions of Black slaves? Didn't society shove women into a separate and subordinate sphere? And what about the Native peoples? De Tocqueville was not unaware of these facts. But he stressed the contrast between America and the old country—his country. The ladder of success was slippery, at times hard to reach, at all times hard to climb, but it was there. Men—and we are speaking here mostly of men—were free to move about, to try their luck in new places and in new occupations, to go up (or come down). They were free to succeed—or fail. Lots of people fell off the ladder of success. The *ideology* of mobility, of opportunity, was a social fact. There was enough basis in reality, enough actual opportunity, so that we cannot dismiss the ideology as pure illusion.

In the middle of the nineteenth century, the United States was perhaps sharply different from England and from Europe, Latin America, and Asia as well. Today, culturally speaking, and in terms of science, technology, and (in many countries) political structure, these differences are perhaps less obvious. Mobility has increased everywhere. This has had a profound impact on *personal identity*, which is our subject. It makes it more of a problem, more of an issue. How this happened in the nineteenth century, and what were its consequences, will be discussed in the following chapters. After that, we will look at more contemporary times.

Chapter 2

An Evil Twin

In 1886, Robert Louis Stevenson published his famous novella the *Strange Case of Dr. Jekyll and Mr. Hyde.* Dr. Henry Jekyll, the leading character, is an Englishman who lives in London; he is a member of the upper class—a man with servants, a man who travels in genteel circles. From birth Dr. Jekyll, as he tells his story, had been endowed with "excellent parts" and with a supply of money that seemed to guarantee "an honourable and distinguished future." Yet he was guilty of "irregularities." He speaks, too, of a "profound duplicity of life" (Stevenson never tells us what these "irregularities" or "duplicities" consisted of). Dr. Jekyll comes to believe that man has a kind of "dual nature." He, and people like him, have both a respectable outer self, and an inner self, more prone to evil. With certain drugs, Dr. Jekyll finds he can "dethrone" the outer self, overcome the "very fortress of identity," and thus release that inner, evil self. He can convert Dr. Jekyll into a dwarfish and sinister creature to whom he gives the name Edward Hyde. Hyde is the very soul of evil. To other people, who see him on the streets, he seems ugly and deformed, although nobody can identify any specific deformity. Hyde prowls the city, committing crimes—all of which, of course, he regrets when he reverts to his other self, the good and respectable Henry Jekyll. This situation ends in tragedy: Hyde commits a murder; the drugs begin to lose the power to reverse the Hyde persona; that persona seems to take over more and more completely; Dr. Jekyll realizes that there is no way out for him; both Jekyll and Hyde must die; and so, they do.

This brilliant story can be interpreted in many ways. On one level it is about human nature and its combination of good and bad. It is also about what later came to be known as "split personality." Yet it can also be explained as a story of the crisis of identity in modern society. Those who only see the evil Mr. Hyde, who pass him on the street, who encounter him as he prowls about, do not know, and cannot know, that there is, in a way, no such person as Mr. Hyde. He is, rather, an aspect of the well-to-do and respectable Henry Jekyll. Similarly, friends, servants, and colleagues of Henry Jekyll, people who thought they knew the man, never dreamt that there was another self, another personality—they had no clue that Jekyll was, at the same time, the evil Mr. Hyde. In short, they never knew the "true" identity of either Jekyll or Hyde and they (and the rest of us) could never really say that he was "really" Dr. Jekyll or "really" Mr. Hyde, or both of them, or neither. Jekyll and Hyde lived in a modern, "anonymous," and socially mobile society, one in which "distinctive dress, appearance, and accent were losing their power to convey social status at a glance." These societies were "brimming with people who were strangers" and in which "the most heinous criminal could appear in the most innocent guise."[1] Mr. Hyde did not "appear" in an "innocent guise," but his looks, his manner, his behavior, gave no hint that he was also Dr. Jekyll, or, to put it another way, another aspect of Dr. Jekyll.

In Oscar Wilde's famous novel, *The Picture of Dorian Gray*, a noted artist, Basil Hallward, paints a portrait of Dorian Gray, a young, handsome man from polite society. In a kind of pact with the devil (the details are naturally obscure), Gray achieves an unusual status: he will remain young and handsome, but his likeness in a portrait, hidden in Gray's house, will grow old. And indeed, the image in the portrait does grow old, becoming more and more hideous and unsightly while Gray himself remains young in appearance. Gray, meanwhile, falls under evil influences, his life turning into a sinful search for pleasure. Hallward, the artist, visiting Gray at his home, is horrified at what he has done—the portrait is now ugly, disgusting. Gray and Hallward quarrel and Gray stabs Hallward to death. After eighteen years of crimes and debauchery, Gray comes to regret his sinful life. In the end, remorseful and full of despair, Gray takes the knife he killed Hallward with and slashes the portrait. He has now, in fact, killed himself. Gray is found dead with a knife in his body, his face old and ugly. The portrait, meanwhile, reverts and shows a young, handsome man, Dorian Gray, as he was, and as he appeared to the outside world more than eighteen years prior.

Wilde's novel was published roughly at the same time as Stevenson's novella. It is a complex work that touches on many themes: the nature of art and the artist, the nature of good and evil. But in one sense, too, the novel can be looked on as a kind of upside-down version of the Jekyll-Hyde story. The deformed, ugly portrait is one aspect of Dorian Gray—it is, in a sense, the *real* Dorian Gray, corresponding to the evil Mr. Hyde. In a way, too, there is no Dr. Jekyll here—the young and handsome man that everybody sees, the outer identity, is not the genuine Dorian Gray. Dorian is, or becomes, a thorough-going villain—a murderer in fact. Yet the puzzle of personal identity is salient in this book too. Meeting Dorian Gray on the street, or in a drawing-room, nobody could be aware of his secret—the portrait, hidden in the depths of his house, growing old and ugly with the passage of time. And, like the Jekyll-Hyde story, the tale of Dorian Gray was bound to end in tragedy. Oscar Wilde's own life took a tragic turn because of a split identity in real life: Wilde, the well-born and famous man of letters and Wilde, the closeted gay. Or perhaps the gay who was not closeted enough.

Like all literature, these two works reflect the society in which they were written. Victorian literature, in general, is obsessed with dualities of identity, with people who were not what they seemed, with skeletons in respectable closets. All this reflects the blurred, confused, complex world of the nineteenth century. A world in which traditional village society was disintegrating, in which more and more people moved from farms and towns to big and anonymous cities. The actions in Stevenson's novella, and Wilde's novel, took place in London, a huge, swollen megalopolis, an anthill of vast anonymous masses. London was, and still is, the seat of England's government, the location of Parliament and Buckingham Palace. Many members of the aristocracy had homes in London. Members of the landed gentry often came to London for the social season. London was also the home of merchants, tradesmen, members of the middle class, members of the profession, and, very notably, masses of the poor who lived in squalid, unhealthy, and crowded slums, and who scratched out a living as best they could. At night, the streets of London were dark and dangerous. Like all big cities, it harbored millions of secrets. Secrets—and crimes.

Crime and punishment, like blurred identity, were constant themes of Victorian literature. Crime is at the heart of the Jekyll and Hyde story and the story of Dorian Gray. The novels of Charles Dickens contain an "astonishing" number of "murders and otherwise unnatural deaths." In *Oliver Twist*, for example, there is "a murder, an accidental death by hanging, an execution" and "a dog's brains are smashed out." In *Bleak House* there is both murder and suicide.[2] Crime was also at the heart of the so-called sensation novels of the 1860s.[3] Outside of literature and quasi-literature, there was also enough real crime and real murder to feed the vast public appetite for crime and punishment, and the more lurid the better. Londoners consumed pamphlets, brochures, and mass-market newspapers that featured tales of murders and other crimes, and also trials, imprisonment, and (especially) executions. Plays based on famous crimes frequently were performed in London's theaters. Horse thief Richard Turpin, who went to the gallows in 1739, had an "onstage incarnation, as *Richard Turpin, The Highwayman*" in 1818. Dozens of such plays found audiences in the Victorian era.[4] All of this was part of the cultural milieu that gave birth to the "mystery story," or "detective story," which we will discuss in a later chapter.

In August 1888, one particular series of murders in the Whitechapel neighborhood of London particularly enthralled and horrified Londoners. A prostitute named Mary Ann Nichols may have been the first victim of this series of brutal, savage killings (the exact number is unknown). All of the victims were women, mostly prostitutes. They were killed and mutilated by someone whose identity is still a mystery, a man (almost certainly a man) who prowled the dark, fog-shrouded slums of London. Nobody knows his name, but everybody knows his nickname: Jack the Ripper.[5] The London newspapers of the time reveled in these crimes, which sold tons of newspapers.[6] The crimes remain unsolved. Today, they are the coldest of cold cases. Nonetheless, an immense literature has been devoted to Jack the Ripper. Theories have piled on top of theories. Book after book has trotted out this or that "solution" to the mystery, sometimes with wild guesses about his identity. No theory has won anything close to general acceptance. No Sherlock Holmes, no Hercule Poirot, has ever stepped out of the pages of books to unravel this mystery. After all these years, we will probably never know the answer. Jack the Ripper apparently got away with his hideous crimes.

Thus, we do not know the true life story of Jack the Ripper. Yet that story, if we knew it, might resemble, in a way, the (fictional) case of Jekyll and Hyde. Jack the Ripper might have been someone who, in daylight, seemed normal, harmless—someone who lived a middle-class life, perhaps even an upper-class life. He may have been a local butcher, tradesman, or a doctor—maybe even an aristocrat who haunted the neighborhood at night. At one time, a finger of suspicion even pointed at a member of the royal family: Prince Albert Victor, grandson of Queen Victoria, the oldest son of the Prince of Wales, second in line for the throne. The prince, who died at the age of twenty-eight, was clearly *not* Jack the Ripper. At the time of the murders, he was hundreds of miles away. Still, it is intriguing that his name popped up at all—that people could suspect a prince of the royal blood, a prince who, people imagined, crept secretly and in disguise out of his palace into the London fog, where he brutally and savagely murdered women. The very rumor says something about identity and its ambiguities in Victorian times.

This ambiguity, this mystery, is surely part of the reason why Jack the Ripper was and is so fascinating, why unsolved mysteries in general have such a grip on the imagination. These are mysteries of identity. These mysteries assume that people we meet, see, and deal with every day, are not who we think they are. Their outer surface conceals a dark, Satanic underbody, a Hyde inside their surface Dr. Jekyll, a Dorian Gray with a rotting portrait hidden in his house. Even the rich and the famous, men like Prince Albert Victor, might have split personalities, men with dark secrets, men who are definitely not what their outer skin suggests, what their speech, manners, and behavior suggest, what their position in society suggests.

The ambiguity of personal identity in modern times has had a major impact on the history and structure of criminal justice. This ambiguity reveals key fault lines, flaws, and pathologies in society and the ways in which they could be hidden or disguised. It has been a source of uneasiness, fear, and at times paranoia and moral panic as well. Moral panics—"witch hunts"—are not random and reflect real controversies and real issues.

The title of this chapter, "An Evil Twin," is a well-known trope of popular culture. Identical twins are genetically the same person, split in two in a way. They look alike and at times dress alike, act alike, and in some cases, it is difficult for anyone to tell them apart. In the Hollywood movie *Dark Mirror* (1946), one of two twin sisters is guilty of a crime, but no one can be sure which one was the evil twin. This is, in a way, a variant of the theme of Jekyll and Hyde: the mystery and ambiguity of personal identity; the difficulty of reading someone's personality, of looking into a person's soul, in a society that brings people in daily contact with strangers.

THE BIG TRIAL

The question of identity and the mystery and ambiguity that comes with it, hangs like a black cloud over many famous and sensational criminal trials. Indeed, the mystery of personal identity is what makes these trials so fascinating. There were, of course, trials before the nineteenth century, and some were notorious and attracted wide attention. But the blurring of identity—and, of course, the emergence of a mass-market press—spread knowledge and awareness of these trials, far beyond the immediate neighborhood and also heightened the element of mystery behind them. In the mean streets of cities, under the cover of darkness and fog, there were many sudden and unexplained deaths—murders that had no eyewitnesses like the crimes of Jack the Ripper. The cheap, lurid press whipped up public interest and excitement. Sensational coverage of scandalous trials paid off handsomely for publishers. The public eagerly bought what the popular press served up.

Most criminal trials are small-scale affairs. A long, drawn-out process of jury selection is rare. Usually, these trials have no witnesses or cross-examination. There is no big issue for a jury to resolve. Indeed, in the United States, for most defendants, there is no trial at all. Most felony cases end with a plea bargain. Plea bargaining began in the nineteenth century. In the twentieth century it became totally pervasive in felony cases all over the country.[7] But even before the age of plea bargaining, most "trials" were quick and barely contested. Real trials, trials with lawyers arguing on both sides, where the outcome was uncertain, were always a small minority.

Few in number, but uncommonly interesting and significant, and not only to the mass public.[8] Most major trials, but not all, take place in big cities. The trial of Lizzie Borden, one of the most famous in American history, took place in Fall River, Massachusetts.[9] On August 4, 1892, someone bashed in the heads of Andrew and Abby Borden, Lizzie's father and stepmother, in their own home. It was a bloody and revolting crime. The Bordens were leading citizens of Fall River—locally prominent, well-to-do, upright, solid church-going people. Andrew Borden had been married twice. After his first wife died, Andrew remarried. He and his new wife, Abby, and two daughters from his first marriage, Emma and Lizzie, lived together in Borden's comfortable home.

The crime, quite naturally, horrified the community. Suspicion fell on Lizzie. Why had she burned one of her dresses in the extreme August heat? On the other hand, she was a respectable woman, a church-goer, upstanding, a woman with no blemish on her record. Nonetheless, Lizzie was arrested, charged with murder, and put on trial. The trial was more than just a local sensation; it became national news. Reporters swarmed over the courtroom, sending out thousands and thousands of words for the hungry public to read. The defense contested every facet of the prosecution's case. At the heart of the case was the mystery of Lizzie Borden. Who was she really? Was she Jekyll or Hyde? The defense hammered home that Lizzie belonged to a solid, respectable family, people of faith, people devoted to their community. Could she really be a murderess? A heartless criminal? A psychopath who brutally murdered her own father? A killer hiding in the disguise of bourgeois respectability, hiding beneath the veneer of her upper-class status? This seemed impossible. The defense, in summary, emphasized that a verdict of guilty meant that Lizzie was "a fiend. Does she look it?" During the "long, weary days" in the courtroom "have you seen anything that shows the lack of human feeling and womanly bearing?"[10] Her attorneys appealed to context rather than evidence: Was it even thinkable that Lizzie Borden led a double life? A crime of this nature was "morally and physically impossible for this young woman defendant."[11] Their argument seemed to resonate with the jury. They reached a unanimous verdict in about ten minutes. Lizzie Borden was not guilty. She was free.

Jurors rarely talk openly about their decision. We have no way of knowing what went on in their minds during the trial. Perhaps they felt that the evidence was not quite strong enough. Or, perhaps, they were swayed by the defense's argument. They could not conceive of Lizzie Borden as a brutal murderess. She was a "gentlewoman," a virgin of spotless reputation, a pillar of the local community. She could not be the evil Mr. Hyde. Still, the question of Lizzie's identity was at the very heart of her trial. It is what gave the trial its buzz, its notoriety, a notoriety which has never quite gone away. No American murder trial, perhaps, has been so famous and given rise to so much speculation. The Borden case has been "explored in fiction, reimagined as ballet and opera, and dramatized in films, plays, and even musicals." People are still trying to "solve" the mystery. It has been argued that Bridget Sullivan, the Borden's Irish maid, was the actual killer or Lizzie's sister, Emma, or a stranger, or somebody else—anybody but Lizzie.[12]

Of course, the most likely answer is the obvious one: Lizzie was guilty. She did in fact kill her father and stepmother. Only the motive remains obscure. Money may be at the root of the crime. When Andrew Borden and his second wife died, Lizzie and her sister were no longer locked into a stifling and suffocating life—they had become heiresses, women of wealth.[13] In any event, the mystery surrounding this trial has intrigued people for decades. In general, the mystery at the heart of sensational trials is what draws people to them, like moths to a flame. The mystery of identity is the reason why swarms of reporters write up and report accounts of these trials for newspapers, and feature them on television. Murder sells. Unsolved and mysterious murders sell even better. The trials themselves are public spectacles. They are also dramas. The two sides, defense and prosecution, paint radically different pictures of reality. If the defendant *seems* respectable, benign, socially prominent—like Lizzie Borden—the jury is told to follow its instinct and acquit. There is no secret pathology. What you see, they claim, is what you get. There is no Mr. Hyde underneath the surface of Dr. Jekyll's life. The prosecution makes the opposite argument. However innocent defendants may appear, they are really villains, murderers, deformed personalities—they are hiding a malevolent identity. The jury must decide who these people really are. Are they Jekyll or Hide? Or both?

In 1849, the trial of Professor John Webster, a Boston brahmin, was the most sensational trial of its day. Webster was on trial for the murder of another brahmin, George Parkman, a professor of medicine at Harvard University. Webster was charged with chopping up Parkman's body in the basement of Harvard's medical school. Money was the likely motive. Webster was deeply in debt to Parkman. Parkman held promissory notes, which Webster could not pay off. He faced financial ruin. The chief justice of the commonwealth, Lemuel Shaw, presided over the trial. The courtroom was jammed every day. Reporters from Boston and out of town flocked to the courtroom to see, hear, and spread the word to an eager public. The evidence against Webster was strong. But was it possible for this man, this paragon, to commit so foul a crime? In summation, one of the defense lawyers described Webster as a man who "for more than a quarter of a century" had been "a respected professor" at Harvard, "the pride of our state." He was also a family man: indeed, "the very center" of his family, an "object" of "idolatry" to his loved ones, subject of their "purest and holiest affections."[14] Could such a man really be, at base, an evil Mr. Hyde, capable of this atrocious and disgusting act? For this jury, the answer was clearly yes. They found Webster guilty as charged. In accordance with Massachusetts law, the punishment was death. John Webster died on the gallows in Massachusetts on August 30, 1850.

To this day, identity questions—identity mysteries—are what provides the spice to headline trials. The question in these trials is the familiar one: Who were these defendants, really? The trial of Dr. Sam Sheppard was perhaps the most sensational trial of the 1950s. Sheppard was accused of murdering his pregnant wife, Marilyn. This, like the Borden trial, seemed to violate the natural order. Sheppard was a respectable man, a professional, an osteopath, who lived in a comfortable home in the suburbs of Cleveland, Ohio. He seemed to be devoted to his family. But could he also be a vicious killer? He claimed he was innocent; the murder (he said) was actually committed by a bushy-haired stranger. Sheppard was convicted in an atmosphere of frenzied publicity. Later, he won a new trial. The Supreme Court of the United States found that the first trial had been such a wild publicity circus, so unruly, so tainted with media madness, that it reached the level of unfairness.[15] At the retrial, Sheppard was acquitted. In all likelihood, Sheppard, unlike Lizzie Borden, was in fact innocent. It appears that there really was a bushy-haired stranger who had killed Sheppard's wife.[16]

Lizzie Borden, John Webster, and Dr. Sam Sheppard had been high on the social scale. When a defendant is an actual celebrity, the trial is even more likely to be sensational.[17] In the 1990s, O. J. Simpson's trial transfixed a worldwide audience of millions. Simpson was a sports hero, a hall-of-famer, a celebrity of the first rank. But was he also a killer? Was he the man who murdered his ex-wife, Nicole, and one of her friends, in cold blood? Many facts pointed squarely to Simpson as the killer. He pleaded not guilty, and his case went to trial—not only before a crowded courtroom, but also to a vast television audience. Simpson is African American, and his lawyers accused the prosecution of racism. The jury found him not guilty. Most Whites thought the jury reached the wrong conclusion. Most Blacks felt otherwise.

Simpson's lawyers made race a central issue in the case. In a sense, they put the criminal justice system on trial. Moreover, Simpson was rich and famous: a racial role model. The trial made his identity an issue.[18] In the Lizzie Borden case, bourgeois society was in a way on trial. In all these cases, a terrifying question was posed: Could outside appearances be a fraud, a veneer, a Potemkin village—a stone which, if you turned it over, all kinds of vermin might crawl out?

Character and class were on trial in many headline cases. In 1860s England, Samuel Kent, a factory inspector, lived in a comfortable house, with children from two marriages, and three live-in servants. One night someone abducted his three-year-old son, Saville, from his bed, murdered him, and stuffed his body in an outdoor privy. Suspicion fell on Constance Kent, the teenaged half-sister of the victim. The authorities decided not to prosecute. Any case against her, in the words of her barrister, would be "unjust" and "improper"; a "young lady in the position of life of Miss Constance Kent" simply could not be a murderess. Yet in fact, later on, after experiencing a kind of religious conversion, Constance confessed to the crime.[19]

Dr. Harvey Crippen was the defendant in a famous English trial.[20] Crippen was an American-born osteopath who moved to England with his second wife, Cora. Cora mysteriously disappeared in 1910. Crippen, meanwhile, had acquired a mistress. Crippen told people his wife had gone back to the states. But people became suspicious. Scotland Yard found a human torso buried under the floor of Crippen's basement. (The rest of the body was never found.) Meanwhile, Crippen was on a ship bound for America, together with his mistress (disguised as a boy). Authorities arrested Crippen (in Canadian waters), and shipped him back to England. He was charged with murdering his wife and put on trial. Crippen insisted he was innocent, but the jury, after a short period of deliberation, found him guilty. He was hanged in November 1910.

Crippen was always described as mild-mannered. He seemed perfectly ordinary, far from the usual image of a murderer. In appearance and habits he seemed bland and benign. Was it possible that this doctor, this little man who wore glasses, was in fact a murderous fiend? A man who could kill his wife, chop her to pieces, and bury part of her body underneath his basement floor? Like Lizzie Borden and Constance Kent, it was hard to think of him as a vicious killer. Unlike the dwarfish and malevolent Mr. Hyde, you could pass him in the street and never know his secret. But not every Mr. Hyde reveals himself outwardly. Jury and public alike found Crippen guilty as charged.[21] One element of the trial was similar to the Lizzie Borden case: the clash between the appearance and habits of the defendant and the facts of the crime. In this case, the jury said yes.

THE SHOCK OF NONRECOGNITION

Most homicide cases are not dramatic. The police make a quick arrest. Factual guilt is rarely an issue. Major trials are different. Each big trial has its own dynamic and tells its own story. But many of them have a common theme, a common issue: Who are these persons on trial? What is their true identity? In modern society, what you see is not always what you get. What seems benign may be deceptive. A smooth surface with darkness underneath. The trial means creeping into a dark room to look at the picture of Dorian Gray. It means questioning the probity, the ethics, even the sanity of prominent people, respectable people, people who show the world only their good side.

The Loeb-Leopold case from 1924 has been called the trial of the (twentieth) century[22] (there have been other candidates for this title). In Chicago, two rich young men, Richard Loeb and Nathan Leopold, university students, men who had every advantage in life, murdered a boy named Bobby Franks. Franks was a cousin of one of the killers. Loeb and Leopold came from similar backgrounds, were classmates at university, and had formed a strong bond, perhaps one with sexual overtones. Leopold, in particular, was a brilliant student, a master of languages. He was also an expert on birds. The two men apparently thought they were special beings, free from the ties of ordinary social norms. They committed a series of minor crimes, then decided to move on to something bigger—murder, in fact—either for the thrill of it or to pull off the perfect crime. The crime, as it turned out, was far from perfect. Suspicion fell on them quickly: a pair of glasses left at the scene of the crime was traced to Leopold. Confronted with the evidence, both men confessed. Thus, there would be no trial in the usual sense. The real issue was the punishment: Would they be sentenced to death? Their families hired Clarence Darrow, one of the most famous trial lawyers of the day. The hearings were a media sensation. Darrow made an impassioned argument against the death sentence. For whatever reason, the judge did spare their lives. He imposed a life sentence on Loeb and Leopold. Loeb was later slashed to death in prison by an inmate. Leopold was eventually released and lived quietly for the rest of his life in Puerto Rico, doing good deeds and compiling a catalog of birds of Puerto Rico. He died in 1971 at the age of sixty-six.

The trial of Loeb and Leopold enthralled the public. The facts were not in dispute. The real puzzle was something else, at the very heart of the case, something we might call the shock of nonrecognition. In Lizzie Borden's case, her very identity was at issue. Was she guilty at all? Here the puzzle was different, in one sense, but similar in another. How could these two young men have gone so badly off the rails? Who were they really? Was something corrupting the young? Was something rotten in society, eating away at members of the privileged class? In both this case, and the Lizzie Borden case, bourgeois society was, in a sense, on trial. Loeb and Leopold were young men of wealth and education, brilliant students, men with bright futures. How could they have killed an innocent boy? What led to this hidden element, this Mr. Hyde inside their souls?

In the 1950s, two teenaged girls from New Zealand, Pauline Parker and Juliet Hulme, were put on trial. It was something of an echo of the Loeb-Leopold case. Parker and Hulme killed Parker's mother, Honorah Rieper, with a brick wrapped in a stocking. The girls were very close friends; their families had plans to separate them, which was apparently the motive for the killing. The girls claimed that Honorah had fallen and hurt her head, but the truth came out quickly and they were put on trial. The girls were minors, which ruled out a death sentence. The trial was, quite understandably, sensational. Like Loeb and Leopold's crime, what the girls had done was taken as a sign of "moral rot afflicting adolescents." The "fetid secret lives" of the girls "were clear evidence of a sickness infecting youth."[23] The main defense was insanity, but the jury returned a verdict of guilty. The girls were released after spending five years in prison. Apparently, they never saw each other again. Ironically, Juliet Hulme later enjoyed a successful career as a crime novelist, writing under the name of Anne Perry.

It would be rash to generalize from extreme and unusual cases or to assume that these crimes reflected, in some special way, the massive changes in society and in culture in developed countries in the nineteenth and twentieth centuries. But one trend does seem clear and relevant: during that period, authority structures became more horizontal. Parents, kings, popes, teachers, and leaders exert vertical authority. The authority of friends and peers is horizontal.[24] The shift from vertical to horizontal authority is, of course, not only a relative shift, but a striking one. In both Leopold and Loeb, and the New Zealand case, crimes were committed by young people tightly bonded to each other. In a social order in which vertical authority has weakened, the formation of such bonds is a crucial aspect of self-definition and a way of coping with a world of strangers, a world of loose connections.

BEWITCHED

The longest, and perhaps most expensive, criminal trial in American history was the McMartin day care trial, which took place in Southern California in the 1980s.[25] Judy Johnson was the mother of a child in a day care center run by the McMartin family. Johnson made wild accusations against the McMartins and their staff; she claimed that they were sexually abusing the children. Other even more fantastic claims were circulated: for instance, Satanic rituals and secret tunnels underneath the center, where fiendish events took place. Children, it was claimed, were innocent victims of these horrors. On the surface, the McMartins seemed to be kind and caring people, people who loved children. But was this only a mask? A veneer? Underneath, were they child abusers, Satanists, or worse? Were they more like Mr. Hyde than Dr. Jekyll?

The original accuser, Judy Johnson, was not a well woman—she was a paranoid schizophrenic and a chronic alcoholic who died of liver disease a few years after setting in motion the attack on the day care center. But why did anyone believe her? In some ways, the McMartin case was quite different from Lizzie Borden's, Loeb-Leopold, or the New Zealand child-murderers. In those cases, the crime—murder—was real enough. There were fundamental questions about the true identity of the defendants, about their motives, and beyond that, questions about society itself. In the McMartin case, almost certainly the "crime" never existed at all. The main evidence against the

McMartins, if you could call it that, came from small children. They were questioned by psychologists who used dubious techniques, which probably put ideas into the children's minds that were never there in the first place. Meanwhile, other parents piled on with accusations of their own—hysterical accounts of baleful practices that spread like wildfire.

In the process, the lives of the McMartins were ruined. In the end, after this extraordinary trial had dragged on and on, nobody was convicted. All the defendants went free or were set free. One defendant, Ray Bucky, a grandson of Mrs. McMartin, had spent years in jail before the case collapsed and he was released. Meanwhile, in other cities (and even in other countries) copycat accusations and trials took place. Some trials ended in convictions, with long prison sentences for men and women accused of carrying on Satanic rituals and sodomizing children. In 2004, John Stoll was released after nearly twenty years in prison in Kern County, California. He had been accused of being the "ringleader of a band of child molesters and pornographers." His conviction had been based on the testimony of children, who, according to defense attorneys, "had been badgered and brainwashed by overzealous investigators."[26]

Why did anybody believe these wild accusations? In hindsight, they seem truly preposterous—modern versions of medieval witch hunts. It was a kind of moral panic—a madness that spread like a virus, infecting parents in city after city. The testimony of the children should have been suspect from the start. What "came from the mouth of babes were juvenile renderings of grownups' anxieties . . . adult projections and fantasies."[27] These "projections and fantasies" reflect the uncertainties of life in the modern world. They are living embodiments of the mystery of Jekyll and Hyde.

In one regard, the McMartin trial shared an important trait with, say, Lizzie Borden's case: a kind of smell, a dark suspicion, a notion that something was wrong, something was awry, something was rotten in the social order. It shared, too, the puzzle of identity that has haunted modern society and which makes it possible for these suspicions to flourish. The sources of the unease are different, but the unease is a common factor. The changing social role of women, the strains of family life, the crisis in gender relations hung over the trial like a deadly chemical fog. In contemporary times, women by the millions have entered the work force out of choice or necessity. Many have children too young for school. Somebody must care for them. Day care is one option, but many parents (mothers and fathers alike) may feel racked by feelings of guilt and insecurity when they choose this route. The children, for hours and hours, five days a week, are left to the care of strangers. The day care workers may seem innocent, loving, devoted to the children. But how can we be so sure? Do they have a secret life? A secret identity? This is basically the same question that suffuses sensational criminal trials: the defendants in the dock, who are they really?

The McMartin trial was a strange episode and one that took place not in the distant past, but in recent years. It reflected, as we mentioned, a particular modern issue involving child-rearing practices. Moral panics have a long history. In 2021 and 2022, the antivaccination movement has had something of this flavor. During the Cold War, there was a kind of moral panic over communism: spies and hidden foreign agents were thought to be everywhere, hiding their true feelings, infiltrating Hollywood, the universities, branches of government, and even the armed forces. To be sure, spies did exist, but the moral panic went beyond any actual danger from these internal enemies.

Fears of witchcraft, of dark, evil forces, of Satanism, have a long history, which has survived, to an extent, in the modern world. At one time, millions of devout people believed in demons and devils. They believed in the existence of a secret and malevolent subworld. Witches and creatures possessed by the devil could take the form, at times, of regular people. Particularly in the sixteenth and seventeenth centuries, an epidemic of witchcraft trials broke out all over Europe. These trials were particularly prevalent in Germany. In England, too, there were trials. In 1612, twelve people (mostly women) were accused of witchcraft in Lancashire. Ten were found guilty and executed.[28]

The witchcraft trials in Salem, Massachusetts, in 1692 and 1693 are a particularly well-known American example. The term "witch hunt," which refers to these trials, has gone into commonly used language and speech. In February 1692, two young girls from Salem began acting peculiar. Many people became convinced that the community was infested with witches. Eventually, twenty people were convicted of witchcraft and put to death. Prominent religious leaders, like Cotton Mather, supported these trials. Mather believed the devil was hard at work in Massachusetts, trying to corrupt society. The very godliness of New England made the devil all the more eager to subvert the colony. New Englanders, Mather wrote in 1692, "are a people of God settled in those, which were once the *Devil's* Territories." This "irritated" the devil who "immediately try'd all sorts of Methods to overturn this poor Plantation."[29]

The witchcraft hysteria eventually died down in New England and elsewhere. In 1735 England, the Witchcraft Act put an end to witchcraft trials, and indeed, outlawed accusations of witchcraft. But the belief in demons, devils, and witches never disappeared, it merely went underground. Many people still believed in "wonders of the invisible world"—secret, hidden forces that could corrupt the souls of human beings, take them over, and force them to join the army of the damned. In 1822, in Norfolk County, Virginia, a man named Joseph Lewis shot an African American, Jack Bass, to death. Lewis suspected Bass of bewitching him and his wife. A female fortune-teller had told him his suspicions were well grounded. In 1905, a florist in San Francisco, Louis De Paoli (his specialty was violets) beat his sister-in-law to death with a chair. De Paoli and his wife were convinced the woman had bewitched them and their children.[30] Catholic priests can perform rites of exorcism, procedures for driving the devil out of persons believed to be possessed. Exorcism still exists, in theory at least. In 1999, the Vatican issued a "revised Catholic rite of exorcism." Evangelical and charismatic preachers perform "spiritual-cleansing ceremonies."[31] Witches, historically, were considered evil, but today, wiccans and covens practice a harmless form of neo-paganism. Pacts with the devil are not part of their stock in trade.

The Jekyll and Hyde story can be seen, among other things, as a secular tale of witchcraft. Dr. Jekyll used science, not the devil, to transform himself, to release his hidden but evil self. The story in a sense reflected a persistent belief in the dark underbelly of society. This belief lies at the base of one of the most sinister and enduring figures in late Victorian literature: Dracula, the vampire from Transylvania. Bram Stoker's *Dracula* was published in 1897.[32] This was not the first tale of a vampire,[33] but has been the most enduring. Dracula, a monster of evil, sometimes took the shape of a giant bat. He slept in a coffin by day; daylight was his enemy. He stalked his victims at night. His sole food was human blood. Not only did he drink the blood of his victims, but his bites could transform his victims into vampires so that they became part of the army of the undead, creatures like Dracula himself.

Stoker's book had strong sexual overtones (or undertones). Dracula seemed to prefer the blood of young, attractive (and virginal) women. His bite can be seen as a kind of sexual initiation, which robbed these women of their primal innocence and led them into a more sinful, evil—and sensual—life. Transylvania, the site of Dracula's dark and mysterious castle, was (for the English) remote and exotic, shrouded in mystery, a place of sinister legends and folklore. *Dracula* was written in the form of journal and diary entries. It begins with the journals of Jonathan Harker, a young Englishman who has traveled to Dracula's castle on real estate business. In Stoker's book, Dracula has a plan (which he carries out) to leave his ancestral home in the Balkans. He gets himself transported by boat (and in a coffin) to England, along with fifty boxes of Transylvanian soil. Once in England, he planned to find new victims and fresh blood (why this could not be done in Transylvania is left unexplained). He succeeds in ravishing (with his fangs) a young woman, Lucy Westenra, who dies and comes back to life as a female vampire. Harker and the other heroes in the book, good, solid, dedicated Englishmen, become aware of Dracula's secret and learn how to master antivampire techniques and foil his evil plots. They succeed in saving the life and soul of the book's heroine, Harker's wife. Dracula, in the end, tries (unsuccessfully) to make his escape back to Transylvania with his one remaining box of Romanian dirt (all the rest have been destroyed by our heroes). But, as he lies in his coffin, they cut his throat, his body crumbling to dust.

Dracula was a huge success. It has fascinated readers for years and inspired a classic movie (1931) starring Bela Lugosi as Count Dracula. The tale has an obvious affinity to old tales of witchcraft, evil, and the supernatural. It nods to a specific genre of English literature, the gothic novel, which flourished somewhat earlier. Ghost stories were prominent in Victorian literature. By inserting his sinister vampire into England, Stoker in a way invoked the Victorian duality that underlay the Jekyll-Hyde story. English society was, on the surface, placid and prosperous, yet underneath there was a dark, mysterious, and unseen layer of society, a kind of verminous cellar below the polished floors of a bourgeois household. Count Dracula, in a way, was part of the mysterious criminal world—he prowled the streets of London, just as Jack the Ripper had done and all the dual personalities of Victorian literature. He symbolized the darkness under the surface of the great metropolis. Moreover, the subtext of the book hinted at another notable Victorian secret: sexual habits and behaviors that were officially taboo and subject to rigorous censorship and repression. We will return to this theme later.

Stoker never expected that his readers would actually *believe* in Count Dracula, the vampire from Transylvania. The thrill of a horror story does not come from belief.[34] It comes from the spell of the unknown and the unknowable. It is, above all, entertaining. Yet, even in this modern and (supposedly) rational world, there are believers—if not in Dracula, then in even more far-out phenomena. A kind of psychological underground persists—people who still believe in devils, or in aliens from outer space, in vast conspiracies, giant hoaxes, and sinister forces that hide below the surface of society. Social media acts to promote and encourage fringe groups of believers. This is especially true in this age of horizontal authority. Believers can communicate with each other, form virtual groups, find like-minded people, and reinforce the most paranoid of fantasies. The internet opens the door to kindred spirits who believe, from the bottom of their hearts, that the world is flat, not round; that the moon landing never took place; that a flying saucer crashed in 1947 near Roswell, New Mexico, only to be covered up by the United States Air Force. Some accept as gospel the *Protocols of the Elders of Zion*, an anti-Semitic forgery. Some believe in giant plots to destroy the hegemony of White people. Some accept cults that preach messages about a coming Armageddon or who are sure that some giant cataclysm is about to end life on the planet as we know it. Afterward, only a few of the chosen will survive. In short, belief in the "wonders of the invisible world" has never ended. It may have diminished somewhat, but it is still a powerful force to be reckoned with—even politically. The continuing ambiguity of personal identity—the fact that we cannot really know the people we see every day, that we cannot be sure that surface reality reflects some kind of true or inner reality—means that the "invisible world" will not run out of believers.

Chapter 3

Crimes of Mobility

In the nineteenth century, growing cities, with their masses of strangers and the anonymity of streets and alleys, produced new types of crime, or made old kinds more common. Cities were, and still are, critical sites of crime: theft, robbery, burglary, rape, and assault. Indeed, these crimes flourished in the dark streets of fog-bound London and the slums of New York. In addition to these common crimes were those that depended on the specific fact of modern, urban society—crimes that depended on mobility and were rooted in the ambiguity of personal identity.

Bigamy, the crime of marrying someone when you are legally married to another, is very much a crime of mobility, for example. In a small town, with a stable population, it is almost impossible to become a bigamist. Joe cannot propose marriage to Anne if he is already married to Emma, because everybody in town knows that Emma is his wife. In olden times this must have been a rare crime indeed. Simulated identity, in general, was rare.[1] Bigamy becomes much more likely in a mobile society where many, or even most, people in town have been there only a short time, or in a city so large that it is awash with strangers—where people can take on an identity and discard it, much like a reptile shedding its skin and growing a new one.

Bigamy is not a crime on the scale of, say, robbery, or assault; it does not make an impact on crime statistics. It was surprisingly popular as a plot device in Victorian fiction, in part due to the influence of a sensational upper-class bigamy trial.[2] Bits of evidence suggest that bigamy was on the rise in the nineteenth century.[3] In England and Wales, 5,327 bigamy trials were reported between 1857 and 1904, an average of 98 a year. Most bigamists, it is likely, got away with their double life. Probably only a small minority, of perhaps unusually brazen men, ended up in court. Only one out of eight cases of bigamy, cited as grounds for divorce, was actually prosecuted.[4] Unfortunately, there are no reliable figures for the United States. Probably, bigamy was at least as common as in England, and perhaps more common, because the country was so big and restless. One piece of evidence comes out of experience with pensions for veterans of the Civil War: apparently there were a few thousand instances where more than one "widow" claimed a soldier's pension after he died.[5] Mobility made bigamy possible for soldiers (and others) because it was easy to move from one place to another and take on a new identity. These pension files did suggest that marriage was rather "fluid" in the United States and that bigamy was "a practice almost as common as divorce in the nineteenth century."[6] In any event, any such "fluidity" reflected mobility and the problem of personal identity.

Bigamists were, for the most part, men. Of the defendants in a sample of 304 English bigamy cases, 82 percent were men.[7] They also (no surprise) made up about 80 percent of those convicted of this crime in nineteenth-century England.[8] This imbalance probably also held true in the United States. Men were, after all, much more mobile than women: they had more freedom to roam the country. It was "easy for a man to leave town, put some distance between himself and his former life, and assume a new identity."[9] Robert Schmidt, a German immigrant, married a woman named Theresa in 1857. Schmidt then moved to California, called himself Herman Weber, and married a "green German woman" in San Francisco. Unfortunately for him, his first wife caught him. A fortune-teller had told her the two would meet again, and the prediction came true. Theresa moved to California where her husband was living. When she confronted him, he promised that if she kept quiet and agreed not to get him arrested, he would let her have half his pension.[10]

Bigamists can be divided into various types. Some perhaps honestly felt that their first marriage was no longer valid. It was a popular belief that if a couple was apart for seven years or more, it was perfectly legal to remarry. No such rule actually existed.[11] Or a man or woman might think, in all sincerity, that wife or husband number one, missing for a long time, must surely be dead. This was the claim of one of the few women bigamists on record, Mary Vandenwende, in New York in 1885. Mrs. Vandenwende, twenty-four years old, "of fair complexion" with "gold-rimmed glasses . . . rather stout build" and "the appearance of innocence itself," was arrested on a charge brought by her (second) husband. Husband number one, she said, had disappeared "and she thought he was dead."[12] Swindlers made up what was probably a more common type of bigamist. J. Aldrich Brown had, apparently, a flourishing career as a bigamist and swindler. He married at least seventeen times. He never stayed very long with any particular wife. He seemed quite intelligent (crafty is perhaps a better word), and was described as handsome and tall. His specialty was preying on "sewing girls in wealthy families." He would marry them, take their savings and whatever they had of value, and promptly disappear. Another type of bigamist, probably the most common, consisted of restless, dissatisfied husbands. John Wilgen, who worked as a printer, had a wife and two children in Minneapolis, Minnesota. He also wrote letters to a woman named Rena Mead and sent her his picture. They got married in 1897 in Limestone, New York. Wilgen proceeded to live a double life, telling Rena that he often had to go to Minneapolis on business. Another example was one Arthur P. Emery, a "traveling agent for the Chrome Steel Company of Brooklyn," who, in 1876, on one of his long trips, married a woman in Cincinnati, Ohio, even though he already had a wife in Brooklyn. Emery was "middle-aged, good-looking," and boasted of "exploits among the fair sex."[13]

The bigamist was a swindler, whatever he thought of himself. He cheated on both his first wife and any subsequent wives. Wife number two was even more of a victim than wife number one. The original wife was, to be sure, cheated and abandoned. But the result for the second and later wives was even more disastrous if the truth came out. Under the law, a bigamous marriage was utterly void and wife number two was simply living in sin. Most of these women were probably completely in the dark about their husband's past. But whether they knew it or not, these women were now, in Victorian terms, "ruined." The scoundrel had perhaps taken their virginity; he certainly impaired their chances for a regular and respectable marriage, perhaps beyond redemption. They were, in short, damaged goods. It is not surprising then that in the actual prosecutions the party who complained was more often a second wife than a first wife.[14]

Bigamy is a crime of mobility—mobility within countries, but also internationally. The nineteenth century was an age of immigration. Tens of thousands of men left the old country for the United States, Argentina, Canada, Australia. Many left wives and children behind. Often, the plan was to get established and then bring the rest of the family to the new world. A certain number of men, however, ignored these families back home and decided a new country deserved a new wife. This was the fate, for example, of a Jewish woman who wrote her sad story to the advice column of the *Jewish Daily Forward* in 1906. Her husband had emigrated to the United States and married again. Later, she arrived only to discover the sad truth. Her husband was arrested and went to jail.[15]

Bigamy was also a crime of mobility for women, in a way, even though they were victims. To be sure, most women who fell into the clutches of the bigamist were women who stayed home in their town, village, or city. Yet they had their own kind of mobility. They married men who were essentially strangers. Traditional marriage was a union of families, often arranged by families; and took place within a narrow circle—the families of the bride and groom might have known each other for years. The women who married bigamists did not follow this pattern. They married newcomers, not neighbors—strangers, not husbands chosen by their families or approved by their families.

Bigamy is, in a sense, a kind of middle-class crime. To commit bigamy, you have to appear to be married; you go through a ceremony that at least *seems* legitimate. "Living in sin" would be, for respectable Victorians, completely unacceptable. Certainly, a woman who lived with another man as his mistress would not be welcome in polite society. The bigamist's second wife was "living in sin" without knowing it. Her groom had defrauded her. He clothed himself in the appearance of respectability—a status that, legally speaking, he did not deserve, nor did she, in fact. Of course, there were also many couples who knowingly "lived in sin," falsely claiming to be married. They were not bigamists; but they were, in fact, violating the official code of morality. Mobility smoothed the way for this kind of violation, as well as for bigamy. In a village, everybody would be likely to know that John and Mary, who shared a household, were not really married. In the big city, in neighborhoods full of newcomers and strangers, and in the raw new towns of the frontier, this was not the case, and it was easier to pretend to be a status one did not deserve.

Blackmail is another crime of mobility.[16] It is a crime that depends on double lives—on the mysteries of personal identity. The classical blackmailer is a person who knows a secret—something criminal, or embarrassing, hidden in the victim's past. The blackmailer threatens to expose the victim unless the victim pays off the blackmailer. It is in some ways a puzzling crime. Some scholars (notably economists) wonder why it should be a crime at all. One scholar asked why is blackmail—selling silence in exchange for money—any "different from an ordinary bargain."[17] If I know one of Joe's secrets, a skeleton in his closet, and Joe is willing to pay me to keep my mouth shut, why is that a crime? Knowledge is power, and it is or can be an asset as well. Why is it wrong to exploit this asset? Unethical maybe, but a crime? Scholars have advanced a number of reasons, more or less plausible, as to why blackmail is and should be a crime. In fact, most blackmailers are thoroughly disagreeable people, or even worse, people threatening to ruin a life or reputation out of sheer malice or greed. Certain kinds of blackmail might constitute fraud or extortion, but these are already crimes in themselves. Other instances are simply nasty behavior, but nasty behavior is not a crime. Arguably, if you know that Joe has committed a crime and has gotten away with it, society benefits if you "sing," and society loses if you keep quiet. But if the secret is not a crime, if it is simply something embarrassing—Joe, a married man, has had an affair outside of marriage—why should the blackmailer go to jail?

The history of blackmail sheds some light on the question of why this is a crime.[18] Blackmail, in the modern sense, became a crime in the first half of the nineteenth century. A few English cases in the eighteenth century were, in a way, protoblackmail cases. In these cases, the blackmailer (the courts did not use the term) accused a "victim" of homosexual advances and threatened exposure. In 1779, the "victim" was Charles Fielding, the son of an earl. One James Donnally threatened to take Fielding before a magistrate and accuse him "of an attempt to commit an unnatural crime" unless he paid up. But it was Donnally, not Fielding, who ended up in court accused of a crime. The judge called Donnally's action robbery. Robbery, the judge felt, did not have to be a violent act—there was or should be such a thing as "constructive violence." This was, legally speaking, something of a stretch. But the judge was so outraged by the defendant's conduct that he was willing to make the stretch. Similarly, in a case from 1776, one Thomas Jones accused a respectable man (a man of "extraordinary good character") of taking "liberties" with him in a theater. Jones demanded money in exchange for silence. The judge called Jones's behavior "highway robbery."[19] These attacks on the "victim's" reputation, the judge felt, deserved the utmost severity. Sodomy was a very serious crime. Threats of exposure, if based in any way on a plausible story, gave blackmailers a powerful weapon for squeezing money out of their "victims."[20]

Blackmail flourished in roiling, crowded cities, with their floating populations, their vice districts, and gambling dens. It never made much of a mark on the criminal justice system, but the practice may have been more common than statistics suggest. Blackmailers were often a subspecies of swindlers known as "confidence men." Con men preyed on their "mark," the victim, by pretending to be something they were not. The victim of blackmail might be, for example, a respectable merchant from a small town. He comes to the big city and decides to taste forbidden fruit. He goes, perhaps, to a house of prostitution. Once there, he falls into a trap set by blackmailers. An account published in 1880 tells the following story: A naïve clergyman, on a visit to New York, gets a message to come and attend to the spiritual needs of a dying woman. When he arrives at the address, he discovers that he has entered "one of the most notorious houses in New York." The people there tell him that his "midnight visit" could be easily proved. They demand money as the price of their silence.[21]

We can sympathize with the minister (assuming he was telling the truth). Bad people had lured him into a delicate situation—one that could ruin his reputation back home. Blackmailers were experts at ensnaring naïve, gullible people. The clergyman was perhaps an innocent lamb who had done nothing wrong. But this was not necessarily the case. The "victims" were often victimized precisely because they were guilty of something wrong or disreputable. Thus, in New York City, in 1923, authorities arrested members of a "shakedown club." Members of the "club" posed as federal enforcement agents and collected money from people who were violating Prohibition laws.[22] In blackmail cases—and this is significant—nobody cares (legally speaking) whether the "victim" is telling the truth or not. The blackmailer would be just as guilty if the good minister in 1880 had gone to a brothel not to give spiritual comfort, but for the usual reason: illicit sex. Nothing in the case would hinge on his motive for visiting a brothel. Indeed, most "victims," one would guess, are vulnerable precisely because the blackmailer's claims are not only scandalous—but also quite true.

The key to understanding blackmail is to ask: Who are these people? The answer lies in the class difference between blackmailer and victim. Almost always, the victim has a higher rank in society than the blackmailer and is richer. There would be no point to blackmail a pauper or a ditchdigger. They have no money, no reputation. The blackmailer thrives on the social gap between him and the victim. The blackmailer is a threat to the social order insofar as he can expose, and ruin, people who are his betters, people who have important roles in society. He threatens to reveal their guilty secret, their feet of clay. And this is dangerous—not just to the "victim," but to society at large. Blackmail is not only a crime of mobility; it is also a crime of identity. The blackmailer's weapon is secret knowledge (or claimed knowledge) about the victim's "true" identity—who he (or she) really is—about a hidden and compromising identity. The blackmailer is the man who knows that Dr. Jekyll is really Mr. Hyde or if not exactly Mr. Hyde, then someone who seems to be Mr. Hyde. The blackmailer's crime is his possession of power over important people, rich people, elites, spiritual leaders, men high up in society. He claims to know that what you see is a veneer, people flying under false colors. Their reputation, their place in society, their position of respect are based on lies or half-truths. The blackmailer will reveal the truth—unless his victim pays the price.

Making blackmail a crime is an attempt to protect the reputation and position of elites. And this reputation, arguably, is crucial to social order. In a society in which identity becomes blurred and problematic, in which confidence men ply their trade, in which traditional values are (perhaps) under threat, trust in elites makes a difference, or at least leading citizens can *think* it makes a difference. In a traditional, hierarchical society, what the masses think of nobles, bishops, and kings, is less crucial than what the masses think of their leaders in a more open, mobile society. And the leaders, in turn, might imagine that their authority depends on respect and trust. Otherwise, the system could crumble into dust. The blackmailer, then, represents a real threat. In fact, leaders and elites may not *deserve* the respect they enjoy. There *are* hidden identities, skeletons in closets, guilty secrets—ministers who visit brothels, men who have guilty pasts. But (one can argue), better to repress and suppress these secrets. Better to keep them buried underground.

Actual blackmail cases may seem counterproductive. After all, what the victim wants is silence—going to the police means telling the story to outsiders, and an actual trial is about as noisy as one can get. The dirty story gets broadcast to the whole world. For this reason, many blackmail plots probably never come to light. Making blackmail a crime might conceivably have some deterrent effect. It also gives the authorities a weapon they can use in egregious cases. They could break up some of the worst of the blackmail rings without sullying the reputation of any particular victim.

Blackmail forms a part (admittedly a minor part) of what I have elsewhere called the "Victorian compromise." By this I mean acceptance of vice, sin, and bad behavior, so long as it remains safely underground and does not run rampant. The blackmailer threatens to expose what should stay hidden. The Victorian compromise meant, in essence, the ability to hide occasional sins or confine sin to specific locations. Cities tolerated so-called red-light districts, areas where brothels—officially illegal—stayed in business, helped along by bribes and occasional fines, which almost amounted to a license to continue to operate. The Victorian compromise also found its way into official law codes. In the American colonies, adultery had been a crime, sometimes severely punished. In the nineteenth century, in many states, adultery as such was no longer a crime; instead the law penalized "open and notorious" adultery. Or, as in Alabama, not simply adultery, but *living* together in adultery. Quiet, sporadic, clandestine adultery was not punishable by law. The act was a crime, in other words, when it amounted to a "course of conduct," when it flaunted itself, when it became an "outrage upon decency and morality."[23] This quote comes from an Alabama case reported in 1848. The defendant, Collins, used to visit his paramour and spend the night with her once a week. This, the court said, was enough to make their affair open and notorious. Only what was open and notorious was any kind of threat. Society was not threatened by the evil Mr. Hyde so long as he kept himself mostly under wraps.

Blackmail, whatever its role in the criminal justice system, was, and is, a popular element in literature. It has been, for example, a staple of the detective novel or "mystery," a new genre which arose in the first half of the nineteenth century, and which we will discuss in a later chapter. In many mysteries, the murder victim is a blackmailer. The killer kills to get rid of him. Bigamy, too, was hardly a major factor in the criminal justice system, but it was a staple of much Victorian literature.[24] It was particularly common in so-called sensation novels, wildly popular best-sellers in England in the 1860s and later.[25] These novels had convoluted plots, lost and contested identities, missing heirs, mix-ups at birth, dead husbands who turned up alive at inconvenient times, and similar plot twists. In Mary Elizabeth Braddon's hugely successful novel, *Aurora Floyd*, published in the early 1860s, the heroine, Aurora, is the only child of a wealthy banker who adores her. But Aurora has a guilty secret. When very young, she had become besotted with Conyers, a handsome scoundrel and one of her father's servants. She elopes with him. Later, she comes to think that Conyers must be dead, and that her secret is safe. She marries a rich, sweet, but bumbling Yorkshireman, John Mellish, who worships the grounds she walks on. He knows nothing of the sins of her youth. Of course, as the reader surely guesses, Conyers is not actually dead. He shows up and, scoundrel that he is, attempts to blackmail Aurora, who is, of course, guilty of bigamy. Then, Conyers is murdered. This is convenient because it ends Aurora's bigamous state and frees her to marry Mellish. Less convenient is the fact that the shadow of suspicion falls on poor Aurora. But she (and the readers) know that Aurora is innocent. The real killer is later exposed, and the novel has a happy ending.

An even more famous novel in its day was *East Lynne* by Ellen Wood (1861). The main character, Lady Isabel Carlyle, is another high-born woman who falls in love with a thoroughly rotten man, Francis Levison. Isabel abandons her husband and children and runs off with the scoundrel. Levison impregnates her but refuses to get married or take responsibility for the child. He leaves her to face her fate alone. But life has other things in store for her. Lady Isabel is badly injured in a train accident, her baby dies, and she is so disfigured that she becomes unrecognizable. Isabel returns home and gets a position in the household as a governess, caring for her own children. Her husband has remarried and is living a happy life. Nobody recognizes Isabel (this is hard to believe) and her true identity remains unknown to everybody in the household. The book ends tragically. Lady Isabel dies; only as she is dying is her secret revealed.

In this novel, Lady Isabel moves through a series of identities, one after another, and she shifts from social class to social class. She was born into the English upper class. When she runs away she forfeits her position in society and becomes a fallen woman, a woman in disgrace, a woman much lower in the social order. Later, she gets a position (in her old home) as a governess. Governesses are common figures in Victorian novels. For women of the upper class, who had no money and no husband to support them, who were penniless and friendless, a job as a governess was one of the few options open to them. It was a job, after all, that called for a good education and good manners—culturally and behaviorally. It was a kind of half-way house between social classes.

Critics sneered at *Aurora Floyd*, *East Lynne*, and others of the so-called sensation novels. But the public loved their melodrama and the twists and turns of their plots. In *Aurora Floyd*, the main characters (except for various servants and the scoundrel that Aurora married) were all members of the landed gentry. The same was true for many of the characters in *East Lynne* and other sensation novels. The characters often had secrets—and secret identities. In *Aurora Floyd* and *East Lynne*, it was a secret about women whose love life crossed class lines. These novels depended on one aspect of social mobility: boundaries between social classes had become somewhat more brittle and porous. Bigamy and false identities were frequent plot devices. The novels turned on skeletons in the closet of gentlefolks—on aspects of personal identity that had to be kept hidden. Such devices are found in virtually all major Victorian novels—in the works of Charles Dickens, for example, and in Charlotte Bronte's *Jane Eyre* (1847), one of the masterpieces of the period. Jane Eyre herself rises and falls in the social scale, works as a governess, and almost enters into a bigamous marriage with her employer whose own guilty secret is that he has been married to a madwoman hidden away in his house.

THE CONFIDENCE GAME

Blackmail and bigamy were, and are, interesting and revealing crimes. But they never amounted to major social problems and never loomed large in the working system of criminal justice. A more serious crime of mobility and identity was the "confidence game," and its practitioner, the "confidence man." These broad, and somewhat vague, terms refer to a class of swindles. In a confidence game, a clever trickster lies, cheats, and dissembles in order to get money from the victim, or "mark." The term may owe its name to the doings of one William Thompson, a swindler of the 1840s. Thompson posed as a rich merchant. He wheedled well-dressed people into lending him money, or a watch. He convinced them to trust him—in short, to have confidence in him. Of course, they never got their money back.[26] The Oxford dictionary traces the term to the 1840s. The first entry in the dictionary is from 1849. Herman Melville's novel *The Confidence-Man* was published in 1857. By that time, the term had become firmly established.

The typical confidence man was an impostor of one kind or another. He pretended to be rich, noble, a member of the clergy, or a respectable businessman. He took on whatever disguise or identity fit his scheme. Henry Mayhew, in his classic study of London life in the middle of the nineteenth century, describes some of the "swindles" practiced in London. One confidence man, for example, pretended to be a German baron who had "received goods in a large amount from merchants in Glasgow." He was accompanied by a young lady. They were both "well-educated people, and could speak the English language fluently." Another man, who called himself the Rev. Mr. Williams, was "adept in deception." He even managed to get himself appointed a country curate. He boldly celebrated marriages and "obtained many articles of jewelry from firms in London, who were deceived by his appearance and position."[27] America swarmed with confidence men in this period—and indeed, in later periods as well (the confidence game is by no means obsolete). There are many nineteenth-century accounts and descriptions of confidence men, confidence games, and their various plots and tricks. For example, fake gold bricks made out of lead, plated in gold, with a small amount of gold at their core could be passed off as a brick of solid gold and peddled to gullible people. In the "green goods swindle" the "mark" thinks he is buying something valuable (often counterfeit money) and puts up cash. The cash goes into the pocket of the confidence man and the mark ends up with a "bundle of worthless sheets of green or brown paper."[28]

The confidence game depends on a certain amount of skill. As one writer in the late nineteenth century put it, a successful confidence man was "the most accomplished" of all the "different types of rogues. . . . It is a criminal calling that an unpolished man cannot successfully follow." Success depended on the ability to lie successfully. The "rascals" who worked the confidence game took "a fiendish delight in outwitting men illustrious in the higher walks of life."[29] Confidence men were thus not "crooks" in the "ordinary sense of the word." They were "suave, slick, and capable." The confidence man did not get money from a victim crudely, like a thief or a robber; rather, the "trusting victim literally thrusts a fat bank roll into his hands."[30] Confidence men were skilled swindlers, men who knew how to worm money out of foolish and gullible people. They were men like "Hungry Joe," a "personally remarkable" man, a college graduate who apparently spoke seven languages. Joe was "always well-dressed . . . about the last man in New York that anyone would take to be a swindler."[31] Or the man who passed himself off as "Norman LaGrange," supposedly a member of Queen Victoria's elite guard. "Norman" frequented the Waldorf Hotel in New York City in 1894 (but of course never paid his bill).[32]

The confidence man flourished in a mobile society—mobile both spatially and socially. For his tricks to work, he needed a society of strangers—he needed cities and towns full of people who did not know each other, places where you could easily pretend to be something or someone you were not. He also needed a socially mobile society where the boundaries between classes had become more indistinct than in the past, where it was possible for a clever rogue to pretend to be a German baron, or a reverend, or a member of high society, and get away with it.

Pretending to be what you are not is a tool of smooth impostors. Beggars could dress in rags and claim to be destitute and blind. They made a living by appealing to the sympathies of passers-by. One New York crook, described in 1895, claimed to have a wooden leg. A rattlesnake had bitten him in Nebraska, according to his story. But he was a "fraud" who had not lost his leg at all: a "piece of board tied to his leg sounds very wooden when rapped with a cane." He collected a good deal of money from kindhearted strangers.[33]

In George Bernard Shaw's great play *Pygmalion*, which we mentioned earlier, Professor Higgins, a speech expert, makes a bold bet. He can, he says, take a wretched flower girl from Covent Garden, Eliza Doolittle, who speaks Cockney English, and turn her into a woman who can pass for a member of the upper class simply by teaching her how to speak proper English. He successfully gives her, in short, another identity. He transforms Eliza into an elegant and well-spoken woman, one who can move easily in high society. One point of the play, then, is its insistence that upper-class identity is not inherited or inherent—it is an artifact, something that can be manufactured. Professor Higgins, of course, is not a confidence man, but like the confidence man, he has a scheme, and a successful one at that. His creature, Eliza Doolittle, after his training, successfully "passes." At the end of the play, she may be about to marry into the upper class. There will be no return to Covent Garden.

Victorians talked a lot about "breeding" as if in some sense manners and gentility were almost a matter of genetics and not simply ways of behaving, something that could be learned or taught. Yet social class was demonstrably fluid. Some English families had distinguished family trees, perhaps traceable all the way back to the Norman conquest. In the nineteenth century, however, a class of the nouveau riche rose to prominence. If you had enough money, if you were successful enough, you could even buy land and join the ranks of the landed gentry. You might even earn a title and enter the world of the English nobility. In Anthony Trollope's great novel, *The Way We Live Now* (1875), one of the central characters, Melmotte, is a financial schemer who crashes into high society, entering Parliament, buying a country estate, and plotting to marry his daughter off to an English aristocrat. Melmotte himself appeared out of nowhere, and his family background was, to say the least, dubious. Melmotte's schemes fail, and he comes crashing down to earth. In the end he kills himself. But the novel tells a story that resonated with late Victorian society. Members of the upper class like to think their class identity was something fixed and inborn. Yet money could buy status. Status was, to be sure, a matter of speech, mannerisms, attitudes, and behaviors. Nonetheless, schemers with money could buy their way in and clever people, like the typical confidence man, could, and did, pretend to be what they were not. There were social gate-crashers who had learned how to pass themselves off, even without the intervention of the likes of Professor Higgins.

In *Pygmalion*, Professor Higgins, in a sense, perpetrated a fraud: he led people to think that Eliza was a member of the upper class, perhaps even royalty, rather than a flower seller with raucous and uneducated speech. He was playing games with the outer forms of identity. Fakes, frauds, schemes of all sorts were extremely common in the nineteenth century for the reasons already mentioned. Some of these schemes could be classified as confidence games. Others were less obviously so. This was the age of P. T. Barnum, the great American showman and faker. He is supposed to have said that a sucker is born every minute. Whether or not he actually said these words (probably he did not), he certainly believed them, and he acted accordingly. Early in his career, in 1835, he passed off an old Black woman, Joice Heth, as a former slave, 161 years old, who had been George Washington's nurse.[34] People paid money to see this woman, who of course had nothing to do with George Washington, and was about half as old as Barnum claimed. Throughout his career, Barnum made money exhibiting freaks and oddities, some of them genuine, many of them not. The "Feejee Mermaid," put together with the head of a monkey and the tail of a fish, was another one of his blockbusters.[35] A gullible public eagerly patronized his shows.

Most of those in the confidence racket, and most impostors and fakes, were men, but there were also occasional women in these dubious businesses. One of them was Loreta Velasquez (this was not her real name, which nobody in fact knows). "Loreta" wrote a book, *A Woman in Battle*, published in 1876, in which she told about her exploits during the Civil War. She claimed she fought in the war, dressed as a man, and passed herself off as Lieutenant Harry T. Buford of the Confederate Army. None of this was true. Later, she hatched scheme after scheme for squeezing money out of gullible investors. She ended up an inmate in St. Elizabeth's, a mental hospital in Washington, DC, a victim of dementia.[36] Confidence men and women often used blackmail as a tool. In 1857, Mary Hill, together with her husband John, introduced the "badger game" to Chicago. In this "game," a woman induces a man to come to her room (for sex, of course). Her accomplice storms in, announces himself as the woman's husband and expresses outrage. At this point, the victim is eager to pay and escape their clutches.[37] A popular account of New York's "high and low life," published in 1882, claimed that the blackmailer is "generally a woman" and that young men "about to make rich marriages are the favorite 'game' of the female blackmailer."[38] The writer assumes that these young "victims" are as innocent as the driven snow, but one has to wonder.

Bigamy, the confidence game, and blackmail are crimes of mobility in the sense that they depend on mobility, and indeed, a mobile society gives birth to these crimes, which cannot flourish outside of a mobile society. Classic crimes—murder, armed robbery, and burglary—have older historical roots, but they, too, are influenced by a mobile society. Small, traditional villages are poor places even for traditional crimes. It is easy to point a finger at likely thieves and killers in these towns. In cities like London or New York, giant human anthills full of strangers, finding and catching thieves is much more difficult. Burglars can change neighborhoods, sneak into houses, steal what they can, then retreat to their own turf, or otherwise disappear into the jungle of the city. An evil Mr. Hyde can prowl the streets, without any fear of recognition. Jack the Ripper can kill and escape exposure.

Mobility produced victims as well as criminals. Jack the Ripper murdered and mutilated prostitutes—women at the bottom of the social ladder. But prostitutes, of course, are not born into the trade. They each have some sort of background story—a childhood, a family, a series of life events. Theirs is a story of dislocation and economic privation—of downward mobility. Once many of them were part of the great migration from countryside or village to the city—from a small community to a new identity and life in the metropolis. There, they lost their way in a harsh environment, a world without a social safety net.

Victims of con men were a varied lot. The victim of the "badger game" was, perhaps, some poor soul who came to town as a tourist or on business. In their home community, they might have been the very picture of virtue. In the big, anonymous city, they could shed that identity and look for adventures impossible at home. Other victims were themselves morally dubious. There is an old saying: You can't cheat an honest man.[39] Some of the victims were looking for easy money, perhaps fraudulent money. In 1929, John B. St. Clair, a real estate broker from Massachusetts, fell in with men who said they were "connected with a horse racing syndicate." They told him they could teach him how to win big at the races—winning would be a sure thing. And indeed, it was. He won a great deal of money (he thought), just as the men had promised. But before paying up, they insisted on "evidence to show that he could have paid . . . had he lost." This seemed fair enough to him; he produced $40,000 and paid the men who promptly (of course) disappeared.[40]

According to a book on the confidence game by Edward H. Smith, published in 1923, mankind "likes to take a chance." People like to rebel "against workaday order and conservatism." To take a risk, "no matter how quixotic, is the color and thrill to light the drabness and dullness of life." People "who work hard for small pay" will spend money on lottery tickets or put a few dollars down on "the most outrageous gambles, the most impossible speculations." They bet on "oil wells in Timbuktu, pirates' treasure in the Caribbean, the hoard of the temple of Quetzalcohuatl, the gold dust from the loins of El Dorado."[41] The same psychic narcotic that animates confidence men intoxicates the victims too—the chance to shed an impoverished, niggling, miserable life, for a life of glamor and success. Other victims, like St. Clair, are successful men, who cannot resist the temptation to make a dubious killing. Both con men and their victims reject traditional ethical values, not to mention fatalism and acceptance of the status quo. For confidence men, the dishonesty of their victims is something of an insurance policy. If the scheme itself seems crooked or illegal, the victims may be unlikely to complain when it goes awry.

Today, the traditional village is at the opposite pole from the boiling complexity of big cities. But in immigrant countries, like the United States,

Australia, Canada, and Argentina, even "villages" and small towns were not ingrown, gossipy places, where everybody knew everybody else and everybody else's business. Outside of, say, old settlements in New England, American small towns in the nineteenth century were apt to be raw new places, full of strangers, full of people who came and went, Villages that grew up almost overnight, like mushrooms. In the 1830s and later, towns in Illinois, Montana, and California, places like Dodge City or Tombstone, were full of strangers, newcomers, and rolling stones lured by land or gold, and at the pale of settlement or communities of squatters on public lands. In these towns, nobody knew anything about you: what kind of family you came from, what sort of background you had before you arrived, what secrets lurked in your past. Personal identity in a town in Wyoming in the late nineteenth century was as problematic as identity in New York or Philadelphia, and just as prone to crime and pathology.

IMPOSTORS

The con man was, in a real sense, an impostor with a fraudulent identity. The confidence man flourished, as we saw, in the nineteenth century. In a few instances, there were impostors on a more sensational scale, grander than cheating a "mark" out of some cash.[42] In past periods there were, for example, "pretenders"—false claimants to the throne of some country. Conditions in the nineteenth century were fertile soil for impostors. One of the most famous was the so-called Tichborne claimant. Roger Tichborne, from an upper-class English family, was lost at sea in 1854 and declared dead. His grieving mother refused to accept the fact that he was dead. She clung to the hope that he had somehow survived and offered a reward for any information about his fate. A man appeared out of Wagga Wagga, in New South Wales, Australia, who claimed to be the lost Tichborne heir. His claim was far-fetched to say the least. A number of people were taken in by him. In particular, Roger's grieving mother desperately wanted to believe this was her son. The claimant was, in fact, one Arthur Orton, an impostor. He eventually went to prison for perjury. Still, even after his trial, some people refused to be convinced. They still thought Orton was the genuine article, that is, the real Roger Tichborne.[43]

A twentieth-century impostor of some note was a woman who claimed to be Anastasia, daughter of the last czar of Russia. The Soviets, during the Russian Revolution, had seized the royal family—Czar Nicholas, his wife, son, and daughters—and imprisoned them. In 1918, as civil war raged in Russia, the Bolshevik government decided it was dangerous to keep the royal family alive. They had the family murdered, and buried the bodies. Somehow, rumors arose that one of the daughters, Anastasia, had miraculously survived.

A number of women came forward claiming to be the lost princess. The most well-known was a woman who called herself Anna Anderson.[44] Her story was as far-fetched and as bogus as the Tichborne claim. She was apparently a Polish factory worker, perhaps mentally ill. Members of the czar's family never recognized her claim, but many people seemed eager to believe in "Anastasia," the princess who had dramatically escaped the fate of her family. At any rate, in 2018, DNA evidence showed, once and for all, that Anastasia was dead, and that Anna Anderson's story was pure fiction.

There is, of course, something romantic about the very idea of a Tichborne or an Anastasia coming out of the murk to claim their true identity—much more romantic than the idea that the claimant is a shameless impostor. A common theme in literature is equally romantic—the foundling who turns out to be an heir or even a prince or a princess. In Charles Dicken's *Nicholas Nickleby* (1839), for example, Smike, a sad and pathetic orphan, turns out in the end to be the heir of the rich miser, Ralph Nickleby. In *The Trail of the Serpent*, one of Mary Braddon's "sensation novels" (1861), the evil villain, who we first meet as a lowly clerk, schemes and murders his way into high society. He succeeds in becoming a nobleman (in France), by virtue of his connections, and marries a woman from the nobility. At the end of the book, we learn that he was in fact son and heir of a nobleman—but too late: he must pay for his crimes. Lost heirs, mysteries of paternity and maternity, people of ambiguous or misleading class or stratum are staples of nineteenth-century literature.

On the other hand, in Victorian literature, as in Victorian society in general, class and rank are assumed to be essential markers of identity. The gulf between true "gentlemen" and "ladies," on the one hand, and the rest of society on the other, is thought to be unbridgeable. Money and position, of course, are as important for the "gentleman" or the "lady." But behavior and attitude are also important, and so is "good breeding," which shows itself through manners, education, and deportment. Family also matters—whether one can trace family history back through the centuries. Still, many members of the elite believed in something else, something almost indefinable, which set "Thoroughbreds" apart from the common masses. Melmotte, the crooked and ambitious financier in Trollope's novel *The Way We Live Now*, seems to be enormously rich, but he is definitely not a gentleman. Nobody knew where he came from or was certain of his family background. In an age in which identity was muddled, in which impostors thrived, many elites continued to believe nobody could falsely pretend to be a "gentleman" or a "lady." It is this notion that Shaw tried to puncture in *Pygmalion.* And Trollope punctures it, too, in *The Way We Live Now*: the novel brilliantly satirizes the aristocrats who fawned on Melmotte when he was riding high. Money corrodes caste and class. In the end, Melmotte is revealed to be nothing more than a con man, committing crimes of mobility on a gigantic scale.

THE BIG HOUSE

As we have argued, identity in the modern world had become fluid, a quicksilver product. Relatively speaking, it is more like putty than concrete. People could change their identity more easily than before. They could leave the place they were born and move to a new city, a new country. They could sometimes take on a new persona. This could mean, of course, a fresh start, a new life, new opportunities. It could also, in some cases, mean a false and fraudulent identity. In either case, individuals were making these decisions for themselves. But society, or the state, could also try to *impose* a new persona. It was thought possible, and sometimes desirable, to reshape personality, to create a new self out of an old one.

This change had long been a goal of the criminal justice system.[45] In the English colonies like Massachusetts Bay, unlike today, imprisonment was not the main way to punish serious crime. Jails did exist, but they were for the most part ramshackle houses. Inmates were debtors who could not pay, or people accused of crimes awaiting trial. The system leaned heavily on bodily punishments—whipping, for the most part—and on stigma and shame: the stocks, the pillory, the "scarlet letter." Stigma and shame are *community* punishments. In colonial times, they were also *public* punishments. The whipping post was public, and so was the gallows. Punishment was, in a very real sense, didactic theater. The point was to teach moral lessons to the offender and also to the community at large. This was even true—perhaps especially true—of hangings. The person hanged is, of course, beyond redemption; but the audience is not. The community can still learn the straight and narrow way, can still avoid the fate of the person in the shadow of the gallows. Hangings took place in full view of the townspeople—in the public square. Sometimes the condemned man or woman even made a speech from the gallows, explaining that person's dismal journey through life, and warning the audience to avoid descent into crime and eternal punishment.

Thus, in the colonial period, the community was part of the solution, not part of the problem. Shaming and stigma can be effective strategies in small, face-to-face communities, where people know each other, and where lines of authority are clear and well accepted. But by the nineteenth century, the old system had lost much of its bite. In a mobile society, a society of cities and strangers, the old techniques do not work. Cities were, in the first place, breeding grounds of idleness, intemperance—and crime. They were also large and anonymous. Public shaming fell into (comparative) disuse. In a mobile society, people can move from place to place, can escape their neighbors, can put a shameful past behind them. In the cities, public hangings no longer served as didactic theater. Respectable citizens, on the contrary, saw them as barbarous spectacles, lurid events that incited the blood lust of the urban mob. New institutions and systems were needed.

In the nineteenth century, imprisonment became the dominant form of punishment. The penitentiary replaced the whipping post, and to an extent, the gallows. The new American penitentiaries, like New York's Sing Sing, and Eastern State in Philadelphia, were huge, walled citadels of punishment. Prisoners lived in individual cells; guards patrolled the perimeter of the prison. Inside the penitentiary, prisoners led lives of total regimentation. They were stripped of their old identities and reduced to a common mass. They dressed in drab uniforms, ate coarse food, and walked in lockstep. The rhythm of the day was the same for everyone, a kind of sullen regularity. Prisoners were not allowed to talk to each other. The interior of the prison was as soundless as the grave. It was a world of complete isolation, totally cut off from the world outside the walls. As the term "penitentiary" suggests, the point was penitence. Prisoners were to be reformed and reshaped. Prison would wipe out their old identity and create, through radical means, a new one with new habits, a new personality, and a new and better character. At least this was the theory.

What prison life was actually like, and what it accomplished, was far distant from what theory suggested. The classic penitentiary was soon forced to compromise with reality. Penitentiaries were expensive. Solitary confinement made them even more expensive, and the states were not always willing to pay. Once prisoners were doubled up in cells, the silent system became impossible. Still, the theory tells us something about society and its social norms. The penitentiary reflected, above all, a nineteenth-century panic among respectable elites, leading citizens. It was as if they asked: What have we done to ourselves? The penitentiary suggests a social order that had turned the colonial system of justice upside down. Migration, city life, mobility, and the identity crisis had given rise to a crisis in criminal justice.

A similar ethos led to a change in the system of welfare. Welfare (poor relief) had traditionally been strictly local—each community took care of its own. The basic contours of the poor law system dated back to the reign of Elizabeth I. The English poor law system was transplanted to the American colonies as well. But in a mobile society, the old system—neighbors responsible for neighbors, local communities responsible for local communities—no longer seemed adequate. State after state shifted poor relief from so-called outdoor relief to indoor relief. Outdoor relief (the term is misleading) meant relief delivered to the poor in their own huts and houses. Indoor relief meant relief given only in an institution: a poorhouse or poor farm. A "pauper" (the term is significant) who needed food, shelter, and medical care (such as it was) had to move into the local poorhouse or poor farm in order to get any help. These institutions became warehouses for the old, the sick, for impoverished families, and the mentally ill. They were as highly regimented as prisons, and perhaps just as degrading.

Again, the mobile society was at the root of the problem. Outdoor relief meant helping out local people who had fallen on hard times. These were people who had spent their whole lives in the community. The poorhouse was a place where strangers could be housed. The system was still local in the financial sense: local communities had to pay for the poor out of local tax money. This meant that strangers who were, or might be, "paupers" were expensive, and distinctly unwelcome. When such people appeared at the borders of the community, they could be (under the law) "warned out," that is, simply ordered to get out of town as soon as possible. They were not allowed to take up residence. And if "paupers" did not go on their own, they could be physically removed and dumped over the boundary line of township or county.

The nineteenth century was also particularly harsh in its attitude toward "tramps," "hobos," and "bums," that is, rolling stones, the driftwood of a mobile society. These were deracinated people (mostly men) who had lost membership in a group, a family, a clan—those without normal, respectable identities. States enacted laws aimed at curbing and punishing "vagrants," a term often vaguely and loosely defined. These laws gave local authorities weapons to use against the floating population. A tramp found guilty of "vagrancy" could be locked up in jail or, even worse, chased out of town (even though the statutes did not mention actual banishment). In Wisconsin, for example, in the late nineteenth century, vagrants were defined as, among other things, "idle persons who, not having visible means to maintain themselves, live without employment," persons wandering about and lodging in "sheds or barns, or in the open air, and not giving a good account of themselves" and all "lewd, wanton, lascivious" people; vagrants could be jailed, or sent to the poorhouse, to work at "hard labor" for up to six months. In Wisconsin, too, if a male over sixteen fit the definition of a vagrant, and was not an actual "inhabitant" of the town he was living in, he could be labeled a "tramp" and jailed at hard labor.[46] In Rhode Island, jail sentences—six months to three years—could be imposed on "idle" people who were "of doubtful reputation" and had no "visible means of support" and also on every "sturdy beggar" who was asking for charity, along with every "common cheat, vagrant, or disorderly person."[47]

Mobility meant opportunity—a ladder to climb, a chance for a new life and success. But success was never guaranteed. Not everybody climbs the ladder in the first place, and of those who do, some slip and fall back to where they started from or even further into the dark pit of poverty and ruin. The poorhouse and the antivagrant laws were living monuments to American failure. Failure was always a dark and shadowy possibility. Life itself was insecure. Recurrent plagues of incurable diseases ravaged the country. Death was a constant presence. The economy was insecure. There was no welfare state. The blurring of identity only increased social insecurity. The American ideology preached that success came from hard work, from honest effort. Hence, idleness was more than a sin, it was a crime. The "sturdy beggar," the pauper, the tramp, were threats to the American system.

AWAKENINGS

The vast sense of insecurity in the country—the crisis of personal identity—was one source, perhaps, of a notable flight into religion. Waves of religious zeal swept over the country from time to time. Americans are a religious people, compared to other developed countries.[48] And religious ferment is a strong feature of American life—more so than in most other developed countries. Historians speak of episodes of religious fervor as "Great Awakenings." The first (in both England and the colonies) took place in the mid-eighteenth century. Another period of religious zeal, the so-called Second Great Awakening, took place in the early nineteenth century. These were complex movements, with complex roots, but thousands were touched by the new light—men and women with a deep consciousness of sin and worried about the state of their souls.

These were "revivalist" movements. Old religious denominations were "revived," in other words infused with new enthusiasm, new bursts of deep faith. But America was also the birthplace of a cluster of new religions. One of the most notable was The Church of Jesus Christ of Latter-day Saints (the Mormons), founded by Joseph Smith in the first half of the nineteenth century. Christian Science, a religion which rejected modern medicine, owed its prominence to Mary Baker Eddy who published her key work, *Science and Health with Key to the Scriptures,* in 1874. Its "mother church" was built in 1894; by 1936, Christian Science claimed some 270,000 members. Another new religion, also dating from the late nineteenth century, was Jehovah's Witnesses. Another was the Seventh-Day Adventists, a religion that can be traced to 1863. Over the years, conservative, charismatic, and "evangelical" Protestant denominations have steadily gained in popularity, often at the expense of older and more traditional churches. The new churches, in particular the Mormons, actively recruit new members. Missionary work is a requirement for young Mormons. The "evangelical" Protestant denominations also show a lot of missionary zeal; they have, and had, a strong impact in the United States; they have also made great inroads into Latin America, in countries traditionally Catholic.

Those who return to religion, who leave their old faiths, or who had no particular religion before, often describe themselves as "born again" Christians. The phrase is significant. A person who is "born again" has become something new and different, has taken on a new identity, and is conscious of this change. The tens of thousands who embraced the Mormon faith, or who became Christian Scientists, Jehovah's Witnesses, or Seventh Day Adventists, are also, in a way, "born again," whether or not they describe themselves this way.[49] Converts and new enthusiasts embark on a new life, redeemed from the old one. Each "born again" Christian has, no doubt, a unique story. But the social context is also relevant: the world in which they find themselves, a world which is somehow deeply unsatisfying. They may be renouncing a life of drunkenness, debauchery, or crime. For others, their sin was hidden and internal—guilt about the deficiencies of the inner self—almost as if they harbored, hidden from view, an inner Mr. Hyde, a secret identity that was warped and rotten.

People often draw a line between religions and cults, but "cult" is not a precise term, it simply means an unpopular religion, one that the majority refuses to accept, a weed in the garden of religion. What began as a cult can evolve, socially speaking, into a recognized and respected religion. Most Americans considered the Mormons—The Latter-day Saints—an odious cult in the early days of its history. Mormons met with intense hatred and persecution, even violence. Mormon groups were driven from place to place. An angry mob murdered the founder of the religion, Joseph Smith, and his brother.[50] Brigham Young then led the faithful on a long journey to what is now Utah, beyond the reach of the "gentiles." There, they founded a city and proceeded to govern themselves. Formally, however, this promised land was a territory of the United States. They had not escaped the scorn of other Americans. Persecution, legal and nonlegal, continued. One tenet of the church was a particular source of horror and outrage: polygamy. According to the founder, Joseph Smith, a "revelation" in 1843 imposed a doctrine of "celestial marriage." On the authority of this "revelation," Mormon leaders took many wives, and indeed insisted this was a religious duty. The practice evoked extraordinary revulsion throughout the country. The federal government acted. It passed laws and made arrests in order to destroy the power of the church. In the late nineteenth century, the church renounced polygamy.[51] In the years since, the church has thrived in Utah, in surrounding states, and elsewhere. Today, it is an established, recognized, and respected church. In 2012, the Republican Party nominated a Mormon, Mitt Romney, as its presidential candidate. The missionary work continues. Worldwide, the church has millions of members. At home, they have become part of the American mainstream.

The story of the Mormons in America, complicated though it is, is among other things a story of convergence and assimilation. A once deviant group, marginal, isolated, and despised, is today a normal and accepted religion. Most members of its community were born into the church, but others are converts who represent the restless element in modern society, those who are looking for change, for something new, for a more satisfying identity. Today, in all established churches, there is considerable ferment. Members enter by one door and leave by another. A shifting, kaleidoscopic search for religious identity, for spiritual meaning, is a big factor in American life, and in other societies as well. We will take up this theme, and what it means for personal identity, in a later chapter.

Chapter 4

White Lies

Ernest Torregano was born in New Orleans, Louisiana, in the late nineteenth century.[1] His family was African American. Ernest was light-skinned. Socially and legally, however, he was classified as Black in the state of Louisiana. He married a Black woman and produced a daughter, Gladys. Ernest got a job as a Pullman porter—an occupation open to African Americans (indeed, most porters came from this community). At some point, Ernest pulled up his stakes and moved to San Francisco, where he passed for White. He went to law school and became a member of the California bar. One day, his mother came to visit him and told a tragic story: his wife and daughter were dead, carried off by disease. This was simply a lie. His mother went back to New Orleans and told the wife and daughter that *Ernest* was dead—another lie, of course. Why would she tell these stories? Most likely, she wanted to protect Ernest's new identity, and prevent his past from catching up with him. Years went by. Ernest remarried, but the new marriage was childless. After he died, the truth finally came out. Gladys Torregano somehow discovered that the father she thought was dead all those years had really been alive and practicing law in San Francisco. Now, however, he had in fact died. Gladys filed a claim against his estate. Ernest's will (naturally) made no provision for the daughter he thought was dead. In fact, it specifically stated that he had no children and gave a nominal amount (one dollar) to anyone who claimed a relationship to him (this was a common clause in wills at that time). In the end, Gladys won her case, despite the specific wording of the will. But she had to fight all the way up to the Supreme Court of California before it was finally decided.[2]

The story of the TorreganoS has a certain soap-opera quality to it, but "passing," the behavior that underlay the case, was by no means rare. During the time of slavery, White masters and overseers notoriously took advantage of female slaves. Children born to these women were legally defined as slaves. Their White fathers, with some exceptions, paid little or no attention to them. The children, of course, were half White. These births continued for years, so in the end, slaves on some plantations were only one-eighth Black, or one-sixteenth, or even less. These slaves looked White and could easily "pass," which some of them eventually did—if they had the chance. This was true, for example, of some of the slave children of Thomas Jefferson, third president of the United States. Jefferson, a widower, had a long-term relationship with a slave named Sally Hemings. No images of Hemings exist, but she was obviously light-skinned—she was, in fact, the daughter of Jefferson's former father-in-law, John Wayles, who had many children by a slave woman, Elizabeth Hemings. Elizabeth (Sally's mother) was herself half White—her father was a ship captain, and her mother was a slave.[3] Sally, then, was at most one-quarter Black and her children with Jefferson at most one-eighth. When Jefferson set free his children by Sally Hemings, his son Beverly passed for White and married a White woman in Maryland. Jefferson's daughter Harriet married a White man in Washington. She, too, slipped easily into the White people's world. According to the memoirs of her brother Madison, she and her family "were never suspected of being tainted with African blood" in the community they lived in.[4] In Mark Twain's classic novel, *Pudd'nhead Wilson* (1894), a slave and her master's wife both gave birth. Somehow, the two babies change places. The slave grows up thinking of himself as a master and the master's baby grows up thinking of himself as a slave. Clearly, this plot would make no sense, unless there were many slaves by the middle of the nineteenth century whose skin was light enough for them to pass for White—slaves who could lay claim to a White identity.[5]

"Passing" was not a crime, but like crimes of mobility, it depended on social mobility, on a context in which people moved from place to place and could move up and down the invisible social ladder. A former slave, or a light-skinned Black, had to change physical locations in order to pass. Slaves had no way to pass on the plantation; everybody there knew who they were. Jefferson's children with Hemings had to wait until they were set free and could move away from the plantation before they could successfully pass. The story of the Healy family is another vivid example of the prevalence of "passing." Michael Morris Healy was an immigrant from Ireland. He settled in Georgia before the Civil War. He entered into a long-term relationship with one of his slaves, Eliza Clark Healy. Together they had nine children. Healy sent his children north to be educated in Catholic schools, and incidentally, to pass for White, which some of them (not all) succeeded in doing. Two of Healy's daughters became nuns. One son became a ship captain. Two sons became priests. One of them rose high in the ranks of the church and eventually became Catholic bishop of Portland, Maine. The other priest became president of Georgetown University in Washington, DC, a Catholic institution. Few people knew the secret of their birth. Revealing it would surely have cost them their positions. The ranks they achieved were reserved for Whites only, even in Roman Catholic circles.[6]

Passing was perhaps peculiar to societies like the United States, with its jagged line between Black and White. Many people straddled the line: on one side whiteness meant a privileged identity and an open door into respectable society; on the other side was subordination, a life subject to insult, segregation, and worse—poverty, and, in extreme cases, death at the hands of lynch mobs. Ernest Torregano crossed over the line and became a lawyer, an honored member of San Francisco society. Before that, he had been Ernest Torregano, a Pullman porter on interstate trains, with no chance of rising in society. Father Healy, distinguished head of a Catholic university, had once been a slave and the son of a slave. The contrasts were stark and pronounced. But passing was also, as Allyson Hobbs points out, a kind of "exile."[7] The Ernest Torreganos of the country, to preserve their new identity, had to say goodbye in effect to friends and family, wiping out their childhood and all its memories; they had to pass through a kind of looking glass into a different world.

Passing was also fraught with danger long into the twentieth century. People who passed could never be sure that their secret was safe. According to one account, in the 1890s two "mullato clerks" managed to get jobs that had been reserved for Whites because they were "passing." When "their colored wives would come to bring them lunch" they had to pretend the women were "servant girls."[8] If the truth had come out, they would have been fired. As long as virulent racism was epidemic in American society, betrayal of someone who was passing could lead to serious consequences. A Black man "outed" a woman who worked at Mandel Brothers, a department store in Chicago. She lost her job. She went to work for another company and again, someone told her employer that she was Black; she was asked to resign.[9] In 1945, years before integration reached the University of Mississippi, Harry Murphy, who was African American, entered the university, passing for White.[10] If his secret had come out, there would have been hell to pay at Ole Miss. Fortunately for Murphy, nobody discovered his hidden identity.

People who passed were hiding their background. Sometimes, when they formed families, they kept their past status secret. In many states interracial marriage was forbidden. For someone passing, a new marriage (to a White person) might even be a crime and the marriage itself would be void. But many people did cross the line; and in time, for some families, all memory of a Black heritage might disappear. Daniel Sharfstein has chronicled three such families: the Gibsons, Spencers, and Walls. Hart Gibson, writing in the 1890s, expressed the belief that Blacks in the United States could never compete with Whites, would always be inferior, and should be sent back to the Congo. Yet Gibson himself had a Black ancestor—a fact he was totally unaware of.[11]

Probably thousands of Americans, especially in the South, had some amount of African ancestry.

A White person, conceivably, could also pass, that is, pretend to be a light-skinned Black. But to do so would have grave social consequences. This behavior was surely rare. The most prominent case of reverse passing, perhaps, was that of Clarence King (1842–1901), geologist, explorer, and author—a man who could, and did, dine at the White House on occasion, a prominent scholar, a man with powerful friends in high places. Yet King had another secret life. He had fallen in love with a Black woman, Ada Copeland. They married and had children. King told Ada his name was James Todd; he claimed to be a light-skinned Black. He told her that he was a Pullman porter—a job that explained why he was so often away from home. Only when King lay dying did he tell his wife the truth.[12]

Mobility made passing possible; "passing" also reflected the strange and extreme definition of race in American law and in American social customs. Local records, for much of American history, were weak and incomplete. This made it difficult at times, especially in the South, to know whether a man or woman was "really" White or "really" Black. The answer to this question was vitally important: it affected inheritance claims, life-situations, even freedom itself. Courts were sometimes asked to resolve this issue.[13] How a person looked was important though not crucial, since many Black people looked White and many White people looked a bit dark—perhaps they had a dash of American Indian blood or were of Portuguese descent (a common claim). More significant was behavior, including social behavior: Who did people or their families associate with? What church did they go to? Who were their friends? Did they *act* White? In the 1840s, one celebrated case concerned a woman who called herself Sally Miller. Was she White? Yes, according to her lawyer. He referred to her "perseverance," her "good conduct," her "quiet and constant industry," all of which showed, he felt, that "there is nothing of the African about her."[14]

COURTSHIP AND MARRIAGE

Another issue that turned on race was the right to interracial marriage. Well into the twentieth century, many states (as we mentioned) prohibited marriage between Whites and Blacks. Some states went even further. In 1866, a law in Oregon outlawed any marriage between a "white person" and "any negro, Chinese, or any person having one fourth or more negro, Chinese, or kanaka blood, or any person having more than one half Indian blood." A marriage that violated the statute was not only illegal, but was also, as a marriage, "absolutely null and void."[15] In 1939, in a trial in California, the issue was whether Marie Antoinette Monks had rights to the estate of her late, rich husband, Allan Monks. She supposedly told Monks she was a French countess. The wedding took place in Arizona, a state where interracial marriages were illegal. Allan Monks was White. But what race was Marie Antoinette Monks? Was she a "Negro" or not? Her hairdresser said she was, by virtue of the "size of the moons of her fingernails," the "ring" around the palms of her hands, and her "kinky" hair. A physical anthropologist also mentioned her "protruding heels" and a surgeon brought up the "contour of her calves and heels" and the "peculiar pallor on the back of her neck." There was also vigorous testimony for the defense. But in the end, the judge ruled against Ms. Monks. She was "one-eighth negro" thus her marriage was a violation of the law of Arizona. Moreover, by telling her fiancé she was French, she had committed a serious fraud—enough in itself to make the marriage void.[16]

Racial identity was also an issue in a famous case in the 1920s, this time in New York, rather than the Deep South or the West. Leonard Rhinelander ("Kip" was his nickname) came from an old, rich, and distinguished family. He was listed in the *Social Register.* Kip met a woman named Alice Jones. She was dark and pretty. Her background was entirely different from his—her father was a taxi driver. Alice and Kip began an affair, which was kept a secret at first, but Kip's family found out and packed him off on a six-month cruise. Nonetheless, when Kip came back, he married Alice. The Rhinelander family was bitterly opposed to the marriage. They hired detectives to find out more about Alice's background and put enormous pressure on Kip to end the marriage. Under family influence, Kip left his wife. He went to court and asked for an annulment. But on what basis? Alice, he said, had hidden her real identity: she was a woman of color. Hence, the marriage had been tainted from the outset with fraud. The Rhinelander trial was something of a sensation. It made front-page news and the courtroom was packed every day. At one point, Alice had to take her clothes off in front of the jury to give them a closer look at her body: Did she seem to be Black or White? In the end, Rhinelander lost the case. The jury decided against him. The marriage remained valid. Alice Jones was Kip's legal wife. Very likely, the jury did think Alice was a woman of mixed race; she practically admitted as much, and members of her family were obviously Black. But for Kip to get an annulment, he had to show fraud on her part; he had to show that she had deceived him. On this point, the jurors were probably unconvinced. They may have suspected that Kip knew his wife's racial identity from the start; that it was never hidden from him. But though Alice won the case, the two never lived together again.[17]

The Rhinelander marriage crossed class as well as race lines. Such a marriage was never illegal, but it was frowned on by society. To be sure, occasionally in Victorian England, some rich, well-born man actually married a woman in domestic service; once in a while a rich, well-born woman eloped with a footman or a groom. Such marriages scandalized polite society.[18] More common, of course, were well-born men who kept mistresses, or who had long-term relationships with women who were lower on the social scale.[19] In the United States, too, marriages across lines of class, race, and ethnicity were once uncommon. The same for marriages across religious lines: Jews marrying Gentiles, Protestants marrying Catholics, agnostics marrying the devout. Like tended to marry like. But over time the pull of inherited race, religion, and ethnic identity weakened. Mobility and other factors allowed men (and some women) to pry themselves loose from their inherited status. Inherited identity blurred. This opened the door to a wider menu of marriage choices. In traditional societies, marriages were in a sense, family affairs: almost treaties and compacts between families. In nineteenth-century literature, it was taken for granted that a man and a woman could not marry without the consent of their families (chiefly the fathers). By the late twentieth century, this kind of filial piety was close to extinction. Free choice of marriage partners replaced marriages within a narrow, family-dominated circle. Of course, romantic love as the basis for marriage was an old theme, both in literature and life. Romeo and Juliet, for example, were passionately in love. Their love was star-crossed precisely because it violated the wishes of their families.

In the period of the civil rights movement, laws against interracial marriage began to vanish from the statute books. In 1948, in *Perez v. Sharp*, the Supreme Court of California struck down the California law against miscegenation.[20] These laws survived longest (no surprise) in the South and in border states. The Supreme Court, however, in *Loving v. Virginia* (1967)[21] finally put an end to all laws against interracial marriage. Richard, a White man, and Mildred, an African American woman, had gotten married in the District of Columbia, where such marriages were legal. But they were Virginians. When they returned to Virginia, and lived together as husband and wife, they were tried and convicted for violating Virginia law and sentenced to prison. In a unanimous decision, the United States Supreme Court reversed the decision and declared all such laws unconstitutional.

Marriages across racial, religious, and ethnic lines reject the inherited identity of both partners. The partners abandon the pull of their own tribe, clan, race, or system of belief. In a way, they abandon their very backgrounds. They choose, in a sense, a new identity. Over time, this became more and more possible, then acceptable; the law followed the changes in social norms and practices. In the late twentieth century, and into the twenty-first, the element of personal choice, in marriage, and in ways of life, has assumed greater and greater importance. This means that individuals are allowed to choose (in some ways) the very markers of personal identity. We will return to this subject in a later chapter.

PASSING: HERITAGE AND FAITH

Passing as White is only one of many forms of passing. Everyone is in some way passing; is in some way presenting to the outside world an image which a person deliberately works at and shapes. But passing is a deeper necessity for those who want to hide, or need to hide, a disfavored or dangerous identity. Faith is a key form of personal identity, but if the faith is unpopular, or is considered a "cult," or (worst of all) heresy or apostasy, passing can be a form of self-protection. In Nazi Germany, during World War II, to be Jewish was virtually a sentence of death. In occupied Poland, the Netherlands, the Baltics—in every country under the heel of the Third Reich—the Nazis and their local allies murdered every Jew they could lay their hands on, including women and children. A small number of Jews escaped, temporarily or permanently, by going into hiding (Anne Frank is the most famous example). Some Jewish children, harbored by Gentile families, were passed off as Christian. In the United States, passing for Christian was never a matter of life or death, but it could, in the past at least, open certain doors that were otherwise closed—doors to jobs, to certain towns or neighborhoods, to certain schools and professions.

Religious passing has a history that goes back much further. In the Middle Ages, Jews and heretics were persecuted, and sometimes killed. In fifteenth-century Spain, King Ferdinand and Queen Isabella offered the large Jewish community a choice: convert or leave the country. Thousands of Jews left Spain. Those who elected to stay converted to Catholicism: the key to survival. Some of these "conversos" became sincerely Catholic; others secretly kept the faith of their fathers. Conversos ran the risk of falling afoul of the dreaded Inquisition. It was not always easy to tell who was a crypto-Jew, and who was not. As one seventeenth-century document put it, if people did not work on the (Jewish) Sabbath, if they "deveined the meat they are preparing to eat, soaking it in water to remove the blood," if they removed "the sciatic vein from a leg of mutton," or celebrated "the Festival of unleavened bread, beginning by eating lettuce, celery or other bitter herbs" they were demonstrating that they were not truly Christian.[22]

Most conversos were not found out. Indeed, over the generations, many of these families, in Europe and in the Americas, tended to assimilate, and to take seriously their Catholic faith. But even some of these families preserved practices that were essentially or historically Jewish, perhaps without realizing that these were not simply family customs. One woman, in Mexico, recalled that her "grandmother lit the candles on Friday night, and she never ate pork."[23] In recent years, in a more tolerant age, a few of the descendants of conversos have returned to their ancestral religion; most, no doubt, simply see it as an interesting aspect of their family history.

For decades in the United States, many Chinese in America indulged in a form of passing—they passed for citizens. In the late nineteenth century, the Chinese suffered from virulent discrimination, especially on the West Coast. From the late nineteenth century on, Congress enacted a series of laws directed against the Chinese. With some exceptions, no Chinese would be allowed to enter the United States and no Chinese was allowed to become a naturalized citizen. But under the Fourteenth Amendment, anyone born in the United States is automatically a citizen—the Supreme Court said as much in 1898.[24] A traveler from China arriving in San Francisco harbor, who claimed to be a citizen by birth, could not legally be excluded. In practice, the authorities were skeptical of travelers who made this claim. They felt Chinese people at the gates of the country were simply telling lies. In fact, many of the stories *were* lies—travelers showed birth certificates that were not really theirs or told false stories about documents destroyed in the San Francisco earthquake and fire of 1906. Papers that belonged to citizens were sold in China to people who wanted to enter the United States. The immigrants who bought these papers or told these lies were, in short, passing for citizens. If they were successful, they had to live the rest of their lives pretending to be somebody else; they had to keep on passing as members of somebody else's family, claiming an identity that did not belong to them.[25]

Today in the United States, millions of men, women, and children live in limbo as undocumented aliens with no legal right to stay in the country. One estimate claims that there are as many as eleven million noncitizens living in the United States, most (but by no means all) coming from Mexico and Central America. Many others have entered legally on tourist or student visas and simply stayed on after the visas expired—people from Ireland, Thailand, Africa. Others somehow have slipped across the southern border undetected. Meanwhile, once in the country, they pass. They live and work in the United States. They drive cars, rent apartments, shop in stores. They marry and have children (who are citizens by birth). How to deal with the undocumented has become a burning political issue: one that divides the country into bitterly opposed factions. The status of these millions is extremely insecure. They live in fear of immigration authorities. Thousands have been deported either because they have committed crimes or because their luck ran out, and government agents, trawling through neighborhoods, caught them in their nets.

The "dreamers" are a special case. These are young people whose parents brought them to the United States when they were children. Many of them have no experience of life outside the United States. Nonetheless, they have no legal status and are subject to deportation. The Obama administration overlooked their status and allowed them to stay, work, and receive an education. The Trump administration reversed this policy and called on Congress to act. No action was taken. And as of this writing, though the Biden administration has been sympathetic, no decisive action to legalize the status of the "dreamers" has been taken. They continue to live and work freely, but in a kind of limbo.

The mobile society has worked in favor of people who passed, including light-skinned Blacks in the age of segregation, Jews hiding from Nazis, as well as people today who are passing as citizens. Most were mobile in a literal sense: they left old locations for new ones and took on a new identity. The conversos were an exception: they passed by staying where they were, taking on a new identity in their homeland. All the men and women who passed did, however, take advantage of a kind of psychological or social mobility: they were able to pretend to be something they were (in some sense) not. It takes talent to play Hamlet convincingly on the stage, but people who pass have learned to play a part off-stage. They have learned how to cross the invisible lines of culture, speech, behavior, race, or ethnicity.

PASSING FOR HEALTHY

If you ask people who they really are, and what their true identity might be, they might find it hard to answer. The gulf between (say) Jekyll and Hyde is stark and extreme. But there are many gradations and nuances in between, just as there are between honesty and criminality, men and women, and other forms of identity. Nature makes us who and what we are—or so it seems—and for most of us male and female seems something completely fixed, something that cannot be undone, something we do not want to be undone. Yet more and more one learns that gender is not as binary as most people think. Probably it was always true that some born (apparently) male think this was some kind of mistake; and some who are born (apparently) female also suffer from a sense that nature got it wrong. Today, hormones and the surgeon's knife can alter gender; but this was not possible in the past.

Gay and straight are also two ends of a continuum. At a time when same-sex behavior was the "love that dare not speak its name," when vice squads prowled the streets, when sodomy was a crime, gay people had to walk carefully through life. Many hid their sexual identities and passed for straight (more on this later). Cross-dressers and drag artists do not fool anybody, or try to. But this was not the case with Billy Tipton, a well-known jazz musician who was assigned female at birth but began presenting as Billy by the mid 1930s. Whether it was to succeed in the world of jazz, which was heavily male, or simply a personal preference, he took on a male identity. He married and, as a man, had sex in total darkness, using an artificial penis.

Apparently, his sex partners were also "in the dark." At least so they said. Billy adopted three boys who considered him their father. When he died in 1989, his secret was finally exposed. A French diplomat in China, Bernard Boursicot, lived for years with one Shi Pei Pu, a male who performed female roles in performances. Shi Pei Pu posed (successfully, it seems) as a woman. He and Boursicot, like Billy Tipton, had sexual relations of some sort. Shi Pei Pu even pretended to become pregnant and give birth. He also turned Boursicot into a spy, which led to Boursicot's undoing.[26]

In traditional society, gender identity was more firmly fixed. Everybody in town knew your gender, or what it was supposed to be. Here, too, social and geographic mobility made a fundamental difference. Billy Tipton emerged from the cocoon of birth only when Tipton changed communities, when he moved to a place where nobody knew him. Billy also crossed *social* lines—lines that defined what women do and are supposed to do. In the nineteenth century that line was comparatively firm. Women were not allowed to play a man's role in politics and only rarely in business or the arts. In the United States, no woman before the 1860s could, or did, practice law. Occasionally, a woman could break through barriers that defined a woman's "sphere."

Today, in the developed world, women vote, hold office, and legally can do whatever men are authorized to do. They can be police officers, pilots, brain surgeons, major league umpires, secretaries of state, and heads of government. The United States Constitution has been interpreted to require legal equality of the sexes. The founders, and the men who drafted the Fourteenth Amendment, never imagined a world with a woman as vice president or secretary of state, or for that matter as a member of a jury. Of course, this is not only a legal transformation, it is a cultural transformation. Since the 1870s or so, women have been able to study law and become members of the bar. But few of them did so, at the time. What changed most dramatically was a sense of personal identity and the magic of social mobility. A woman, more and more, can change her *social* space; can escape from her separate sphere. Women now make up half of all law students. They are a slight majority of medical students and a clear majority in veterinary school. They lag behind in dental school, but their numbers are growing steadily.

Arguably, Billy did nobody any harm—except perhaps to the women he lived with and deceived. There can be real harm, however, when people hide an infectious disease from the rest of the world. Especially if he (and it is usually a man) hides a disease that he could pass on to sexual partners (more on this later). Each of us has a genetic and medical identity. Scientists have peeled away more and more of the secrets of human genetics. Is it wrong to suppress a medical identity? Suppose you discover that your genes condemn you to disease, dementia, or early death: Do you have a duty to tell people? Should a potential sex or marriage partner know? If you apply for a job or an insurance policy, how much do you have to reveal? Is it wrong to "pass" for healthy?

Today, many of these questions have no definitive answer. Here, science can blur the issue of human identity. Inside Dr. Jekyll a genetic Mr. Hyde may be lurking—not a hidden stratum of evil, but a stratum of dangerous disease. Today, social norms tend to exalt personal choice, but many choices can, and do, affect the people around us. Sexual choice can collide with another crucial concept of the day: informed consent. Worldwide, during the pandemic of the 2020s, controversy raged over the right to resist vaccination and the right to refuse to wear a mask. COVID-19 is like all such pathogens, microscopic and invisible. The person you pass on the street may be a deadly carrier, the medical equivalent of Mr. Hyde.

SPIES AND MOLES

A popular form of fiction is the spy novel. Its popularity dates from the late nineteenth century, though earlier examples can probably be found. The spy, unlike the detective, practices a profession with a long history. Spies are even mentioned in the Bible. Medieval and Renaissance rulers had spies who reported to them about conditions and situations in foreign countries. Spy novels came into their own in a period in which real spies had become more important. Eric Ambler (1909–1998) was one of the most significant writers of spy novels. His first novel—probably his most well-known—*A Coffin for Demetrios*, was published in 1939. An earlier example was *The Scarlet Pimpernel* (1905) by Baroness Orczy. The novel is set during the time of the French Revolution. The main character, Sir Percy Blakeney, presents himself as a fop, a mindless fool. In France, the guillotine is devouring its victims, among them members of the French nobility. The daring exploits of the notorious "Scarlet Pimpernel" rescues many lives. Nobody knows the hero's real identity. In fact, it is Sir Percy himself. Who could have guessed that Sir Percy was a bold and notorious spy? His success depended on his ability to play a part, to fool the world about his true identity. In short, the spy novel, like the detective novel, depends on the hidden self.

Sir Percy was fictional. Some real-world spies—for example, the notorious Cambridge Five, who spied on England in the service of the Soviet Union—were like Sir Percy, men of culture and social position—men who seemed unlikely traitors. The spies who spied *for* England and against the Soviet Union also lived double lives. Spies are men and women who are passing as patriotic citizens. They are living a dangerous lie, and one with high stakes. The punishment, especially in wartime, can be death. From the nineteenth century on there were critical "advances" in the technology of war. To learn an enemy's secret plans, or to find out what weapons an enemy was developing, might make the difference between victory and defeat.[27]

Spies lead perilous and precarious lives. Every spy is, almost by definition, a person with a double identity, both Jekyll and Hyde. No spy is more dangerous than the so-called mole. Moles are spies who have burrowed their way into a high government position, which they can then exploit on behalf of a foreign power. Moles are favorites of spy fiction, most notably in the work of John le Carré (born David Cornwell). Le Carré may be responsible for the term "mole" itself, or at least for making it popular. In *Tinker Tailor Soldier Spy* (1974), the main character, George Smiley, searches for a mole who has wormed his way into the highest circles of British intelligence. Like the Scarlet Pimpernel, the mole's success, like the success of all spies, depends on his ability to deceive the world about his true identity. Oleg Gordievsky, high up in the Soviet Union's KGB, was in fact an agent for the British—he passed important secrets and inside information to Western allies. His story has been called "the greatest espionage story of the cold war."[28] There are also double agents, spies who work both sides, take money from both sides, and perhaps fool both of their foreign contacts.

In the period of the Cold War, the threat of Soviet espionage became a major political issue in the United States. Left-wing groups, and the local Communist Party, were objects of suspicion. But those who were secretly spying for the Soviets, cloaking their activities, were thought to be more dangerous than those who were overtly pro-Soviet. One of the most sensational trials of the 1950s was the trial of Julius and Ethel Rosenberg, accused of giving atomic secrets to the Soviets. The Rosenbergs were convicted and sentenced to die in the electric chair. Despite a huge national and international campaign to save them, they were put to death in 1953. The Cambridge Five in England were eventually exposed—at least two of them fled to Russia and avoided prosecution. In the United States, Aldrich Ames, a CIA agent with access to important secrets, spied for the Soviet Union (he was perhaps the man who betrayed Oleg Gordievsky). Ames was convicted of espionage in 1994 and sentenced to life imprisonment. In fact, every major power tries to spy on other countries, even friendly countries. Every major power is in turn itself spied upon.

Spying is serious business. "Intelligence" is a major function of wartime government, and peacetime politics. Most "spying" goes on quietly. Not all of it is cloak-and-dagger material. Today, there are all sorts of tools the intelligence community can use, gathered through satellites, wire-tapping, and even from reading newspapers and other public documents. All this probably far outweighs the use of actual human spies who do the sort of work that lights up the pages of spy novels. And even some of the human spying, by actual agents, can be fairly humdrum. In 2010, Americans learned that a pair of Russian spies had been unmasked, who were completely unlike the sinister and dangerous spies of fiction. They were almost laughably inept—and it was not at all clear what use they were to their Russian masters. Richard and Cynthia Murphy lived in suburban Montclair, New Jersey. On the surface, they had little or nothing in common with James Bond, or the spies John le Carré wrote about, or for that matter, with Oleg Gordievsky or Aldrich Ames. The Murphys lived quite ordinary lives. They went to block parties and school picnics. They grew hydrangeas. They had children (two daughters) and raised vegetables in their backyard. Their "deep cover" consisted of a life of boring anonymity, deep in the wilds of an American suburb.[29]

The Russian government had trained the "Murphys," who were from Russia (that was not their real name, of course), in espionage techniques and language skills before they moved to the United States. Their false identity allowed them to bore into American society. Marriage and children were part of the cover story. The Murphys were not supposed to steal secret documents, rather, they were expected to "infiltrate" American institutions.[30] Presumably, they could provide their Russian handlers with insights into American society and some of its institutions. An intercepted email explained that their mission was a form of "long-term service." Their "main mission" was to "search and develop ties in policymaking circles" and send back intelligence reports.[31] These unlikely spies were arrested, pleaded guilty, and were quickly whisked off to Moscow as part of a "swap" of spies.[32]

The Murphys hardly seemed like real moles: their espionage had a certain low comedy element. The Murphys' neighbors were flabbergasted when they found out the couple were spies: to think that these people next door, with their kids and their hydrangeas and their vegetable garden, were really Russian agents concealed in plain sight was unbelievable. They were like aliens in a science fiction movie who descend to earth and take over the human forms of friends, neighbors, and relatives.[33] But they seemed far less threatening than an invasion of aliens. That the family next door, so bland, so ordinary, was a pair of secret agents was fascinating, but, as one neighbor said, "more bizarre than scary." Another neighbor said, "I'd rather have Russian spies as neighbours than a paedophile."[34]

All spies have double identities. They work in secret. The stakes are usually higher than insights into suburban life in New Jersey or whatever else the Murphys might have uncovered during their careers. The suburban moles in Montclair do remind us how little we actually know about the "real" identities, not only of strangers, but even of neighbors, of people we see every day. Most people would agree with the neighbor who said better a mole than a dangerous criminal next door. But in either case, who can tell? Sometimes that *is* the case: a dangerous criminal *is* next door. And sometimes the neighbors (interviewed on TV) express total shock. How could it be that Mr. X, in the house on the corner, so quiet and ordinary, was a serial killer? How could it be that Mr. X, like Jack the Ripper perhaps, led a second life of rape or murder? How could this man, who seemed so ordinary, bury dead bodies in his cellar or fill his freezer with body parts? These incidents are, indeed, Jekyll and Hyde come to life. They reflect the mystery of personal identity in everyday life.

The moles in New Jersey went to picnics, they grilled hamburgers on their deck, one daughter won second prize in a spelling bee at school. Yet they had a secret identity, which nobody guessed. And the neighbors of the man who turns out to be a serial killer, who are quoted as shocked or surprised: Are they themselves so innocent? Is their outer life a game, a show, a masquerade? Who people "really" are can be an irreducible mystery—even for those we live next to and even for those who live in our very own house.

LIFE IS A CABARET

All of us are passing in one way or another. People play roles throughout their lives. They present themselves in different ways to different people, and in different situations. This was a central insight in the work of Erving Goffman. For Goffman, life was a kind of performance, or rather a series of performances. People create impressions, deliberately. They act parts, they provide other people with cues and hints about who they are. *The Presentation of Self in Everyday Life*, the title of Goffman's book, says it all. It is a study of how people interact with other people—what identity they project. "Presentation of self" is universal, but there is also "misrepresentation," that is, giving out a false or "phony" impression. Goffman mentions impostors, confidence men, and those who tell "open," "flat," or "barefaced" lies about who they are or their status in society.[35]

Humans, no doubt, have always been concerned with "presentation of self." Perhaps it was something that mattered even to the hulking Neanderthals. But "presentation of self" is different in the modern world, the world described in this book. People in villages or closed communities like the Amish, or the classic Israeli kibbutz, are also concerned with impression—they may pretend to love this or hate that, but conditions of life in big cities (or small frontier towns for that matter) magnify the issue of self-presentation and make identity and its projection more problematic. Impostors and con men have a difficult time in the enclosed and cocooned world of face-to-face societies—for that matter, the whole cast of characters described in this chapter could hardly flourish in that kind of environment.

Playing a part is not always easy. And not always possible. It depends on skill. Role-playing comes naturally to some people, and not to others. Class and background matter. Only an expert like Professor Higgins could transform Eliza Doolittle from a guttersnipe into a woman who could "pass" for a member of the British upper class. Appearance, speech, and behavior are crucial, as Professor Higgins understood. In the city, well-dressed, respectable people, can stroll into the lobby of a downtown hotel and use the restroom. Nobody questions who they are. A young Black man might find this somewhat harder. Neat clothing would help. Women evoke less suspicion than men. And a grizzled, homeless man, dressed in dirty clothes, would be totally unwelcome and might very likely be thrown out.

Hotel clerks use appearance as a clue to identity—to caste and class. The homeless man has no way to manage "presentation of self." Context is important. Patients in a mental institution are all assumed to be insane; the staff interprets the actions of each patient in this light. This was the conclusion of a famous study from 1973. In this experiment, perfectly sane people "gained secret admission" to mental hospitals. Once admitted, the "pseudopatients" stopped showing signs of mental disorder, but somehow nobody noticed. Once the label of insanity was pinned on the subject, there was "nothing the pseudopatient [could] . . . do to overcome the tag." The tag profoundly "color[ed] others' perceptions."[36] The validity of the study and its data has come under question. It may well be that the author played fast and loose with the data, that he "exaggerated and fabricated parts of his . . . story."[37] But the basic point may still be valid: the paper, though it was "exaggerated, and even dishonest . . . touched on truth as it danced around it."[38] Labels and appearances do matter. "True" identity is in many ways unknowable.

Race in the United States (and elsewhere) is itself a clue, a tag, a label. Racism is deeply entrenched and systemic. An African American who dresses "White" and behaves "White" can try to neutralize the labels. But this does not always work. African Americans complain, justifiably, about racial profiling. They talk sarcastically about the crime of "driving while black." The police, too, often make assumptions about people of color—assumptions that can be lethal at times. The problem goes far beyond police behavior. In April 2018, two African American men, sitting quietly in a Starbucks restaurant in downtown Philadelphia, Pennsylvania, waiting for a friend, were asked to leave. When they refused, the police were called. The incident was a profound embarrassment for Starbucks. The company ordered all of its employees to undergo training on issues of racial bias.[39] A well-dressed White man, displaying an air of confidence, can open doors that are closed, or partly closed, to people of other races. Yet this White man may be playing the role: he may be passing. He might be a swindler or a confidence man. When he confidently enters a hotel lobby, he might not be a guest, or someone looking for a restroom. He might be casing the hotel, in preparation for a burglary. He might, in other words, be some sort of secret Mr. Hyde, biding his time and scouting for victims.

Chapter 5

The Dawn of Mystery

The first half of the nineteenth century was a period of rapid social change; it was the age of the railroad, growing industrialization, and rising cities. It was also a time that we might call the age of the mystery story;[1] the age in which a new literary genre sprang into life: the detective story, or "mystery."[2] It is possible to dredge up examples here and there, from Rome or ancient China, for example, that could be described as "mystery stories." But as a genre, a type, it cannot be traced further back than the first half of the nineteenth century. Once these stories were introduced to the world, their popularity exploded. Even today, they are enjoyed by millions. Hundreds, maybe thousands, of novels and short stories, which can be described as "mysteries" or "detective novels," are published worldwide. The taste is global. People talk about a Scandinavian school of mysteries. There is a huge audience in Japan, in Germany, in Latin America.

Edgar Allan Poe is often considered the father of the detective story. His short story, "The Murders in the Rue Morgue," appeared in *Graham's Magazine* in 1841. It is widely accepted as the first true detective story.[3] The story takes place in Paris. A woman and her daughter have been savagely murdered. The daughter's body was stuffed into a chimney; the mother's body was tossed out the window. The police are baffled. Witnesses heard strange voices spoken in a language they could not understand. In the end, an amateur, C. Auguste Dupin, solves the mystery. Dupin, a "young gentleman," from a good family (though living in genteel poverty), unravels the puzzle, with his extraordinary powers of deduction. Dupin sifts the known facts and comes to the conclusion that no human being could have committed this crime. The "killer," in fact, was an animal: an orangutan. A sailor, it turns out, had caught the animal in Borneo and brought it back to Paris. It escaped and ended up in the Rue Morgue, where it killed the mother and daughter.

One year later, Poe published another story, "The Mystery of Marie Roget," which was based on a real and dramatic case. In 1841, a young, attractive woman, Mary Rogers, disappeared. Later, several men saw a body floating in the Hudson River, near Hoboken, New Jersey. It was the body of the missing woman, Mary Rogers, the "beautiful cigar girl."[4] The police were unable to solve the crime. Her boyfriend, a suspect, had an unshakable alibi. He then died under mysterious circumstances—very possibly by suicide. Poe was enthralled by the case and saw a chance to make money from it. He claimed he knew the answer, and that his story would demonstrate the truth. Once again, he would attribute the solution to the great Auguste Dupin with his almost magical brain power. Poe transferred the story to Paris, changed the name of the victim, but kept many of the details of the case intact. Unfortunately, his conclusion was almost certainly wrong, at least as far as the real Mary Rogers was concerned. Chances are that Rogers died as a result of a botched abortion and that her boyfriend, father of the child, committed suicide out of guilt.[5]

Poe may have been a pioneer in this genre; he certainly had no way of knowing that these rather overblown short stories were only the beginning of a vast new form of literature. *The Notting Hill Mystery*, published in 1862 by Charles Warren Adams, is said to be the first full-length mystery novel. The plot is fairly thin.[6] More, and better, examples were soon to come. In Mary Elizabeth Braddon's novel, *Henry Dunbar* (1864), a murder is the pivotal event, and though readers with a grain of sense will guess the culprit, in the novel a detective named Carter solves the mystery.[7] In France, Emile Gaboriau was a huge success. His first important mystery novel was *The Lerouge Case: The Widow Lerouge* (1866). The widow Lerouge was murdered in her home. Only in the final pages of the book do we learn who killed her. An amateur detective, Tabaret, plays an important role in the book.[8] Gaboriau's later novels feature a police officer, LeCoq (LeCoq appears in the *Lerouge* book, but in a very minor role). Willkie Collins, a friend and colleague of Charles Dickens, and a novelist of real distinction, published *The Moonstone* in 1868. The crime in this book is the theft of a fabulous gem: a diamond stolen from India and brought to England. Here, too, the mystery is not solved until the final pages. One of the characters is Sergeant Cuff, portrayed as an actual detective. *The Moonstone* is a genuine classic, one of the best of Collins's novels—rich in humor and populated with interesting characters; it is still very much worth reading.

There are elements of the mystery story in a number of Dickens's works as well, for example, in *Bleak House*, published in 1852–1853. Late in his life, Dickens turned fully to the genre in his last novel, *The Mystery of Edwin Drood* (1870). There is a double mystery in this novel. In the nineteenth century, authors often published their novels as serials, in magazines, before releasing them as novels. Dickens died halfway through serial publication of *Edwin Drood.* The world was left with two mysteries: First, who killed

Edwin Drood and second, how did Dickens plan to end the novel (and solve the mystery)? The answer to both questions is a matter of sheer speculation.

In the United States, the first crime novel is said to be *The Dead Letter* (1866), written by Seeley Register, a pseudonym used by Metta Victoria Fuller Victor, a pioneer female author of detective fiction. In this novel, young Henry Moreland has been murdered. A private detective, Burton, solves the mystery, but, as usual, we have to wait until the end for the solution, which is, frankly, not much of a surprise.[9] In the late nineteenth century, Anna Katherine Green was the most notable American who specialized in mysteries.[10] *The Leavenworth Case: A Lawyer's Story*, published in 1878, was a huge success. The plot conforms to what was becoming a common pattern in mysteries. There is a murder—in this case old-man Leavenworth—and no one, at first, knows who did the bloody deed. Suspicion falls on his two nieces who lived in his household. In the end, they turn out to be innocent and the true culprit is unmasked. As in *The Moonstone*, a character described as an actual detective plays a decisive role in the novel: Ebenezer Gryce of New York. Green went on to write many more mysteries and enjoy considerable financial success.

THE DETECTIVE: REAL AND FICTIONAL

In short, the mystery novel became extremely popular quite quickly in the nineteenth century. It also became somewhat stylized, developing its own norms and conventions. But why did this precise form of literature arise, and why at this precise point of time? What aspect of the social context was the soil in which the mystery grew?

To begin with, the nineteenth-century public found crime endlessly fascinating. Huge numbers of pamphlets and broadsides recounted tales of blood, gore, vile murders, executions, and great horrifying crimes. Mass-market newspapers contributed their share as well.[11] Cheap and accessible, they fought each other for circulation and the attention of readers. Coverage of crimes was sensational, and wildly inaccurate. Crime news was also a staple of such periodicals as the *Police Gazette* in the United States, founded in 1845, and the *Illustrated Police News* (from the 1860s) in England. Crime and punishment fascinated the public, and the more lurid the case, the better. The appetite for what we would now call "true-crime" material was enormous. It was also featured in dozens of plays in London's theaters. For example, the smash hit *Jonathan Bradford, or the Murder at the Roadside Inn,* was performed on stage in 1833. It derived its plot from a notorious eighteenth-century case. It ran for some 160 performances.[12] As early as the

1830s, "gaffs," cheap, improvised, sometimes temporary theaters, charging a penny and seating 100 to 150 people, performed scenes from local accounts of horrible crimes. Accuracy was rarely a criterion. Even puppet shows acted out crimes for the general public.[13]

Crime fiction developed along with changes in the system of criminal justice. The creation of the detective story coincides with the establishment of the actual detective, that is, a new professional force, the detective squad. Before the nineteenth century, in both England and the United States, a fairly crude system of constables and night watchmen was responsible for law and order. As cities grew, they became more violent and unruly. London was a gigantic metropolis. In the United States, New York, Philadelphia, Boston, and other cities grew rapidly. These cities were full of new people, immigrants from other countries, and refugees from rural life. In the 1830s and 1840s, riots erupted in cities and mobs ran wild in the urban slums. Anti-Catholic toughs burned the Ursuline Convent, near Boston, in 1834.

The old system was pathetically unable to cope with urban crime and disorder. A new system replaced it: the police force, a more or less professional, uniformed, paramilitary outfit. Police officers were on duty twenty-four hours a day. London was the first city in the English-speaking world to organize such a force. The London Metropolitan Police came into existence in 1829, under Sir Robert Peel (hence the nickname "peelers," or, more commonly, "bobbies"). New York City's police department dates from 1844. Soon, there were departments in Baltimore (1853), Philadelphia (1854), and other cities.[14]

Policemen wore uniforms and badges, advertising exactly who they were. This was deliberate. An organized police department was meant to control and prevent urban crime and disorder. Cities were raucous, dangerous, and disorderly places. The more obvious the presence of the police, the better for crowd control and riot prevention. The organized police force was soon supplemented with a corps of detectives. In England, the first detective squad was formed in 1842. It consisted of eight men. American cities soon followed: Boston in 1846 and New York in 1857. Thus, the introduction of the detective roughly coincides with the introduction of the detective story. The profession and the literary form grew out of the same cultural soil.[15] And real-life detectives, like Jonathan Whicher in England (one of the original eight detectives of 1842), served, at least in part, as inspirations for the genre.[16]

A detective's job was different from that of the ordinary policeman. Policemen were on the streets, working their beats: uniformed, obvious, and a visible deterrent. Detectives never wore uniforms or badges. They worked, in fact, in the shadows. They were not concerned with rioters, barroom brawls, or gangs of street hoodlums. Their job was to ferret out the secret violators, those who worked with tricks and scams, whose weapons were not fists and knives but malevolent brains.

In a sense, detectives were an upside-down version of confidence men. Like con men they too, were "undercover." They hid their true identities from the world. A detective's work made him a kind of spy whose target was the underworld. Through clever tactics, secrecy, and stealth, he was able to fight against fraudsters and impostors. Detectives were confidence men: working, however, on the other side. Their job was to discover secret identities—to find the Hyde inside smooth-talking Jekylls, the men who preyed on members of respectable society.

Detectives of course did more than this. They were experts, for example, at detecting pickpockets. They were engaged in a kind of arms race against their enemies on the other side. Since hidden and shifting identities were an aspect of crime in the nineteenth century, there was an eager search for new and better ways to label and detect criminals. In an age of mobility, confidence men, and criminals in general, could easily transfer from places where they were known to places where they were strangers. This was a special problem in the United States, where criminal justice systems were radically decentralized.

Photography, an invention of the first half of the nineteenth century, proved to be a useful tool for fighting crime. As early as 1857, Sergeant Lefferts, stationed at the headquarters of the "Detective Police" of New York City, put together a "Rogue's Gallery," a collection "of daguerreotype portraits," in which the "likenesses" of known criminals were displayed. This gallery allowed departments to share these photographs. In the late nineteenth century (from about 1880), police departments also began to use a new technique called the Bertillon system, named after a young clerk in the Paris police department, Alphonse Bertillon. This system was used as a way to identify criminals systematically. Bertillon's method, "anthropometry," rested on precise body measurements—the length of the middle finger, the length of the left foot, the color of the eyes, the dimensions of the head. Photographs of criminals supplemented anthropometry. Bertillon even devised a special chair for his subjects to sit in while being examined. He standardized the camera work, in the interests of exactness, and to make comparisons easier. Many police departments adopted the Bertillon system,[17] which was an improvement on earlier methods, but was hardly fool-proof. A much better method soon came along: fingerprinting. The prints of no two people are exactly the same. Fingerprint identification (for criminals, or people applying for pensions) actually began in India. In 1877, William Herschel, a district administrator in Bengal, proposed fingerprinting as a tool to fight crime.[18] Later, in the twentieth century, a system for classifying fingerprints developed and the Bertillon system was discarded. Fingerprints soon became an essential tool of crime detection and a method of proof: the "ultimate achievement in transforming the body into a text."[19] Over time, law enforcement agencies built up fingerprint databases. Today, police labs have many other tricks up their sleeves. Moreover, forensic information can now be shared across state and national borders in societies which are, if anything, even more mobile than societies of the nineteenth century.

CRIME SOLVERS

Fascination with crime led to fascination with police and detectives. Some detectives cashed in on their fame by writing memoirs: books in which they touted their accomplishments and recounted exploits in which they caught sly and slippery crooks.[20] As mysteries became more popular, they often included (fictional) detectives. This was true, for example in *The Moonstone* with Sergeant Cuff, Gaboriau's LeCoq, and Ebenezer Gryce in the works of Anna Katherine Green.

But most fictional detectives are not members of the detective squad at all. The most famous of them all, Sherlock Holmes, was definitely an amateur, a lone wolf with no official status at all. *A Study in Scarlet*, by Arthur Conan Doyle, published in 1887, introduces Holmes to the world, along with his faithful friend, Dr. Watson. All the Holmes stories are still in print, and in an important sense, he has never died. Nor has the genre. Since the nineteenth century, tens of thousands of mysteries have flooded the world's presses, billions of copies have been sold, and the popularity of the genre is global. Very little of this is "literature" in the usual sense, but the fans do not care. They come from all walks of life, and for many of them, this is one of life's great (though somewhat guilty) pleasures.[21] W. H. Auden called the "reading of detective stories" an "addiction like tobacco or alcohol."[22] If so, millions are addicted. The "mystery," in the world of books, has achieved the same kind of astonishing success that ants and beetles have achieved in the natural world.

The detectives in all these books can, of course, still be actual detectives They may also be private detectives, or "private eyes." Professional private detectives came into existence shortly after the introduction of the public detective. Allan Pinkerton was an outstanding example. His agency, whose motto was the "eye that never sleeps," protected Abraham Lincoln from assassination plots early in Lincoln's presidency, and operated a network of spies for the Union forces. His agency grew into a big business, with a somewhat dubious reputation for strike-breaking.[23]

Yet in most mystery books, the solver is neither a member of the detective squad or a private eye, but someone entirely different—an amateur, like Sherlock Holmes—and sometimes an unexpected or improbable character. The detective can be a mute, a blind man, a priest, a rabbi, an accountant, a stockbroker, an English lord, a village spinster, a college professor, a member of an American Indian tribe—in short, practically anybody. They can grow orchids, play the violin, or pursue any conceivable hobby or avocation. They can represent any nationality and race. The thousands of mysteries have explored almost any situation a person can think of. Within this gargantuan mass of books and stories, you can find almost any pattern, any twist, any gimmick you might imagine, any possible variation on any possible theme.

One might think, then, that all these books, tumbling off the press every year, could not possibly have anything in common. And in a way, this is true. There are, of course, patterns, and a standard plot. But the majority do share one significant feature: the problem of *personal identity.* If we can describe any mystery as typical, it would be something along the lines of *The Leavenworth Case* or the novels of Agatha Christie or other popular novelists. In the beginning of any of these books, a murder is committed. We are introduced to a number of people who are, or could be, suspects—they have, perhaps, both motive and opportunity. There are twists and turns along the way. The path is strewn with red herrings, but real clues may also be scattered here and there. Suspicion falls now on this person, now on that. Finally, in the last chapter, the true killer is unmasked. In any event, if the writing is skillful, the solution comes as a great surprise.

Consider, for example, most of the novels written by Agatha Christie. Christie is perhaps the most successful mystery writer ever, with the possible exception of Arthur Conan Doyle. Apparently, more than two billion copies of Christie's books have been sold. They have been translated into more than a hundred languages, including Icelandic and Sinhalese. Wildly successful movies have been made from her novels as well as popular television programs. A Christie play, *The Mousetrap*, ran on the stage in London longer than any other play in history.

Christie's success is due in part to her talent for fooling the reader—for providing an ingenious twist at the end. In her novels the guilty party is likely to be somebody you never suspected. In one, the narrator himself turns out to be the killer. In another, *all* the suspects are guilty. In *And Then There Were None*, the suspects are isolated on a lonely island. They are killed one by one. It seems as if no one could have carried out the crimes. In this book, as in all the others, there *is* a solution, just not the expected one. The surprise ending has been an abiding trait of mysteries. This was true as early as *The Moonstone*: most readers may not have guessed the name of the thief who stole this fabulous jewel. This kind of surprise is still a feature in countless mystery novels.

But *why* does the solution surprise us, as it should, if the book is successful? Why is it so hard to guess, to find the answer to the mystery, even if the author has dropped subtle clues along the way? Because the authors *want* to deceive us. They want to lead us astray. They want us to think that X, who had a powerful motive, was the one who (say) killed his crusty old uncle, the skinflint, who was about to change his will and disinherit X. It turns out, though, that X was not the killer at all. The killer was Y, an entirely different person, somebody we never thought of as a killer, whose guilt we never guessed. The author has kept us confused and uncertain as we turn the pages eagerly, until the mystery is solved in the final chapter. It was Y who committed the crime: a surprising turn of events. Someone unexpected. A person we thought was innocent turns out to be guilty. It was someone, in other words, whose true *identity* eluded us. A person we thought was Dr. Jekyll turned out, instead, to be Mr. Hyde.

This writing technique was used early, as in *The Moonstone*, for example. Another notable mystery of the nineteenth century was *The Mystery of a Hansom Cab* (1886), by Fergus Hume. Melbourne, Australia, is the setting of this well-written and ingenious novel. In it, a man named Oliver Whyte, dead drunk, is chloroformed to death in a horse-drawn cab. Suspicion falls on a young man, Brian Fitzgerald, an Irish immigrant. Brian is engaged to the daughter of one of the richest men in Melbourne. The evidence seems quite overwhelming. Brian insists he is innocent, but refuses to cooperate with the defense for reasons he will not divulge. A clever detective named Kilsip comes to the rescue. Brian is put on trial, but in the middle of the trial, a surprise witness appears and provides an alibi for Brian. The jury acquits him. But if Brian did not commit the crime, then who did? From this point on, the plot weaves in and out with more surprises at the end. (It would be cheating to give the secret away.) Australia, the locus of the book, was a raw, new country (relatively speaking). Virtually all the characters are immigrants or have immigrant backgrounds. They came to Australia and created new identities for themselves. Dark secrets and old identities, buried deep in past lives, are the key to the mystery.

This, as we said, is a frequent trope of mysteries: hidden identities, characters hiding some vital fact of their past. A prospective bridegroom is, in fact, already married. A married woman is, in fact, not validly married. Some of the characters are not what they claim to be, but something entirely different. In short, there are characters who conceal their true identity. Above all, there are characters (or at least one key character) who pretends to be innocent, who "passes" for innocent and successfully, until Miss Marple or Sherlock Holmes or Perry Mason or Nero Wolfe pierces through the lies and unveils their true identity.

In many English mysteries, especially those of the "golden age" of the genre (the period between the two world wars), the characters are, as we said, rich and well-bred (or appear to be). They are drawn from the elite, the landed gentry, country squires, clergymen, members of the rising middle class, men and women of fashion. One of Agatha Christie's novels, *The Murder at the Vicarage* (1930) introduces Miss Marple, a village spinster, and one of

Christie's most famous "detectives." Miss Marple succeeds, in novel after novel, in solving mysteries that baffle the bumbling authorities. Lord Peter Wimsey, a member of the English nobility, is the "detective" in the novels of Dorothy Sayers, which were written in the 1920s, and considered among the finest of the period.[24] Even in more recent periods, elite households still figure in many novels; murders occur in the quiet precincts of Oxford, among other unlikely places. P. D. James is one of the leading mystery writers of the late twentieth century. Her debut novel, *Cover Her Face* (1962), takes place in an elegant home. The victim, Sally Jupp, is a household servant.

No place can seem as harmless as a country vicarage, in Miss Marple's (fictional) village, but the evils and secrets of the outside world somehow penetrate even this quiet haven. In Agatha Christie's world, village life is changing—subtly at times, more overtly at other times, and the evils of modernity are oozing into its very pores. Yet in some ways the *identity* issue is even more starkly present in these neat and oddly bloodless stories. Despite the genteel surroundings, the very form of the mystery novel demands something discordant: at least one character must have a skeleton in the closet, and very often there are many skeletons and many closets. In the end, the most germane of the skeletons lurks in the closet of the least likely character. The principle of the detective story suggests that some people—perhaps all people—are "acting a part," that things "are not what they seem."[25] Even in those genteel circles we find both Jekyll and Hyde. False presentation of self—false identities—these are the unspoken premises of these works.[26] A murder in the vicarage is also, in a way, a fictional version of the Lizzie Borden case: murder in a quiet, respectable, middle-class environment. It would be hard to find more striking proof that things are not always what they seem, or rather, that people are not always what they seem.

Sherlock Holmes, the brain-child of Arthur Conan Doyle, remains king of the fictional "detectives." Holmes, who (supposedly) lived at 221B Baker Street in London, had eccentric habits, played the violin, and was addicted to cocaine. His powers of analysis were legendary (and scarcely believable). He could look at a hat, a cane, a pipe, and (without seeing or talking to the owner), "deduce" an incredible array of facts about the owner. In his first book, *A Study in Scarlet* (1887), Holmes looks at a corpse and tells the representatives of Scotland Yard that the murderer was a man six feet tall, had small feet, a ruddy complexion, had long fingernails on one hand, and that he smoked a particular brand of cigar. Scotland Yard is, of course, amazed, and skeptical, but Holmes, as always, turns out to be right on every point.

The detectives in mystery stories often have this kind of ability, or something like it. Indeed, Poe's Dupin, the first "detective" of them all, had a mind (as we are told in "The Murders in the Rue Morgue") that could "look right through a man's body into his soul, and uncover his deepest thoughts." Agatha

Christie's Miss Marple, the village spinster, has a profound insight into village life: she knows all there is to know about the quirks of the characters in her town. An inordinate number of murders seem to take place in her village. Miss Marple, with her amazing intuition, has no problem solving these cases. Nero Wolfe, the fictional "detective" created by Rex Stout in the 1930s, is seriously obese; he rarely leaves his luxurious home in New York City, where he grows orchids and eats gourmet meals prepared by his cook. Clients come to see him; his assistants—notably Archie Goodwin—do whatever legwork is needed. Wolfe's extraordinary brain does the rest. G. K. Chesterton created the short, dumpy figure of Father Brown, a Catholic priest, who carries an umbrella. Father Brown, whose exploits appear in a series of stories from 1910 to the 1930s, has an instinctive grasp of human nature, which leads him to the true (and surprising) solution to mysteries. Father Brown is more interested in saving souls than in solving crimes. The Father Brown stories often have a religious twist, or convey a religious (Catholic) message.

Sherlock Holmes, with his clever deductions, and the other brilliant detectives of fiction, convey an implicit message. In modern life, true identity was ambiguous, class lines were blurred; in a shifting, mobile, rapidly changing society, there were many hidden mysteries of character and personality. Only a shrewd detective could penetrate these veneers, see through the disguises, read the secret signs, and expose the "real" identities that lay underneath. Most fictional detectives are amateurs. Indeed, the professionals are often portrayed as incompetent and ineffective. Still, fictional detectives mirror the skills that real-life detectives were supposed to have, the ability to go beneath the surface of society, however ambiguous and deceptive that surface might be.

THE MYSTERY AND ITS RIVALS

Detective fiction, the fiction of Sherlock Holmes, Miss Marple, and Father Brown, stood in sharp contrast to other forms of popular fiction—stories with ghosts, magic, and spirits, in which the supernatural and the magical added spice and fascination. The detective story is a product of the nineteenth century; ghost stories, legends, and tales of the uncanny go back much further in time. Every culture has folk tales, tales of black-and-white magic, frogs that turn into princes, sleeping beauties that a kiss can awaken; Cinderella transformed by a fairy godmother, haunted houses, and ghosts that walk about at night. Science and rationality were on the march in the nineteenth century, but children still found endless delight in fairy tales and adults believed, or wanted to believe, in miracles. Religious faith was one of the strongest bonds in society. If the nineteenth century was the age of science, it was also an age of resistance to science; resistance to rationality. The Bible was still the holiest of books. If Darwin's theory contradicted, or seemed to contradict, the Bible, many believers would choose the Bible over Darwinian heresy.[27] And, as we mentioned, the nineteenth century was also a century of great awakenings, and of new religions, like Christian Science and the faith of the Latter-day Saints. Religion and science stood in a certain amount of tension with each other.

Most people believed in redemption, resurrection, and an afterlife. Many believed, or hoped, that the living might be able to speak to the dead. This was especially poignant in an age in which death was a constant presence. Children died of childhood disease. Plagues carried off adults. During the Civil War, battles and disease ended life for thousands of young men, North and South. Grieving families craved the comfort of belief in the afterlife, and in heaven as "an eternal family reunion," joining them with their dead husbands, brothers, and sons. Spiritualism promised to provide grieving families with communication with the dead, here and now, rather than after death. The Civil War gave spiritualism extra meaning. The "planchette," a wooden board (later known as the Ouija board), was one vehicle for sending and receiving messages from the life beyond.[28] William Mumler, the "spirit photographer," found another way to prey on the grief-stricken. When he developed a photograph of a woman (for example), whose sons had died, the plate "mysteriously" revealed the ghostly image of the sons. In the 1860s, customers flocked to Mumler's studio, hoping they would, in this way, see their beloved dead again.[29]

Ironically, Arthur Conan Doyle's Sherlock Holmes was the most calculating of (fictional) human beings. Yet the detective story was, and is, the very opposite of the ghost story. Sherlock Holmes and his cohorts never indulged in the supernatural. Popular ghost stories in the late nineteenth century and afterwards appealed to an older stratum of literature which flirted with ghosts and demons, magic potions, and miracles at the tip of a magic wand.[30] The detective story is almost obsessively rational; it depends for its very life on rationality. The mystery has to be solved in the end, and solved in a way that makes sense in the real world. It cannot fall back on the supernatural. It cannot pull a spiritual rabbit out of the hat. That would be considered cheating.[31]

This point is powerfully illustrated by one subgenre of the mystery story, the so-called locked room, or locked door mystery. In these stories, the puzzle is not only *who* did it, but how on earth was it done. The crime itself seems impossible. How, for example, could anybody shoot X to death in a locked and sealed room. Suicide is ruled out. In any event, when the door is broken down, and the room searched, there is no trace of a gun. It is as if the killer, and the gun, somehow vanished through the walls. Or seemed to. The locked-room mystery teases the reader: Can this really be supernatural? Is the crime really the work of a ghost, or some ancient curse? No, in the end there is an explanation; what seems to be magic is nothing more than plain human crime.

One of the first examples of this tantalizing art form was *The Big Bow Mystery* (1892), by Israel Zangwill.[32] The victim, Arthur Constant, a young lodger in London, is found dead. He fails to appear at breakfast. This worries his landlady. She is convinced that something is awry. She pounds on his door, but he does not answer. The room is locked and bolted from the inside. The landlady, in a panic, calls in a neighbor and they smash down the door. Inside, poor Arthur is found dead—murdered. His throat has been cut, apparently with a razor. Young Constant had no reason to kill himself. Moreover, there is no trace of the razor or any other weapon in the room. All the windows, and the chimney, are either locked or too small to permit any living creature to enter or leave.

In John Dickson Carr's novel *The Hollow Man* (1935), his detective, Gideon Fell, provides the reader with a kind of lecture on locked room mysteries. Dr. Fell lists various modes of solving these puzzles, some of them rather far-fetched: A dagger made of ice (which kills, then melts, leaving no trace behind) or an "ingenious grandfather clock," which, at one point, starts making a hideous clanging noise. When someone in the room touches the clock to turn it off, it releases a blade.[33] Zangwill provides an ingenious solution in *The Big Bow Mystery* (in keeping with a well-known convention, I will not give the secret away). In every case, the solution emerges. And it makes sense (more or less). Mystery novels, after all, claim to take place in the real world; they tell stories that are often far-fetched, but at least might be possible. And, of course, the real world has its mysteries as well, including mysteries of identity. In the real world, some of these mysteries are never solved, identities are never unmasked, the killer is never found. The identity of Jack the Ripper is still unknown. In other cases, we are left in a state of uncertainty: Was Lizzie Borden really guilty? In the world of fiction, the knots are always untied.

The story of Jekyll and Hyde is not a mystery in the sense of Sherlock Holmes or Edgar Allan Poe. And the "science" in this novella is completely bogus. What on earth could this drug be, that turns Jekyll into Hyde? Still, as we said, this novella, like the mystery story, rests on the puzzle of identity. It invokes the same sense of surprise. Not to the reader, of course; the reader knows all along that Jekyll and Hyde are one and the same. But nobody else even suspected that this was true. Nobody knew the that the good Dr. Jekyll was also the evil Mr. Hyde. As we said, Jack the Ripper was, in all likelihood, a real case of Jekyll and Hyde. The puzzle of personal identity binds them all together: Sherlock Holmes, Lizzie Borden, Jack the Ripper. They share a common theme.

HARD-BOILED

Agatha Christie's small towns and vicarages, and the British mysteries positioned in the comfortable world of the well-to-do, had their American counterparts. Mary Roberts Rinehart was an American writer on the Christie model: very popular and very successful. In her most famous novel, *The Circular Staircase* (1908), the narrator describes herself in the opening sentence as a "middle-aged spinster" with money, and a personal maid. The action takes place in an elegant country house with "extensive" grounds and a staff of servants. The world of the American "hard-boiled" mystery is radically different. The "golden age" of this type of mystery began in the 1920s and could not be more different from the classic (English) golden age, although it was roughly contemporaneous. Raymond Chandler and Dashiell Hammett were the two most noted "hard-boiled" writers. In Agatha Christie and Mary Roberts Rinehart there is violence to be sure—indeed, a murder is what usually sets the plot in motion. But this happens, as it were, off-stage. Nor can one imagine Miss Marple, Lord Peter Wimsey, or Father Brown ever indulging in violence themselves. Nor is there overt and graphic sex in these novels: certainly not for Miss Marple or Father Brown. Sherlock Holmes, Nero Wolfe, and others of the tribe, strike the reader as peculiarly sexless. Occasional "detectives" were (we are told) married. Some even had children. But for the most part, nothing much hinged on their personal lives.

The world of Chandler or Hammett is different: darker, more corrupt, more violent, and more overtly sexual. In an Agatha Christie novel, sometimes the police seem incompetent; they often fail to solve the case. But nobody questions their integrity. In Chandler's novels, on the other hand, the police seem brutal and corrupt. Sex and violence suffuse the pages of these books. The general shape of the novels usually conforms to the common pattern: a crime is committed, usually a murder, and at the end of the book, after many twists and turns, the puzzle is solved, and we learn who committed the crime. But the tone is radically different from that of the English novels. Even the landscape is different. In a typical passage in Chandler's *The Lady in the Lake* (1943), Philip Marlowe, the narrator (a private eye) describes what he sees as he drives: "Behind wooden fences the decomposing carcasses of old automobiles lay in grotesque designs, like a modern battlefield. Piles of rusted parts looked lumpy under the moon." Chandler's characters get drunk, attack each other, take drugs, and have almost random sex. In books like *The Lady in the Lake*, or *The Big Sleep* (1939), it is hard to find a decent, upright character. The key family in *The Big Sleep* is rich and lives in a mansion, but two sisters, who live there and are key players in the drama, are sex-mad and addicted to drugs. Everyone in the book is dark and corrupted, women as well as men.

Nobody can be trusted. Dead bodies pile up. Women throw themselves at Philip Marlowe. He himself has a certain amount of dogged integrity, which he conceals under a tough exterior. And, of course, he carries a gun.

Agatha Christie, and the English (and American) mysteries of her type, imply a specific image of society. It is smooth on the surface, but there are skeletons in the closet and dirty secrets carefully hidden from view. Society is rapidly changing, but the process of decay is subterranean. People in your circle are not always what they seem. Identity is problematic. Rot has set in, quietly, even in the most genteel precincts of the landed gentry and in the homes of the upper middle class. Some of it is invisible to the naked eye. It takes a Miss Marple or a Sherlock Holmes to turn over the stones and reveal the vermin crawling underneath. Yet, for all that, the ultimate message is (implicitly) hopeful: Sherlock Holmes or Miss Marple can restore social order, at least temporarily.[34] Crime in Agatha Christie's novels definitely does not pay: the murderer is exposed and will be duly punished.

America in the twentieth century was more like Raymond Chandler's world than Agatha Christie's. To a degree, reality was masked by prudery and self-censorship. But this was an America of red-light districts, police brutality, municipal corruption, and politicians who were entangled with the mob. Reform movements in the late nineteenth century and the early twentieth century, struggled to clean up the cities, to destroy the red-light districts, to get rid of bars and saloons, and to replace corrupt urban political machines. Yet Prohibition, the jewel in the crown of this movement, was in the end, a political failure—it lasted only a decade or so. Vice was deep-seated, along with corruption The Prohibition years struck many observers as years of rank lawlessness. The decade of the 1920s was followed by years of depression and despair.

In Chandler's world, and in the hard-boiled school in general, traditional society had died, along with the traditional values of traditional society. Chandler parades before the reader drunks, crooked businessmen, predatory women, drug addicts, brutal and dishonest policemen. Private detectives, like Marlowe or Hammett's Sam Spade, succeed because of their cynical grasp of reality, their awareness that they live in an ugly world. The killers in these novels have motives not unlike the killers in Agatha Christie: greed, jealousy, lust for revenge, thwarted love, escape from blackmail. But these motives, in the hard-boiled novels, are rawer, cruder. In these books, one man alone is guilty, perhaps, of the crime that sets the plot in motion. Yet all the rest are guilty too—not of that particular crime, but of something else no doubt. Violence and corruption pervade every page of Chandler's books.

Today, among the thousands of mysteries published each year, there are mysteries of the Christie type and the Chandler type, and every possible variation in between. The old forms persist, but the genre also reflects the "gritty realities of today." Many of these books exploit the "reality and the uncertainties" of the times we live in, times in which people feel "threatened by crime and disorder" and a "constant awareness of the dark undercurrents of society and of human personality."[35] Mysteries appear in many languages and reflect, necessarily, local cultures.[36] One can even speak of national "schools" of mystery writing. Scandinavian crime fiction is so popular it almost constitutes a genre of its own, "Scandinavian noir."[37] Scandinavia itself may be a "beacon of social democracy," but, as one reviewer put it, the "reality of life is darker and more complicated," at least in the novels.[38] Scandinavian noir is like the hard-boiled school, and perhaps even more so. These books seem to come out of grim, dark, northern winters. They are suffused with sex and violence: women are raped, children are abused and murdered. Yet they, too, reflect the common theme of all detective novels: the ambiguity of identity, the duality of modern life. Every society, even rich, tranquil Scandinavian society, is both Jekyll and Hyde.

One more theme is worth mentioning: thrillers which feature the hunt for serial killers. This is true, for example, in the work of Patricia Cornwell.[39] Serial killers are almost always men. They are psychopaths who commit motiveless crimes. They constitute an irrational and murderous fringe of society. Serial killers may have been around for centuries, but there is more awareness of them today; or perhaps they are more common. Modern serial killers, like con men, thrive on anonymity, on the ability to move from place to place. They need this mobility and the cover of darkness that city life affords.[40] Serial killers are hard to trace and to catch. Sometimes they hide in plain sight: their daytime identity, their surface life, seems routine, respectable, nothing out of the ordinary. The wild pathology is hidden underneath: these are dangerous people who hide "their true selves from those around them as they perpetrated . . . crimes."[41] Serial killers may have no obvious reason to kill. They may have no connection of any kind with their unlucky victims who were simply in the wrong place at the wrong time.

Serial killers are rare, but like urban terrorists, they inspire fear far beyond the actual danger they pose. H. H. Holmes, the killer who haunted the Chicago World's Fair of the 1890s, was a notable example from the nineteenth century.[42] Another was Thomas Neill Cream, a serial poisoner, who was tried in the Old Bailey, the Central Criminal Court in London, in 1892.[43] Jack the Ripper was a serial killer. His murders were never solved, as we pointed out. A modern Jack the Ripper might not so easily escape. Victorian England had no forensic laboratories, no database of fingerprints, no way to analyze hairs, fibers, and other residues of crime. There were no surveillance cameras—no eyes on the street. These cameras led to the arrest of two men who exploded a bomb during the Boston Marathon (2013). DNA testing (sometimes combined with genealogical records) has exposed a number of serial killers.

Genetic tools identified the Golden State Killer, who was responsible for more than a dozen murders and dozens of rapes and burglaries in California between 1973 and 1986. In 2018, thanks to DNA, the police arrested the killer, who was by then seventy-two years old and long retired from crime.[44] He pleaded guilty to some of the crimes and was sentenced to life in prison.

There is a kind of arms race between criminals and the authorities. Modern crimes, like Victorian crimes, thrive on conditions of life that make it possible to hide a secret identity, at least for a while. They thrive, in short, on anonymity. But anonymity becomes less and less viable in an age of forensic science, data mining, and massive surveillance. Modern detective literature does not, and cannot, ignore these advances in crime-fighting, including fingerprints. Modern forensic science would have astonished Miss Marple, not to mention Sherlock Holmes. Dr. Kay Scarpetta, Patricia Cornwell's "detective," is a medical examiner; Cornwell's books deal with issues of medical science, autopsies, and elaborate descriptions of the condition of dead bodies.

Similarly, the "police procedural," another common subgenre, emphasizes the way real police and detectives go about their work. Agatha Christie paid no attention to the actual work of the police. She reveals the name of the killer, but nothing beyond this—nothing about arrest, trial, and punishment or whether her clever deductions really amount to "evidence" that would prevail in a court of law. The modern "procedural" is a form in which the "actual methods and procedures of the police are central to the structure, themes, and action." These novels are more "realistic" than other forms of the genre.[45] Here, at times, the individual "detective" is replaced or supplemented by the team of police workers. Still, in many of these novels, the basic structure remains: the search for a perpetrator whose identity is hidden (at least from the reader).

In some novels criminal lawyers themselves occupy center stage. Erle Stanley Gardner (1889–1970) practiced law before he turned to detective literature. His novels, starting in the 1930s, featured Perry Mason, a lawyer whose clients, accused of murder, invariably turn out to be innocent (which of course is not that common in real life). In the typical Mason novel, the climax comes during a dramatic criminal trial in which Mason's client is the defendant. In the midst of the trial, Mason surprises everybody by proving that his client is not guilty of the crime. He also exposes the person who actually did the dirty deed. Scott Turow, also a practicing lawyer, scored a huge success in *Presumed Innocent* (1987). This helped set a trend, in which trials and legal practice are at the core of the novel, treated in a way that is legally accurate (generally speaking), and in which the work of criminal lawyers is central to the plot. Today, the "mystery," now almost two hundred years old, shows no signs of losing its grip on its vast and enthusiastic audience. Its form keeps mutating, but certain core aspects remain.

THE WAR OF THE WORLDS

The personal identity issue, in short, reflected great changes in the structure of society and played an important role in both life and literature in the nineteenth and twentieth centuries. Mysteries, spy novels, and sensation novels like *East Lynne* and *Lady Audley's Secret*, often focused on issues of blurred, mistaken, or simulated identity. All of them grew out of a world of mobility, a world of ambiguous identity.

"Science fiction" is another form of literature which became popular in the nineteenth century. The "science" in "science fiction," to be sure, is often not particularly scientific. Mostly, science fiction tries to picture a future transformed by science and technology. Necessarily, it extrapolates from the present, helped along by the author's imagination. At base is a conviction that science and technology can, and will, reshape the planet and human life, sometimes in good ways, but often in dystopian ways. To science fiction writers, the future often seems grim and dangerous, a period in which science and technology threaten to open Pandora's box.

Utopian literature has something of a tradition. Indeed, More's *Utopia*, which gave this genre its name, was written in 1516. Jonathan Swift's book *Gulliver's Travels* (1726) imagined new and strangely different worlds (for satirical purposes). Mary Shelley's *Frankenstein* (1818) is, in a way, a form of science fiction. The older literature did not usually try to predict the future. It imagined alternative ways of life using tools that existed at the time. But when science and technology moved ahead at a dizzying pace, science fiction came into its own. Writers began to imagine transformations that depended on science and technology; for example, life in an amazing submarine in Jules Verne's popular book *Twenty Thousand Leagues under the Sea* (1869). Verne's work also anticipated (more or less) the possibility of travel in space.

In the nineteenth century, science and technology had themselves developed rapidly and dramatically. By 1900, telephones, railroads, steam-powered vessels, and the first primitive automobiles had been developed. Charles Darwin and evolutionary theory threatened to turn the world of faith upside down. Science fiction reflects the danger, uncertainty, and turmoil that the world undergoes, as science and technology race ahead with warp speed: a world in which nothing seems stable, in which the very ground underfoot seems to shake. But science and technology also open doors to vast, new, dazzling possibilities. The literature reflects change, uncertainty, fluidity; in a way, it reflects a kind of social and cultural mobility on a global or even galactic scale. It paints or imagines worlds in which society can move from one state of affair to another in ways that are never truly predictable.

In medical science, too, enormous changes took place. In the long run, nothing contributed as much to human welfare as the germ theory, which destroyed old legends and speculation about the causes of disease, and, significantly, paved the way to conquer many of them. Louis Pasteur, in France, was a major figure in the development of germ theory. If "germs" (microscopic creatures) caused cholera, and if polluted water carried the germs, purifying the water could prevent epidemics of cholera. And, indeed, chlorination of water supplies put an end to this dreaded scourge.

What Pasteur and others proved was that these microscopic creatures, invisible to the naked eye, were at the root of so much human misery; that they could be as malign as any Dracula or Mr. Hyde. They were, in their own way, incredibly powerful. Science also revealed the existence of huge galaxies, infinite numbers of stars, a mysterious uncharted cosmos whose dimensions seemed almost beyond human imagination. One dark dystopian branch of science fiction describes situations in which forces from outer space attack our puny planet. *The War of the Worlds*, a novella by H. G. Wells, published in 1897—the same year as Bram Stoker's *Dracula*—is one example. In Wells's story, monsters from Mars invade Earth (Wells, like Stoker, made his creatures arrive in England, rather than, say, China or Africa). These horrific aliens seem, at first, to be utterly invincible—nothing can kill them. They have death rays and other weapons that destroy everything that gets in their way. Human armies struggle helplessly against them. Alas, civilization as we know it seems doomed. Yet suddenly, Earth is saved: the creatures begin to die, one after another. What caused this miracle? Pathogens, microscopic germs, the smallest living creatures. The aliens had no immunity to these pathogens, which apparently did not exist on Mars. Their invisible but tremendous power saved civilization from destruction.

It may seem fanciful to compare invaders from outer space to threats from Jack the Ripper or Mr. Hyde. What binds all these together is a sense of danger, a sense of uncertainty, an ambiguity between normality and what lies underneath: hidden worlds in outer space and hidden invisible worlds in inner space. In a way, too, science fiction, with its imaginary worlds and visions of strange futures, is a kind of modernization of fairy tales, legends, and ghost stories of the past.

The War of the Worlds had a happy ending: the creatures died; the world was saved. Science fiction does not always have a happy ending. Consider, for example, *Invasion of the Body Snatchers*, a science fiction movie directed by Don Siegel in 1956. The movie was a box office success and is now considered something of a minor classic (another version, with a similar plot, appeared in 1978). In the original film, aliens from outer space swoop down on a California town. The aliens take the form of giant pods that can duplicate human forms, and take over these humans while they are sleeping. In the morning, the pods have become exact duplicates, or clones, of the human beings they replaced. But they are no longer human. They completely lack human emotion. As the movie progresses, more and more people fall victim to the invaders, and become aliens themselves. There seems to be no way to stop this process. At the end of the movie, the body snatchers appear to be spreading, inexorably, from one California town to the next and then, presumably, to the rest of the country, and perhaps, to the rest of the world.

A lot of ink has been spilled over how to best interpret this movie (or whether to interpret it at all). Two strands of interpretation seem, oddly enough, diametrically opposed. We might call one a right-wing interpretation and the other a left-wing interpretation. The movie was made during the period of the Cold War. In the right-wing interpretation, the pod people are a metaphor for the infiltration of Communists and fellow-travelers into American life. Thus, the movie reflects the panic and paranoia of the McCarthy era: Communists and crypto-Communists have wormed their way into society, hiding their true feelings, spreading propaganda, oozing into all aspects of American society, poisoning American institutions, taking over society in the same way as the pod people. Your neighbor, who looks so normal, so ordinary, might be a crypto-Communist, or even worse, a hidden Soviet agent. The left-wing interpretation also reflects the pathologies of the McCarthy era. Senator McCarthy and his backers, and the right wing in general, with their wild accusations and allegations, their claims that those institutions and people that did not toe their line, have betrayed the country—all these have poisoned trust and human relationships, and made ordinary citizens suspect the very humanity of those who did not share their political beliefs. Then again, the movie might be taken as an allegory about capitalism and mass culture—forces that can turn human beings into pod people or perhaps it is about the stifling impact of conformity or, in a way, simply a tale about the mystery of human personality.

Whether any of these themes was actually intended may be beside the point. For our purposes, the movie can be seen as a work of imagination that taps into the main theme of this book. Whatever else it stands for, the movie reflects the continuing crisis of identity. Who are these people, taken over by the aliens? They look like ordinary people, they act like ordinary people, they walk and talk like ordinary people, but they are no longer people at all—they are aliens from outer space. Their true identity is invisible to the naked eye—it is hidden, subversive, unsettling.

What makes this movie so disturbing (and effective) is the way it differs from conventional horror movies. The monsters are not weird creatures with long green tentacles and hideous shapes. They look like us. They *are* us, in a way. *The Manchurian Candidate* (1962; there was a remake in 2004), another famous, eerily effective movie, touches on a similar theme. The Korean War, which began when North Korea launched an invasion on South Korea, is in the background of the original film. A group of allies, led by the United States, fought back against North Korea. The allied armies turned the tide, swept across North Korea, and approached the Chinese border, which brought China into the war. After years of brutal conflict, the fighting ended with an armistice. Both Koreas ended up more or less where they started, which remains true to this day.[46]

In the movie, a group of American soldiers have been captured and imprisoned by the Chinese, who brainwash one of them, Raymond Shaw. The Chinese "program" him to respond when he sees a certain signal (the Queen of Diamonds). Shaw, when he is under the spell of this signal, loses consciousness and does whatever his Chinese handlers tell him to do, with no memory afterward of what he had done. On the surface, Shaw seemed to be a loyal American—a war hero, in fact. But he had a secret identity—one he was not even aware of, which made him, inadvertently, a tool of the Chinese government, and an incredibly dangerous spy. Shaw's mother, brilliantly played by Angela Lansbury, is working secretly for the Chinese. Her boorish husband, Raymond's stepfather, is a US senator. The plan is to get him a Vice Presidential nomination. Shaw, acting under the command of his handlers, would assassinate the presidential candidate, and Raymond's stepfather could become president of the United States, presumably to act in the interests of the Chinese government. In the end, the plot fails. Shaw is somehow deprogrammed. When the time comes for him to assassinate the presidential candidate, he kills his mother and stepfather instead. He then ends his own life with a bullet to the brain.

The Manchurian Candidate is pure science fiction—brainwashing has hardly advanced as far as the film would have it. And the plot is wildly far-fetched. But the movie is intriguing, beautifully made, and well-acted. Like *Invasion of the Body Snatchers*, the movie makes a strong political point. Shaw is (without knowing it) both Jekyll and Hyde. His mother also has a dual personality—she has sold her soul to the Communists. The film takes an everyday fact of life—the ambiguity of identity—and stretches it, exaggerates it, expands it. The movie, at its core, expounds a conspiracy theory, a theory of secret evil. It is also, like *Invasion of the Body Snatchers*, a product of the Cold War. It plays on the public's fear of hidden and disguised enemies, boring from within, on plots, conspiracies, and pathologies that are not visible to the naked eye.

Blade Runner (1962; a later version appeared in 2017), directed by Ridley Scott, is another classic film from roughly the same period. *Blade Runner* is a dark and dystopian movie set in a city of the future. Robot-making has improved (if that is the word) to the point where you cannot tell who is human and who is a robot. There are ways, to be sure, to unmask these "replicants." Replicants are far more human than the pod-people in *Invasion of the Body*

Snatchers. Nonetheless, they lack the full range of human emotions—they are, after all, not people but machines. *Blade Runner* is only one of many movies and books[47] that explore this theme: robots who look like real human beings, and (on the surface) behave like human beings. In a real sense, these robots begin to approximate human beings. The theme of these movies and books is technology run amok. They have many levels of meaning, but all are haunted by one cardinal fact of modern life, and the theme of this book: life in a society of strangers, and the utter ambiguity of personal identity. Family relations, friendships, and human emotions may cushion and cocoon us, but out there, in the big world is a cosmos of strangers. We know nothing of the inner life of the strangers we pass in the street. Can we really know *anybody*? At some point, this ambiguity may reach the ultimate stage where we cannot tell if the "people" we see are even human at all.

The argument in this chapter has been, at its simplest, the claim that fact and fiction are social cousins. The mystery novel, in its classic sense, seemed to spring up out of nowhere, its popularity spread like wildfire. But its origins lay in the very nature of nineteenth-century society. Mysteries, together with spy novels, and (more recently) novels haunted by serial killers, reflect certain basic facts of the world of today. They also reflect the revolution in crime-fighting that began in Victorian times, and especially the invention of the detective squad. Crime-fighting is also the theme of police procedurals. The sheer ambiguity of identity, fostered by a mobile, restless, urban society, the blurring of class differences, the flowering of science and technology—all color both fact and fiction (including science fiction). The world has changed enormously since Edgar Allan Poe, and even since Sherlock Holmes and Agatha Christie, but the main causes and effects are still with us.

Chapter 6

A World of Doubt and Opportunity

In sum, mobility, in its various senses, created a new social situation in the Western world in the period after the Industrial Revolution. Cities swelled in size; they were crowded with newcomers, people who were strangers to each other. Mobility led to a new, or heightened, form of the problem of *personal identity*: it was harder to know what people were really like, because their inner selves, their "real" selves remained hidden. There were also various forms of "passing": people who took on a new identity, a simulated identity, sometimes for reasons we would find sympathetic today. New kinds of fraud and crime also appeared, or became more common: crimes of mobility such as bigamy, the confidence game, and blackmail. Crooks took advantage of a world of ambiguous identity. New forms of literature appeared and new institutions—the detective squad, for example—the police force and the penitentiary. The structural facts of modern life lay at the root of new facts and new forms of fiction.

What was it like to live in a world of strangers, a world of blurred identity, a world in which frauds and fakes flourished, a world of radical uncertainty? How did this affect the culture, and the psychology, of people who lived in this world? Most people were not frauds or fakes. Mobility was their world too, just as much as it was the world of the confidence man. They, too, often had hidden identities—sexual identities and secrets. We will look at this aspect of their lives in chapter 7.

In a mobile world, position in society was, compared to the past, much less a matter of birth, much less fixed and unchangeable. Doors opened that once had been tightly closed. There were rifts in the fabric of society, little openings, places where a man might squeeze through, and go up—or, alas, go down. The role of women, of course, was much different from the role of men. For most women, her role was tied to the role and identity of her husband. Her wealth and status, on the whole, depended on him. For the man, upward mobility was a possibility. It was a difficult and complex process to be sure. But financial success and a good position in society were at the end of the rainbow. Hard work and talent were vital elements. But so was luck. Life was, in many ways, a lottery.

To call life a lottery is a metaphor. There were in fact actual lotteries. The lottery, in fact, has a long history. There were lotteries in Europe and in the American colonies, used for all sorts of purposes: to build a lighthouse in New London, Connecticut, for example, or for the benefit of churches in Philadelphia, and for other worthy causes. Lotteries were particularly common, for some reason, in Rhode Island. The Revolutionary War did not end their popularity: George Washington bought twenty tickets at six shillings each, for a lottery whose goal was paving the streets of Alexandria, Virginia.[1]

Lotteries became controversial in the nineteenth century. Delegates to the Constitutional Convention of New York in 1821 proposed a total ban on them. The subject was vigorously debated. Lotteries, the argument went, were evil. They tended to "promote and encourage a spirit of rash and wild speculation amongst the poor and laboring classes." They filled the minds of ordinary people "with absurd and extravagant hopes," and diverted them "from the regular pursuits of industry."[2]

Why was this so wrong? The New York debate gives us a clue. Lotteries opened a magic door, a chance to become rich, for anybody who could scrape up the money to buy a ticket. Nobody objected to the idea that ordinary people could get rich in the United States. Americans, in fact, boasted of this. Nothing, they felt, stood in the way in the game of life. Talent and perseverance could pay off. But precisely for this reason the game of life needed certain rules. Hard work, innovation, service to society, bold enterprise: these were legitimate ways to climb the greasy pole. Lotteries were not one of these ways. They were illegitimate shortcuts. Lotteries were a gamble, a chance to get rich quickly. They were, in a way, fraudulent—akin to the schemes of con men. Moreover, they took bread from the mouths of the poor. Lotteries held out false hopes and sent dangerous messages.

The debate in New York was echoed in an 1850 Supreme Court case, *Phalen v. Virginia*.[3] At one time, Virginia had authorized a lottery to raise money for improvements on "the Fauquier and Alexandria Turnpike Road." But later, in 1834, a new law sharply restricted lotteries; they were banned after 1840. Phalen, the defendant, was convicted of the illegal sale of lottery tickets. The US Supreme Court upheld Phalen's conviction. The court called lotteries a "pestilence" and the worst form of gambling. A lottery "infests the whole community; it enters every dwelling; it reaches every class; it preys upon the hard earnings of the poor; it plunders the ignorant and simple." As a result of the movement against lotteries, few of them survived by the middle of the nineteenth century. One survivor, the Louisiana state lottery, had a noxious reputation for corruption. In 1895, Congress enacted a Federal Lottery Act.[4] Under this law, it was a crime to import, mail, or carry from one state to another "any paper, certificate, or instrument purporting to be or represent a ticket, chance, share, or interest in . . . a lottery . . . or similar enterprise." In *Champion v. Ames* (1903), the Supreme Court upheld this law.[5] Justice Harlan, writing for the majority, called the lottery "an evil of . . . appalling character."[6]

In fact, many get-rich-quick schemes mushroomed in the nineteenth century and later. Some were outright frauds: pyramid schemes, for example. Pyramid schemes followed a common script. Managers promised quick, but spectacular returns. Supposedly, these returns came from brilliant investments. But there were no investments. Management relied on injections of capital from new investors to make payments to the earlier investors. They sat back and watched as early investors became pied pipers, attracting more and more new money. With this new money, the promoters provided the spectacular returns; meanwhile, the promoters themselves lived high on the hog, at least until the bubble burst.[7] The underlying problem was the same as the lottery problem: a mobile society promised opportunity, but also tempted people to look for shortcuts of one sort or another. The lottery, while it lasted, at least had the backing of state governments. Pyramid schemes of course did not.

Frauds are, of course, social phenomena. Each culture produces its own variety. Many of the crimes of mobility might just as well be labeled frauds of mobility. Bigamy was a crime, and a fraud on both wives. The con game was both a fraud and a crime. Victims of the con game were people who fell for schemes that often played on the lure of easy money and the temptations inherent in a fluid, mobile society.

HARD TIMES

The world of blurred identity, which victims and victimizers shared, was a world of vast uncertainty. To be sure, uncertainty in life is nothing new. Calamities and disasters are as old as civilization, and surely much older. Village life was never truly idyllic; it was always precarious, always subject to plagues, diseases, famines, catastrophic weather, and the ravages of war. The nineteenth century world was perhaps even more precarious than before. In close-knit communities, neighbors helped neighbors; there were helping hands available for widows and orphans, and for the elderly and the ill. But in the slums of London, or New York, or for that matter, in the raw new towns that sprang up like mushrooms in the United States as the tide of population moved westward, the frail, the unattached, and the poor, could not count on the help of neighbors. In every corner of the country, the shadow of disease and financial ruin were a constant presence. Medicine was primitive and ineffective, on the whole. There were no cures for most diseases. Women frequently died in childhood. Infant mortality was high. Cholera epidemics and other plagues swept the country at frequent intervals.[8] There was no welfare system to speak of; no social safety net. Life and accident insurance did not exist for ordinary families. Locusts or drought could destroy a farmer's crops. No government agency, indeed, no agency at all, protected against floods, fires, and earthquakes or provided help or compensation to victims. For many of the old, sick, and destitute, there were friends, relatives, church groups that could help. There was also a primitive system of local poor relief, but more and more poverty meant the poorhouse, or the poor farm, and these were, in effect, a kind of pauper's prison, a last resort for those who had lost everything. In a society of rolling stones, many of the stones rolled inexorably downhill.

Many young men, some of them unattached, went off to seek their fortune on the frontier or in new areas where the public domain was open to settlers. Some went even further afield. Thousands flocked to California during the gold rush. This was a slow and risky trip, either by wagon train through treacherous and hostile territory, or by long voyages at sea. Only a few got rich from gold. Some made money selling miners equipment, or liquor, in businesses in boomtowns like San Francisco. But some found destitution and early death. Human beings, after all, are social animals. A floating life, a life without connections, life as a tramp, a hobo, a pauper, a life torn from its moorings, was a life at risk.

Life had many dirty tricks in store for the unlucky. Nothing was guaranteed. Money itself was radically unsafe. Before the Civil War, there was no national banking system, for the most part, and no national currency. The idea of a national bank was controversial. Andrew Jackson, who was elected president in 1829, vowed to get rid of the Second Bank of the United States and did so in 1833. Jackson had no power to provide a real substitute. The economic system floated on a sea of credit. Hard currency—gold and silver—was in short supply. What counted as currency consisted of bank notes issued by local banks. Incredible numbers of counterfeit bank notes also circulated. The counterfeiters got better and better at their job. As a result, it was almost impossible to know what was genuine and what was not. In Ohio, for example, the Stark County Orphans Institute claimed the right to issue bank notes. Another group set up something called the Orphan Institute's Bank and issued notes cleverly designed to look like notes of the other orphan institute. No matter: neither "bank" ever redeemed any of its notes.[9] Even genuine bank notes were a source of risk and uncertainty—notes issued by banks that actually existed and had the right to do so. How was a merchant in Illinois to know what a bank note from Connecticut was worth, even assuming the note was genuine? The bank might have failed or be tottering on the brink of insolvency. Or it might have shut its doors a year earlier. The best thing to do would be to pass the note on to somebody else, as quickly as possible. The money supply, in short, acted as a kind of Ponzi scheme. At some point, a worthless bank note might end up in the hands of someone who would have to bear the loss.

A sensible and cautious person could probably avoid traps set by a confidence man. It was also possible, by the early nineteenth century, to be vaccinated against smallpox, but there was no vaccination against most other diseases and very little that could be done to protect a family from the other calamities of life. The jerry-built financial and banking system was a peril to big and small merchants. The business cycle was another problem. About once a generation the economy imploded, followed by a period of financial and economic stress. These eruptions in the business cycle ruined the lives and fortunes of thousands of families and businesses. Even solvent companies and well-run banks foundered in the trough of the business cycle. Occasionally, state and federal governments provided some help in crisis times, especially when nature itself was the villain. In 1815, in New Madrid, Missouri, a devastating earthquake prompted Congress to vote funds for relief. There were provisions for victims of fires in Portland, Maine, and victims of the Great Chicago Fire of 1871. In 1875, money was appropriated to pay for seed when a plague of grasshoppers devastated farms. Other grants went to victims of cyclones, floods, and yellow fever.[10] But these grants were sporadic and inconsistent. They never amounted to a general program. No doubt, family, friends, and neighbors were havens for people whose lives careened into difficulties; and religion was a consolation and an anchor for millions. But, on the whole, life in the nineteenth century was like a lottery: a game of chance with winners and losers.

It is difficult to know how life's uncertainties affected personality, attitudes toward life, politics, and society in general, and how the uncertainties of life impacted behavior. Surely there were massive effects. The legal system was not much of a source of relief. People did expect justice in particular cases. The rule of law was relatively robust. But there was no concept of a *social* duty—a state duty, a collective duty—to provide for individual welfare except in the most minimal sense. The poorhouse stood as a symbol of attitudes toward poverty and welfare that precluded any such duty.

How did people navigate the dangerous waters of life? With difficulty. There were reefs, shoals, storms, but many ships did reach harbor. The economy was perilous, unsteady, and rocked with periodic failures; still, it grew; it offered rewards to the winners in the lottery of life. The land was fertile. Government took steps to improve infrastructure. Roads, ferries, canals, and bridges were built, sometimes with subsidies. Then came the railroads. Goods flowed more freely to markets. Immigration and the birth rate guaranteed a growing population—and a growing economy. The Native peoples were sidetracked, defeated in war, cheated, exiled, sometimes murdered, but in any event, the settlers got them out of the way. New areas opened up for a wave of White settlers. The Louisiana Purchase and the spoils of the Mexican War vastly increased the size of the country.

Change and growth were constant. The problem of personal identity never vanished. It was one of the factors that made for uncertainty, and which complicated life. Jekyll and Hyde were issues not only in big cities and not only with regard to physical danger and crime. The same question confronted people in the marketplace: This bank, this endorser, these buyers or sellers: can we know them, trust them, deal with them? The problem changed form over time, but in a bustling, shifting, complex society, it remained a living issue. In the twentieth century, as we will see, science, culture, and government actions alleviated some of the uncertainties of life. New uncertainties replaced old ones. New versions replaced old identities and old personalities. Mobility and the blurring of identity remained powerful social factors. But these played out in different ways in a changing society.

Chapter 7

The Worm in the Bud

The title of this chapter is taken from Roland Pearsall's book *The Worm in the Bud: The World of Victorian Sexuality*,[1] which covers the subject of the secret world of Victorian sexuality. In the United States and the United Kingdom, as well as in other countries, there was at the time a formal and official code of morality, both in law and in the social norms of respectable people. This code reflected a strict and unyielding tradition. Only married couples were supposed to have sex, or even orgasms. It would come as no surprise to learn that people did not always live up to this code. Many people broke the rules, including, no doubt, people who truly believed them to be right and proper, even God-given. Major cities in many countries had brothels. Thousands of women made a living selling their bodies, and thousands of men came to buy what these women sold. Sex outside of marriage was common and was even somewhat condoned in some societies. Masturbation was nearly universal. The flesh is notoriously weak.

Sexual behavior and sexual orientation have always been important aspects of identity. Boys and girls were raised and educated differently. There were different expectations for boys and girls. Attitudes toward sex, and sexual behavior, were also supposed to be different. Respectable women were expected to be fairly passionless. Sex drive was stronger in men, or so went the belief. Respectable men were supposed to marry for love, and to stay faithful. The man was head of the household. He was supposed to be moderate in all his habits, including his sexual habits. Marital sex was indeed a duty, but sex was an exceedingly private affair. It was never discussed in public. In general, sex of any kind was not discussed in public. It was never to be visible to the outside world.

Vast numbers of people, of course, did not live up to these expectations. They suppressed or concealed their sex lives. Most societies, of course—possibly all societies—regulate sexuality (or try to). But Victorian repression—at least at the official level—strikes us today as extreme. Underlying it was an implicit theory about the social order. Society *needed* repression—of vice, bad habits, and many forms of sexuality. In a fluid, uncertain world, men—and to a lesser extent, women—had been set free from tight, ancient chains. But perhaps for this very reason it was vital to keep certain tendencies, including sexual ones, under control, otherwise fires might rage out of control, forces that could damage or destroy society. Each man—and woman—was, potentially at least, a Jekyll and a Hyde. For the sake of society, the Jekyll personality had to predominate. Jekyll wore clothing, Hyde was naked. Hyde was a secret tendency, a part of one's identity that had to be hidden and, in some ways, denied. The outside world never saw the naked body. It was always covered up with underwear, suits, dresses, coats. But it was there. The naked form was a reality. It could not be totally repressed. There was, in short, a sexual underworld: the worm in the bud.

Some aspects of the hidden world were legal and acceptable. They were simply private. Without sexual intercourse the species would go extinct. Other forms of behavior were defined as wrongs, or even as crimes. Many of these behaviors were deep and significant parts of a person's identity. They were, so to speak, in the closet.

In big cities, in a world of strangers, there was space for all sorts of underworlds, including sexual underworlds. "Passing" took place mostly in the cities. It was easier in the cities to pursue forms of sexual identity that were taboo in small places; or easily exposed in those places.

BAD BLOOD

In the nineteenth century, there was a sharp distinction between the middle class and society's "others," the lower orders, the dregs of society. Society had, in a way, its own dual personality: a Jekyll and Hyde social order. Earlier we mentioned hostility toward the unattached—toward tramps, hobos, paupers. Mobility weakened old orders, old hierarchies, old assumptions. The elites, the respectable classes, tried to enforce regimes of protection against people and ideas that threatened social stability. Society needed discipline. It needed moderation. It needed the Victorian compromise. It needed a certain amount of repression. Repression of sexuality. Repression of disorder. It needed a certain amount of censorship, formally or otherwise.

Darwin's theories burst into the comfortable world of religion like a bombshell. Evolutionary theory gave birth eventually to a new science: genetics. Every human being is shaped by invisible forces, at the cellular level. We have no way of knowing the inner nature of a person we pass on the street. And those inner natures include genetic inheritance. In the twentieth century, scientists would uncover more and more of the secrets of genetics.

But genetics, particularly in its early years, had its own evil twin: the eugenics movement, an unholy jumble of junk science, racism, and social prejudice. To eugenicists, heredity—inherited degeneracy and social pathology—was a moral threat to society. Society's Mr. Hyde was the army of low-lifes, criminals, paupers, prostitutes, drunks, bastards, the feeble-minded, and the moronic. Bad seed passed down from generation to generation. In July 1874, the New York Prison Association sent Richard Dugdale on a tour of county jails in New York. To his surprise, he discovered a family with a "long lineage, reaching back to the early colonists"—a family which, generation upon generation, produced criminals, prostitutes, and morons.[2] He called this family "the Jukes." Oscar McCulloch, writing around 1890, described another line of degenerate human beings; he called them the tribe of Ishmael. Members of the tribe lived a life of "inherited parasitism" they were doomed from birth to be part of a "festering mass" from which there was no escape.[3] The Ishmaels had a "pauper history of several generations." They married other degenerates and formed a "pauper ganglion of several hundreds." The Ishmaels populated the "almshouse, the House of Refuge, the Woman's Reformatory"; they were "generally diseased. The children die young."[4] A study by Henry H. Goddard, published in 1912, featured another family he called the Kallikaks. The Kallikaks provided for Goddard a kind of natural experiment. Martin Kallikak, at the time of the Revolutionary War, was married to a decent Quaker woman. But he also had a fling with a feeble-minded woman who got pregnant and produced a child. The descendants of the good Quaker marriage were all respectable people, the descendants of the other woman were the very opposite: they were paupers, mentally ill, feeble-minded, and delinquent.[5] Other researchers found more of these degenerate families, such as the "family of Sam Sixty," for example (the label was pasted on because Sam had only "sixty percent mental equipment" and was a "medium grade moron").[6] Even at the time that these studies were conducted, there were scholars who expressed doubts. Later research showed plainly that both the method and the analysis were totally off base. But at that time, many people absorbed the message from these eugenic studies. The studies gave people something they wanted to hear—something about good blood and bad blood.[7]

The Jukes, the Kallikaks, and the tribe of Ishmael, and all those at the bottom of society, were taken as a warning: they were a threat to respectable, orderly society. Advanced societies, in the eyes of eugenicists, were in danger of committing racial suicide. The advanced societies, of course, were White societies, especially Nordic Whites. The new immigration was a particular problem. In the late nineteenth and early twentieth centuries, there was a flood of poor immigrants from Eastern and Southern Europe. Immigration laws already excluded Asians. In the 1920s, Congress closed the doors to the vast majority of immigrants from Italy, Greece, and Slavic countries. But the danger at home was perhaps just as great. The Jukes and the Kallikaks and the other degenerate tribes were breeding like rabbits; these tribes might eventually swamp the children of good, solid, respectable citizens.

The only way to improve the human flock was "to breed only from *the best,* and eliminate the unfit breeding material."[8] The better classes could do their bit by having more children.[9] Unfortunately, it was not easy to induce "the best" to make more babies. Cutting down on middle-class abortions would help. But on the whole, it seemed much more practical to attack the problem from the other side: that is, by preventing degenerates from reproducing. Tighter marriage laws were a help. More drastic measures followed. Indiana, in 1907, passed the first US statute that authorized actual sterilization.[10] "Skilled surgeons" at state institutions would be allowed to sterilize "confirmed criminals, idiots, rapists and imbeciles." California, as well as a number of other states, followed Indiana's lead. The 1909 California law applied to inmates of state prisons who showed evidence of moral and sexual perversion.[11] California sterilized a record number of its citizens—twenty thousand—before it ended the practice. Leo Stanley, the chief surgeon of San Quentin State Prison, was a sterilization enthusiast: he favored what he called cutting the "G string" of eligible men. Not only would this stop them from propagating, it would actually improve their "general health and vigor." Another technique that Stanley used to improve his human guinea pigs was to inject them with material from the testicles of "recently executed prisoners," together with testicles from goats, boars, rams, and deer. This had good results, he felt. Meanwhile, Stanley sterilized some six hundred prisoners. Some of them, but not all, were volunteers.[12]

Science and politics concocted the eugenics movement and supported its somewhat crackpot notions. Later, science and politics discredited and destroyed the movement. But in the early twentieth century, many prominent men, scientists and scholars like David Starr Jordan, president of Stanford University, climbed on the eugenics bandwagon. There was also opposition from the start. Lawsuits were brought attacking sterilization laws as violations of constitutional right. Most of these lawsuits failed. Very notably, the Supreme Court put its stamp of approval on sterilization in *Buck v. Bell,*[13] a case out of Virginia. Carrie Buck, an unmarried mother, inmate of a "Colony for Epileptics and Feeble Minded," was the victim in this test case. Oliver Wendell Holmes Jr. upheld the law in a short, pithy opinion. It included the famous line, "Three generations of imbeciles are enough." In fact, as modern research has shown, neither Carrie Buck nor her child were "imbeciles" at all, they were simply poor and powerless.

Sterilization was cruel and pointless. It never made much of a dent in the population it was trying to control. Hitler's embrace of the notion did not help its popularity. The Nazis were admirers of American eugenics laws.[14] For the Nazi regime, sterilization was much too tame. The Nazis simply proceeded to murder the mentally ill and handicapped. The Japanese, too, found eugenic ideas intoxicating. Japan passed a law in 1940 that authorized the sterilization of the mentally unfit.[15] Even Sweden joined the crusade. Thousands of Swedes—mostly women—were sterilized between 1934 and 1974; women who were promiscuous or rebellious were the candidates for this drastic procedure.[16]

In 1942, in *Skinner v. Oklahoma*,[17] the US Supreme Court struck down an Oklahoma law that authorized sterilization. The decision in *Skinner* rested on fairly narrow grounds. Under Oklahoma law, a thief could be sterilized but an embezzler could not be. The court found this distinction irrational—a violation of the equal protection of the laws, guaranteed by the Fourteenth Amendment. But the majority opinion, written by Justice William O. Douglas, also included a ringing defense of the right to marry and have children. Douglas also argued that the "power to sterilize" was liable to fall into "evil or reckless hands," which of course had happened in Nazi Germany. State sterilization laws were struck down or repealed, one by one. None of the eugenic laws survive today.

Eugenics was based on a deformed version of the idea of "good breeding." And it was allied to a more important, and sinister, movement: scientific racism. Racism had always been a key feature of American history. The pseudoscience of race was one of the intellectual pillars of slavery. It provided intellectual cover for imperialism; vague notions of racial superiority undergirded the colonization (and oppression) of millions of nonwhites by the British, French, Dutch, and Portuguese empires. But eugenics did not rest only on ideas about higher and lower races. The Jukes, the Kallikaks, and the tribe of Ishmael were White, and so was Carrie Buck. The roots of eugenics lay deeper in society: in the culture clash between old elites and new immigrants, between traditional hierarchies and the discontents of a mobile and rapidly changing order. The mobile society produced winners and losers. It produced great wealth for some and rootless poverty for others. It generated a floating population of tramps and hobos, and a vast slum population in the cities. Traditional society had ways to monitor and confine the deviant and the defective. There was a place in society even for the village idiot. The nineteenth-century world controlled its underclass in other ways, through institutions like the poorhouse and the penitentiary.

These movements—eugenics, social Darwinism, control of deviant behavior—were and are complex, with many sources, many factors. They transcend the problem of personal identity, but that problem does play a role in these, as in so many of the movements and developments of the nineteenth and early twentieth century. Eugenics, for example, proposes one bold solution to the question: Why is there crime, perversion, and social deviance in society? The answer is in the blood lines. People also believed, of course, that criminals could be shaped by their environment. They could learn evil from bad companions, and from liquor and bad habits. They might be condemned and destroyed by circumstances beyond their control. But in addition, there were criminals and deviates who inherited the urge to go wrong. The problem is deep inside the person; it is an inner identity, an invisible identity, which cannot be wished, trained, or reformed away. Criminals are Mr. Hyde, not Dr. Jekyll, in the very core of their bones.

SEXUAL IDENTITY AND ITS DISCONTENTS

In the Victorian era the official code was a catalog of sexual repression. The rules for sexual behavior were clearly and ruthlessly defined. They were also monitored by law. But if you took the formal code literally, you were asked to repress not just behavior, but also attitude and in many ways, free discussion of sex. Social norms amount to a code of censorship. Decent people never talked about sex. Social norms, and public opinion, were probably the most powerful tools of enforcement—more effective than police, courts, and prisons.

The sexual code was particularly severe with regard to gays and lesbians. Their behavior was taboo. Indeed, in both the United States and England (and other countries), homosexual behavior was a serious crime. "Deviate sexual intercourse" or "sodomy" were banned. The "abominable crime against nature" could result in extremely harsh punishment.[18] Most gay men and women were forced to live "in the closet," hiding or tamping down their sexual identity. No doubt many tried to "pass" for straight. But there was also a sexual underground that they could join, though this was both precarious and dangerous. In 1889, the Cleveland Street scandal centered on a male brothel in London. The scandal broke after the police arrested Charles Swinscow, a fifteen-year-old delivery boy. He was suspected of stealing. People reported that he had what seemed an abnormal amount of cash for a delivery boy. Had he stolen the money? No, he explained, the money was not stolen. He earned it from "private work" that consisted of "going to bed with gentlemen" at a brothel on Cleveland Street. Other delivery boys were caught up in the web. They testified that "men in high positions" were among the customers. One nobleman fled the country to avoid arrest. Wild rumors circulated that a member of the royal family was among the patrons of Cleveland Street. Nothing was ever proven, and this particular claim was perhaps all smoke and mirrors.[19] But the laws against "sodomy" were real enough. Famously,

Oscar Wilde fell afoul of these laws. In 1895, after a sensational trial, he was convicted of gross indecency, and sentenced to prison.

Laws against sodomy remained on the books in both England and the United States as well as other countries, until deep into the twentieth century. Indeed, in the twenty-first century in some third-world countries, and in conservative Muslim countries, they not only survive, but take a particularly harsh and unyielding form. In Western countries, enforcement of sex laws was always sporadic. There was a certain amount of implicit tolerance, especially in big cities—a tolerance punctuated from time to time by crackdowns and purges. Violators of the code who attracted attention to themselves, as Oscar Wilde did, ran the risk of suffering severe consequences. Life in the closet could be risky. But as late as the 1950s and 1960s, it was even more risky to display "perversion" openly, or even to hang out in gay bars or work for the government in a sensitive position. Particularly during the McCarthy period there was a campaign against "perverts" in the civil service of the United States. The excuse for this campaign was the rather shaky theory that "perverts" threatened national security. Their hidden identity, it was said, could be exploited by blackmailers and foreign agents.[20]

But even "straight" people were in the closet during the Victorian era. To be sure, what went on in the privacy of the home *was* private. Even outside the home, risks were small. Penal codes prohibited adultery and fornication, but there was at best feeble enforcement, if any at all. What I have called the "Victorian compromise" flourished in the nineteenth century: quiet tolerance of sexual misconduct, on the whole—so long as it was private, sporadic, and did not openly threaten official morality. Sin was forgotten if it stayed in its place. Indeed, as we pointed out, in many American states, adultery was a crime only if it was "open and notorious." The Victorian compromise evoked the old saying: If you can't be good, be careful.[21]

Millions of straight people, no doubt, had their own secrets—sexual practices that were improper, from the orthodox standpoint. Medical literature and advice books in the nineteenth century made it crystal clear that masturbation was a dangerous practice. It was a curse to body and soul. In extreme cases, it could cost a person's life. One book, published in 1892, warned parents to be alert for signs of habits of "self-abuse" in their sons. These signs included "strange appetites for clay, chalk, and slate pencils. . . . Round shoulders; an unnaturally stiff wriggling gait. . . . Bedwetting, palpitations, pimples (especially on the forehead), epilepsy, or wet palms." There were, fortunately, techniques for dealing with this problem, for example, singing psalms or sitting in a bowl of ice water.[22]

"Self-abuse" was blamed for almost everything, "including stooped shoulders, loss of weight, fatigue, insomnia, general weakness, neurasthenia, loss of manly vigor, weak eyes, digestive upsets, stomach ulcers, impotence, feeble-mindedness, genital cancer"—the list could go on and on.[23] Dr. J. Richardson Parke, writing in 1909, claimed that "loss of one ounce of semen equals that of forty ounces of blood." Children who had habits of "artificial eroticism" faced a dreadful future: the child would lose its "rosy complexion," would turn "pale or leaden in countenance," eyes would grow "sunken and dull," the mind would turn "sluggish and indolent." General health would begin to fail, the appetite would go, followed by a long slide into "hopeless neurasthenia, or even imbecility or lunacy."[24] The Reverend Sylvester Graham, a prominent figure in the early nineteenth century, condemned the practice in the strongest terms. (Graham also had serious opinions about food and food habits. His name lives on today as the "Graham" in Graham crackers.) To Graham, masturbation was an appalling practice, "Incomparably the worst form of venereal indulgence." It was secret and solitary, and "wholly unnatural." Its effect on the body was disastrous, resulting in "ulcerous sores" and sometimes "permanent fistulas of a cancerous character. . . . foetid, loathsome pus," all of this ending up, "not unfrequently," with death itself. Along the way the teeth can "decay and become black and loose, and in some instances drop out of the jaws."[25] Obviously, anything that promoted this practice, anything that stimulated "prurient" thoughts or behavior, was itself quite dangerous. A handbook for older boys, published in 1916, told the story of a football player at a big university. Mysteriously, his game began to suffer. The coach looked into the matter and found the answer: There was a "suggestive picture" hanging in the lad's bedroom. The coach ripped it down. Quickly, the player's game began to improve.[26]

Despite all this, "self-abuse" was astonishingly common. An "eminent professor in a Southern College" told Anthony Comstock that most young men (from 75 to 95%) were "victims of self-abuse."[27] College and seminary students (males), in a 1902 survey, were asked to identify temptations that had come their way. More than half of the 232 subjects listed masturbation as the biggest temptation—and 131 out of the 132 admitted they had succumbed to it.[28] The famous Kinsey Report (1948) on male sexual practices went even further. More than nine out of ten males had masturbated at some point in their lifetimes and most unmarried men did it more or less regularly—it was their main form of sexual outlet. Kinsey's report on women in 1953 showed a female rate of masturbation lower than the rate for men, but it was still impressive (and perhaps more shocking): more than 60 percent of the women in Kinsey's sample had "masturbated at some time in the course of their lives." Indeed, women could "choose their masturbatory techniques from a longer list of techniques than males ordinarily utilize."[29]

Kinsey's reports, which claimed to lay bare the real world of sexual behavior, burst like a rocket in to society. Kinsey did not just report, he also made recommendations. The law, he argued, should not forbid behavior that was common, harmless, and normal. Of course, this was galling and unacceptable to the forces of traditional religion and conventional morality. They bitterly condemned the Kinsey reports. Some scholars also raised serious questions about his sampling methods, his statistics, and his overall conclusions.[30] Still, this was a major attempt to explore a dark and hidden subject; to bring light into the real world of sexuality. Millions of people in the United States and elsewhere violated the official norms. They were guilty of "self-abuse," of adultery, of same-sex behavior, and other sexual habits and practices that were legally, morally, or medically condemned.

In the high Victorian period, sex itself was suspect—excessive sex, that is. Sex, in the opinion of some experts, was best taken in small doses, like medicine. Reverend Graham felt that "venereal indulgence" (sex, in other words) brought about "convulsive paroxysms" and "powerful agitation to the whole system. . . . The brain, stomach, heart, lungs, liver, skin, and the other organs, feel it sweeping over them, with the tremendous violence of a tornado."[31] These "paroxysms" were obviously dangerous, unless carefully controlled. How much sex was too much, in Reverend Graham's opinion? As a general rule, even for the "healthy and robust," once a month seemed to be optimal. If you have sex more than once a week you are "impairing your constitutional powers, shortening your lives, and increasing your liability to disease and suffering."[32] After all, the "organs of reproduction" are designed for the purpose of propagating the species; and to do this, their "function" does not need to be exercised very often.[33]

People like Reverend Graham were even cautious in regard to sex between married couples. He was not the only expert who felt these couples should not have sex too often. According to one guidebook, "about once a week or ten days" was ideal for married people, and in fact, those "that indulged only once a month" received "a far greater degree of the intensity of enjoyment."[34] Dr. Frank Lydston, writing in the early twentieth century, thought husbands and wives should try to reduce their "intimate association." The "less knowledge they have of each other's physiology, the better for sentiment." He even thought that married couples should sleep in separate beds: single beds were a temptation toward sexual "excess."[35] Sylvester Graham had a similar view. He did feel, though, that married people were not likely to overindulge in sex: they have "become accustomed to each other's body, and their parts no longer excite an impure imagination." This very dullness makes their sex lives "more natural and instinctive" and when combined with the right diet (Graham was after all a fanatic on this subject), intercourse for these happy couples would be "very seldom."[36]

One has to wonder what married couples actually thought about these ideas. Most of them probably did not read this literature, and its advice in any event might fall on deaf ears. Many men and women had sex before, during, and outside of marriage. Every city and town had streetwalkers and brothels; brothels rarely went out of business for lack of customers. Some of the men and women who indulged in the dreaded practice of "self-abuse" probably felt a certain amount of guilt or felt that their health was at risk. But it is hard to know how many fell into in these categories. Today, Sylvester Graham and Frank Lydston seem ludicrous, but at the time, no doubt, many people took them seriously.

For them, sexual desire, and even sexual behavior, were part of the underworld of their identity. Victorian prudery implies, as we said, that sexual life had to be controlled and monitored. The conditions of life in the nineteenth century, especially city life, allowed people to experiment with identity, putting identities on and taking them off, like costumes and disguises. Hence it was all the more reason why stringent controls seemed necessary. Sexual freedom, to respectable members of society, was like the drug Dr. Jekyll took to unleash his inner Mr. Hyde. That inner self had to be locked, bolted, and kept under strict supervision—exiled, as it were, to the subcellar of society.

TALKING DIRTY

Censorship was part of the system of social control; legal censorship, but also norms about what could and could not be openly discussed. Free talk about sex was taboo. The legitimate press practiced rigid self-censorship. Doctors and medical books, of course, could not totally avoid the subject. Advice books discussed, in guarded tones, topics such as sexual behavior and sexual best practices. Dr. Frederick Hollick, for example, published books on sex and marriage in the middle of the nineteenth century in which he discussed such topics as the "male generative organs," "venereal diseases," and "diseases of woman." He wrote in plain language "for the people" and in a way that was, he felt, "strictly scientific, moral and unobjectionable."[37]

Yet, if aliens from outer space came down in the nineteenth century and absorbed Victorian literature, reading every novel and newspaper, they might have no clue that babies were produced by the union of sperm and egg during sexual intercourse. And a long list of topics like homosexuality, contraception, prostitution, and venereal disease would escape these aliens, unless they were enormously clever at reading between the lines of texts. If the aliens consulted the Oxford English Dictionary—a massive and august work of scholarship, in many volumes, a work that claimed to be totally comprehensive, and to include every English word, and every meaning of every English word, and the origin and etymology of every English word, and the earliest occurrence in print of every English word—they would find thousands of rare, obsolete, and regional words, and thousands of technical words. Yet two common English words, fuck and cunt, would be missing. These words were familiar to every English-speaking male (and no doubt to many women as well). A strong social taboo trumped rigorous scholarship. These words were simply unmentionable.

Similarly, George Bernard Shaw's play, *Mrs. Warren's Profession*, written in 1893, was at first barred from the English stage. Mrs. Warren owned a brothel; and this was not fit for the ears of the theater-going public. Lord Chamberlain, the official in charge of censoring London plays (the office was not abolished until 1968) refused permission to the play. The first production, in 1902, was at a private club. The police stopped a performance in New York in 1905. In 1918, an official in the Lord Chamberlain's office recommended against allowing an English version of a French play, *Maternity*, by Eugene Brieux, to sully the English stage. "In a civilized world," he argued, "we do not discuss openly the *details* of sexual intercourse, of visits to the W. C.," along with such subjects as abortion or venereal disease. These can only be discussed "in privacy with the priest or the doctor."[38] Prudery in language was epidemic in the United States as well as in England. In the high Victorian era, for example, there were people who said "limb" instead of "leg," which was considered a bit coarse. Well into the twentieth century, the postmaster general maintained what H. L. Mencken called a "bureau of snoopers and smut-snufflers" to monitor newspapers and magazines.[39]

Censorship of the written word was nothing new. Most governments, past and present, have tried to squash expressions of political dissent. In some conservative countries, heresy and blasphemy are still severely punished. In the nineteenth century, pornography was outlawed in both England and the United States. Laws prohibited the sale of obscene books and pictures. In response, an underground market emerged for these books and pictures, just as there was an underground market for buying and selling sex. In the early nineteenth century in New York, there was a thriving pornography business. When sellers sensed a threat of crackdowns and arrests, they moved out of state and began to send their wares through the mail in the proverbial plain brown wrapper. One dealer advertised "rich, rare and racy reading," including such works as *The Bridal Chamber and its Mysteries* and *The Wedding Night: or, Advice to Timid Bridegrooms* (there was an extra charge for "colored" illustrations).[40] The solution: national legislation banning such publications. An 1842 law made it illegal to import "indecent and obscene" pictures into the United States.[41] Under an 1865 law, it was a crime to mail obscene books and pictures "knowingly." In 1873, the so-called Comstock Act, also prohibited mailing any devices "intended . . . for any indecent or immoral use" or "for the prevention of conception or procuring of abortion."[42]

In fact, these laws were never seriously enforced. There were only a few postal inspectors, and they were not allowed, as a general rule, to open mail and packages. Moreover, sellers were able to sell contraceptives fairly openly, provided they were careful to describe their products with euphemisms and in guarded language. Buyers surely knew what they were getting when they bought, for example, "sanitary sponges for ladies" as "fine in texture as velvet" in order to keep the vaginal passage "germ . . . free."[43] Or when they bought "rubber goods" advertised in the *National Police Gazette* in 1889, for "25 cents each."[44] To be sure, major companies, after passage of the Comstock Act, shied away from the business. Nonetheless, it flourished.

What explains the explosion of prudery in the Victorian period? Religion and morality provide part of the explanation. There were also considerations of public health. Sex, especially in generous portions, was (as we saw) considered bad for people. And, in truth, venereal diseases were a genuine hazard to public health. Yet even more important, perhaps, was an implicit theory: the idea that sexual excess did not only hurt individuals; it also hurt society. Men were, potentially at least, raging beasts: it was important for society to keep their animal instincts within limits. Women, too, needed to be controlled—and at the same time protected from men. Social advancement, and human progress, demanded a certain degree of repression, a certain degree of monitoring, managing, and controlling with regard to sexual desires and sexual identity. In *Civilization and its Discontents*, (1930), Sigmund Freud implied as much: civilization needed repression, although perhaps at some psychological cost. In the late nineteenth century, laws about sexual behavior were strengthened, with the aim of promoting official norms, protecting the reputation of elites, and buttressing a code of moderate and respectable behavior. Suppression of some forms of sexual identity, and the tamping down of excess sexual desire, was part of the program. Society, in an age of flux and change, felt the need to arm itself against "open and notorious" vice.

Ordinary people—the masses—were in particular need of censorship and control, at least in the view of elites. There was, to a large degree, a double standard. Readers of an English translation of the scandalous works of the Marquis de Sade might suddenly find, to their surprise, a passage in the original French. This was a sign that the text in question was especially raunchy. Presumably, people who knew French were better able to read de Sade without moral injury.[45] The movement to censor movies fed on this impulse. Movies became popular very quickly. By the beginning of the twentieth century, nickelodeons sprouted like dandelions on city streets. In New York City, there were five hundred nickelodeon theaters by 1908. Movies were cheap and accessible. Men, women, and children flocked to them to watch images projected in closed and darkened spaces. Shocked by the scandalous nature of some early movies, the city of Chicago adopted a censorship ordinance in 1907. Many cities and states followed this lead.[46] An Ohio law created a board of censors. Under that law, the board was authorized to approve only movies that were "moral, educational, or amusing and harmless."[47] The Supreme Court of the United States upheld censorship laws in 1915. Movies, the court said, were potentially a "force for evil." Freedom of speech? Not a real issue. Movies were simply a business. Moreover, they could potentially excite a "prurient interest." And there are "some things which should not have pictorial representation in public places and to all audiences."[48] Most state cases, too, upheld the work of the censors. In 1939, New York refused to allow a movie, *The Birth of a Baby*, to be shown to the general public. True, the movie had "scientific value"; it was not "inherently indecent", but showing the "actual birth of a child becomes indecent when presented to patrons of places of public entertainment."[49]

The film industry, in this period when many states and cities censored movies, panicked at the thought that the industry might face national censorship. In defense, studios adopted the Motion Picture Production Code, an extreme form of self-censorship. Under the code, dirty words and themes were completely taboo. In any film, criminals and adulterers had to pay for their crimes and sins. Religions were not to be criticized. Only wholesome values could be shown on the country's screens. As a result, as H. L. Mencken put it, the movies were "cribbed, cabined and confined by regulations that would now seem oppressive in a Baptist female seminary."[50] During the industry's high and palmy days, the code had a powerful impact on the movie industry. Mainstream movies were forced to play by these very strict rules. Under the code, no movie was to be produced, if it would (in the words of the code) "lower the moral standards" of the people who watched it.

The code had a relatively short life. It vanished in the 1950s. Legal blows hammered away at the various censorship boards.[51] The courts expanded the concept of freedom of expression in ways that made the job of the censors more difficult, and ultimately, impossible. In hindsight, the code seems to have embodied the dying spasm of Victorian repression. The so-called sexual revolution overwhelmed it. A new era upended Victorian prudery. Behind the sexual revolution was a larger social movement, a movement which glorified freedom of choice, the right of individuals to express themselves, to choose custom-made paths through life—subject, of course, to limitations—but on the whole, more expansive than in the past. It was a revolution in the way millions of people defined their personal identity. A revolution in a person's sense of what had to be kept under wraps and what that person could see, say, and do.

THE SINS OF THE FATHERS

Ghosts, written in 1881, was one of Henrik Ibsen's greatest and most famous plays. It was also one of the most controversial. Ibsen was Norwegian, but he wrote the play in Danish. He disliked the play's English title. The Danish title had nothing to do with "ghosts," it referred, rather, to people or events that return or repeat themselves. What returned and repeated itself, in the play, was the sinfulness of a father that was visited on his son.

Captain Alving, who never appears on stage, in some ways dominates the play. He is already dead when the play begins. Alving, it turns out, was a kind of Jekyll and Hyde character: widely respected in the community but a man with a secret life, the life of a philanderer, a life of illicit sexuality. His wife, Helen, on the advice of her pastor stayed married to him despite his moral failings, in part to avoid public scandal. Alving, however, contracted syphilis, a dreaded and intractable disease, which he transmits to his wife, and which now threatened to overwhelm his son, Oswald. At the end of the play, the sins of the father have come home to the son in a deadly and horrific way. As the curtain falls, the son's doom has become obvious, and nothing but tragedy lies ahead.

The play scandalized respectable society. Venereal disease was a topic unfit for public discussion, and definitely unfit for the theater. The play, even today, projects a powerful message: in its time, *Ghosts* bitterly attacked the hypocrisy of respectable society. That society (he felt) paid a fearful price for prudery, for its refusal to face the facts of life. The play also attacked the Captain Alvings of the world, the men (mostly men) who hid their secret sexual identity and in doing so, brought misery and ruin to innocent people.

Upton Sinclair, in *Damaged Goods* (1913), adapted from a play by Eugene Brieux, told a similar story. Young George, the main character, is engaged to a wealthy woman from a good and respectable family. George felt he led a fairly virtuous life, but he had consorted with at least two prostitutes. He discovers a "tiny ulcer" on his body. He goes to a doctor and discovers, to his horror, that he has contracted syphilis. The doctor warns him not to marry. The disease can be cured, but it would take several years. If you go ahead with the marriage, the doctor says, "you will be a criminal." George refuses to accept this advice. How would he be able to explain postponing the wedding for years? If he tells the truth, his father-in-law will undoubtedly insist that the marriage never take place. Desperate, George consults another doctor, a less reputable one, who promises to cure George quickly. George marries, his wife gives birth to a daughter, and the nightmares become reality. The daughter is born infected with the disease. When George's wife learns the truth, she takes the baby and walks out on George. But Sinclair provides *Damaged*

Goods with something of a happy ending: George's wife returns; the baby and George will undergo treatment. Presumably, they can ultimately get rid of the disease. Still, George and his wife have gone through hell before they reach this point. The moral of the story is clear: ignorance, and a refusal to face facts, inflicts enormous harm on society. Education, publicity, openness would save people from the fate of George and his wife.[52]

These works dealt with a social dilemma. Secret vice was destructive. Suppression did not work—the sex urge was too strong, prostitution too widespread. Social censorship only made the problem worse. Important subjects were taboo. Many people felt that secrecy and social censorship were absolutely necessary. But prudery exacted a heavy price. Publicity and education were one answer to the problem. The question was which strategy worked best: censorship and silence or publicity and sex education? There was always the danger, of course, that neither strategy would work.

Another strategy was to wage open war on vice. Every big city, and many smaller ones, had a "red-light" district, areas where brothels, low-down bars, and gambling joints were concentrated, virtual shopping centers of vice. The police usually turned a blind (or half-blind) eye to these districts. Payoffs greased the path of tolerance. In some cities, there was an informal licensing system. In Hartford, Connecticut, before 1911, houses of prostitution were "under the protection of a long tradition." They were "raided occasionally," but the houses only paid fines, and then immediately reopened for business.[53]

Corruption alone does not explain why the red-light districts had flourished. They were, after all, part of what I have called the Victorian compromise. They had plenty of customers and many people (not simply the police) felt they served a purpose. Yet in the late nineteenth and early twentieth centuries, a powerful campaign took hold in the United States, a war against sexual misconduct, prostitution, and "debauchery." The leaders of the campaign rejected the old system that tolerated vice. Vice had to be stamped out. In state after state, sex laws were tightened.[54] Communities in the early years of the twentieth century resolved to drive prostitution out of the cities, eliminate red-light districts, and shut down brothels forever. City after city formed vice commissions to study the problem, issue reports, and recommend solutions. Typically, the commissions proposed destroying prostitution root and branch; and close down the "red-light districts," where brothels spread disease and moral decay. In the words of the Minneapolis vice commission (1911), the houses of ill repute were the "source of most of the loathsome venereal disease which afflicts society."[55] Community welfare demanded their destruction.

There was also a demand to do something about the problem of so-called white slavery. Vicious men, it was believed, drugged, seduced, or overpowered innocent girls who came to the city, forcing them into prostitution. This would inevitably end badly for these young women; they would lose their health, their virtue, and their chance for happiness. Congress enacted the Mann Act in 1910, which made it a crime to transport a woman across state lines for purposes of prostitution, debauchery (this splendid word is now almost obsolete), or any other immoral purpose.[56] The war against vice was also a war against the saloon culture and the curse of drunkenness. Waves of temperance and local "dry" laws had swept the country at times, but the campaign in the twentieth century was more powerful—and more successful. In the period just after the end of World War I, an amendment to the US Constitution outlawed the sale of liquor.[57] The "noble experiment" of Prohibition lasted through the decade of the 1920s. This was a time of speakeasies, of bathtub gin, and organized crime. Prohibition gave American society another noxious form of split identity. The saloons did vanish. But the sale of liquor did not. Hundreds of speakeasies replaced them. City people never liked Prohibition, nor did immigrant populations on the whole. Prohibition was a White, Protestant movement, popular mostly in the countryside. It lost whatever luster it had as the years went on. Too many people wanted liquor and were determined to get it, by hook or by crook. Millions saw nothing inherently evil in a beer, a glass of wine, or a cocktail. In the 1930s, a new constitutional amendment put an end to the "noble experiment." The masses got their beer and wine and the elites their highballs and Scotch. When Prohibition died, not many mourners came to the funeral. Prohibition was swept into oblivion.

The antivice movement reflected many social forces, many political forces, and many cultural elements. The demographics of the country were changing dramatically. Immigrants from Southern and Eastern Europe were streaming onto American shores: Italians and Greeks, and Slavs and Jews. A kind of cultural panic gripped old-line Americans. This was one major source of the war on vice. In response, Congress enacted draconian immigration laws, to keep out the "huddled masses" that seemed to be a threat to traditional, old-line Protestant culture. Vice and bad seed were an internal danger; unlimited immigration was an external danger. The goal was to combat both types of threat; and to restore a regime of virtue and moderation. Urban life reflected a kind of split personality: respectable neighborhoods, and red-light districts. Cities, like men, were both Jekyll and Hyde. Vice commissions pointed the way to reform. The cities had to get rid of their corrupt underside. Sexual abstinence had to replace the culture of the brothels. As the Minneapolis commission put it, there was only one way to "absolute safety": young men should "lead clean lives," the lives their mothers and sisters led, the lives they would demand from "the girls they are to marry."[58]

It was, alas, not a practical way. Social duality was not so easily conquered. Ultimately, the war against vice was lost. There was a contradiction at the heart of the war. Censorship and prudery were important because they protected society. But they also harmed society: they were the veil that protected men like Captain Alving, that allowed them their split personalities. Moral leaders insisted on keeping the Victorian code; but they failed. Sexual life, and such topics as contraception, came out of the closet. The dream of conquering immorality turned into a nightmare.

The death of Prohibition was only the beginning. The age of the flapper and the speakeasy evolved into the age of *Playboy* magazine and the permissive society, a drastic turn of the wheel. The Kinsey reports (1948 and 1953) were a single generation later than the Vice Commission reports. The underlying attitude seemed light-years away. The door opened, not just to discussion, but to outright tolerance of ways of life, ideas, and habits that had been censored and suppressed. A time of repression and censorship morphed into a period that exalted free and open choice. Societies were still divided into strata of Jekyll and Hyde, but they were very differently defined and assessed.

Chapter 8

Coming Together and Moving Apart

In the mobile society, some people took advantage of the problem of identity and preyed on fellow citizens. Others masked their personal identity and "passed" in one way or another. Neither group was anything close to a majority. Bigamists were few, compared to the men who stayed married, or filed for divorce. Solid citizens outnumbered confidence men. Most African Americans would not or could not pass.

Not that ambiguous, fluid identity was rare. It was and is a general aspect of life. Jekyll and Hyde were extreme cases. But ordinary people, too, had their hidden side, their role playing. And they lived, after all, in a world of cultural, social, and economic mobility. Personal identity was not simply problematic, it was also prismatic, changeable, and in some ways and some respects, a matter of personal choice.

Mobility opened locked doors. But taking advantage of opportunities was never easy. The ladder of success was available. Individuals and families moved from their homes to new places. Americans were restless, eager for novelty. Millions of Europeans also moved: from village to city or from Europe to America. Personal choice, however, was always subject to severe constraints. Some glittering choices were simply forbidden, by law or custom. Cost and social structure closed many of the open doors. A dense network of rules, customs, and habits, enforced by law, and by gossip, shunning, and other forms of informal punishment, stood in the way of self-fulfillment.

Yet culture and structure both changed dramatically from the nineteenth to the twentieth centuries, and then into the twenty-first. Laws changed—norms and expectations even more so. The menu of choices expanded. The caterpillar, whose sole job in life is to crawl on the ground, munch on leaves, and grow fat, becomes, in the end, a butterfly, a creature with wings, a creature that can fly. Men in developed countries (and, more slowly, women) burst free of the cocoon of custom. Their freedom was both real and illusory. The menu had expanded: customers had more choices and could pick what they wanted. But only if it was already on the menu.

The expansion of choice—of the menu—did not take place overnight. It was, as always, gradual, incremental. Slowly, the sense of who one was, the sense of personal identity, morphed into a new notion: a more voluntary, more personal, more idiosyncratic sense of self. For the Victorians, indeed, identity had become more fluid and open than it had been. This was both liberating and dangerous. The sense of danger led to suppression and control—of sexual life very notably, as we saw. Ultimately, the regime of suppression was forced to retreat. We discussed the war on vice—a war to keep society on an even keel, a war on behalf of some elements of the old morality. Sigmund Freud—at least this is one way to read his work—felt that civilization needed to repress some of its wildest impulses. At the same time, Freud put forward, and made popular, new and fairly radical ideas about sex. His theory of the unconscious seemed to suggest that every Jekyll had its own Mr. Hyde. And one that, perhaps, in some ways needed to be released.

Personal identity had become, well before our times, more fluid. The menu of acts, behaviors, attitudes, and ways of life expanded. The ropes loosened. Old norms decayed. People became freer to indulge in their sexual choices; and in other choices as well: what games to play, what clothes to wear, what places to live in, what hobbies to pursue. We morphed into an age of expressive individualism; an age of what I have called the republic of choice. But always, of course, subject to severe constraints: only someone incredibly naïve or willfully ignorant could overlook how much depended on race, gender, class, wealth, genetic inheritance, family, and sheer luck. Most caterpillars die before they become butterflies. Birds eat them, parasites attack them, food supplies fail them.

Still, the middle class (at least) is freer to choose than ever before. Consider, for example, what we eat. Eating is a basic human need. It is more essential to survival than sexual behavior, and (apparently) much less contested. In some ways, the sociology of food and eating tells an important story about the way notions of personal identity have evolved.

At one time, eating habits were essentially inherited. You ate the food of your community. Italians ate Italian food, Japanese ate Japanese food, Mexicans ate Mexican food. The French, the Chinese, the Japanese, were societies that were fiercely proud of their cuisines (the less said about traditional English food the better; or American cuisine, for that matter). Citizens of country A almost always sat down to dinner eating the customary food of country A. They never considered eating foods of countries B and C, which struck them (if they thought about them at all) as strange, unpalatable, or even disgusting. In California, for example, in the period around 1900, a time of great hatred against the Chinese, the White majority totally rejected Chinese food. Chinese dishes seemed barbaric, nauseating, foul-smelling, unfit for White mouths to chew, White throats to swallow, White bellies to digest. That was then—more than a century ago. If those Californians of 1900 miraculously came back to life, they would be astonished to see crowds of Anglos in Chinese restaurants and even more astonished to see little Anglo children using chopsticks, as if they had been born to it.

Today, of course, Californians—and everybody else—have branched out beyond Chinese food. Some dishes have become almost universal. Pizza, for one. Yes, pizza is Italian—Southern Italian at that, but its origin hardly matters any more. More surprising, perhaps (and more recent), is the international craze for sushi. People eagerly gobble it down—people who, two generations ago, would have eaten raw fish wrapped in seaweed only if they were on the brink of starvation. I learned on the web that, in 2018, there were 203 sushi establishments in Berlin, 437 in Moscow, 281 in Santiago, Chile, and more than 50 in Lima, Peru. In Berlin there were also 300 Vietnamese restaurants, 164 Indian restaurants—"foreign" eateries outnumbered the ones described as "German." In the remote Faroe Islands, there is a restaurant whose sushi is considered "outstanding." And a town in Bavaria not only has sushi but will serve it in a setting that (they say) is more or less very much like an authentic Japanese *onsen*, or bathhouse.

Sushi, of course, is still associated with Japan. Foreigners probably still hesitate to eat some varieties that the Japanese find tasty. It is also still true that the Japanese are proud of their cuisine: sushi, sashimi, and tempura (thought tempura is actually a Portuguese invader), and their grand kaiseki meals. More restaurants in Tokyo have earned stars in the Michelin guide than in Paris. This, of course, is yet another sign of globalization: the French consider their cuisine the best in the world, but they are increasingly willing to treat other cuisines with almost equal respect. Many of the great chefs in Paris are not French at all. In 2016, it was reported that Japanese chefs headed forty of the leading Parisian restaurants.[1]

You can, of course, get sushi in Paris—you can also get Mexican food if you wish, and naturally Italian food as well. Michelin has given stars to restaurants in many countries—Thailand, for example, and the United States. Meanwhile, back in Japan, hip Japanese can choose from many cuisines, and many restaurants, with or without Michelin stars. Today, in Tokyo and other Japanese cities, you can enjoy Korean barbecue, or Chinese food, you can also elect French, Italian, or Hungarian food. Sushi, as we said, at one time must have seemed unthinkable to Americans or Finns. At that time, too, the Japanese and Chinese would have balked at eating a foreign food that consisted, basically, of congealed, evil-smelling dairy fat. Today, this is considered a delicacy in Tokyo, as it is in Paris, and in other world cities. I am referring, of course, to certain types of cheese.

In our times, in short, millions of people—admittedly, mostly middle class and up—have developed cosmopolitan eating habits. Indeed, they take these habits for granted. Two American friends would find it not the least bit peculiar to say, "Let's do Mexican food tonight," or Burmese, or Hungarian. Countries differ in this regard. Italians still mostly eat Italian food (and why not?). Americans are much less fixated on "American" food (again, why should they be?). But food habits, in general, have changed enormously. In every major city in the developed world, as we have seen, dozens of restaurants serve something other than the national food. This is true all up and down the scale of restaurants. If you want Mexican food in Tokyo, you can have it, and if you want sushi in Budapest that, too, is available. And if you fancy McDonalds or Kentucky Fried Chicken, you can have that too.

Food is only one example of an important, and emerging phenomenon. It is the globalization of culture. It expresses the primacy of individual choice; a sense of personal identity that is open to new experiences, and new ways of thinking and acting. Millions of middle-class people in the developed world take vacations in foreign countries. Tourism has a history, but it was, at one time, mostly open to the rich. In today's world, tourism is of major political, cultural, and economic importance. Countries with warm weather or exciting sights, or both, may derive a fat share of their GNP from tourism. Tourist travel is one of the reasons—though not, I think, the primary reason—why food habits have become more cosmopolitan. The crucial factor is a willingness to open one's mind (and wallet) to cultures other than one's own. Some tourists are boorish and thoughtless, others want to see and feel other ways of living, other styles of life—other identities, if you will. People from cold climates flock in the winter to places with beaches and palm trees. This seems only natural; but it is, in fact, not natural at all. The trip takes money, but also the willingness to leave home, try different food, see different surroundings. To be sure, some tourists simply want to reproduce England or Sweden (food and all) in a warmer climate. But the millions gawking at the pyramids or Michelangelo's *David* or a Zen Garden in Kyoto may want something more, something they cannot get at home. Some will even, eventually, "go native" and may go so far as to change, not just landscapes and cuisines, but also, at times, languages, countries, and even ways of life.

Religion itself is an example of how, in the age of expanded choice, inherited personalities, customs, and habits can turn brittle. A 2009 survey on religious attitudes and behavior in the United States by the Pew Research Center turned up an astounding fact: more than 40 percent of all surveyed adults had changed religion at some point in their lives.[2] These were people who no longer felt bound to their inherited religion. You might even call this religious tourism. Just as so many could decide to try Hungarian or even Ethiopian food, just as they could decide to leave their own backyard and visit Istanbul, or go trekking in Nepal, so, too, they might decide to try a new or different religion. The United States is perhaps something of an outlier here. It is, after all, much more diverse, religiously speaking, than other developed countries. Churches in the United States sometimes vigorously proselytize, or, to put it another way, market themselves. Still, religious tourism (if we can call it that) is not just American. Millions of people in Latin America, who used to be Roman Catholic, have now signed on to Protestant evangelical churches. Mormon missionaries radiate out from Salt Lake City to convert people all over the world, and with a good deal of success. In the United States, you don't have to be East Asian to be a Buddhist; you don't have to hail from the Middle East to convert to Islam. Or to Bahai. Or to leave any of these, and choose something else, or no religion at all.[3]

These are examples of what has become so salient in the world of today: the idea that one can *choose* a personal identity. You can get rid of what you were born with and take on new aspects of the self, like a reptile molting and getting a new skin. Eating in a Hungarian restaurant is a mild example, visiting Belgium or Patagonia is fairly innocuous, shifting from country to country, or going from one church to another, is a good deal more drastic.

Perhaps the most extreme example would be to shed the gender you were born with and take on an entirely different one. Most people, of course, would never consider this. But there are those who do consider this move; and they can, and sometimes do, make the transition from one gender to another. Modern hormone therapy and surgery make sex reassignment surgery possible. This was performed as early as the 1930s in Germany. Christine Jorgensen, born a male in the United States, had surgery in Denmark in 1951, and became a woman—and a celebrity.[4] Much less drastic—and more ordinary—are nose jobs, face lifts, and plastic surgery in general. Hair dyeing is even more common. For some young people, changing from brown to blonde is not edgy enough: they choose orange, purple, and other colors not normally found in nature. Socially and psychologically, all these changes—from sex to hair color—reflect a distinctively modern feeling of fluidity, with regard to personal identity. It reflects as well an increase in the range of options. And, more significantly, an increase in the number of people who are willing to take advantage of these options.

ASSIMILATION AND ITS DISCONTENTS

Fluidity and free choice (in certain areas) are striking characteristics of modern society; the idea that human beings can remake the self, can transform their personal identity. Yet one also hears that people in modern societies are terrific conformists—followers not leaders, sheep not shepherds, people whose attitudes and behaviors shift with the winds of fashion. In *The Lonely Crowd* (1950), David Riesman and his associates divided people into three types, each with their own mode of "character": tradition-directed, inner-directed, and other-directed. Tradition-directed people stick to the inherited past. They are born, live, and die in the cage of inherited norms and institutions. Inner-directed people are goal-oriented, but their goals are "implanted early in life by the elders," they obey the rules of society, and are kept "on course" by goals already set. "Self-made men" (and, presumably, self-made women) are inner-directed—they burst free of traditional restraints and climb the ladder of success as much as they can by internalizing a rather rigid set of norms. The mobility of the period set them free, politically and economically. In the United States, however, (and surely elsewhere) a new personality, a new character type emerged and became (according to Riesman) extremely common. These were people "other-directed." They take their cues from their peers, their contemporaries—either people they know or those they are acquainted with "indirectly" through the mass media.[5] Other-directed people are conformists—what other people think and do constitutes their "chief source of direction and chief area of sensitivity." In short, they take their "signals" from other people.[6]

The Lonely Crowd is a complex and subtle study of character and behavior, and it is easy to oversimplify the main line of argument. Still, the authors seemed to identify something that struck many observers as quite real: a fundamental change in character and behavior. Kids, as they grow up, tend to get signals from friends, peers, people they see on TV and in the movies, people they admire. Today, one would add, they get signals from the internet and social media. Signals from parents, teachers, and religious leaders have gotten weaker. To other-directed people, authority is, on the whole, horizontal rather than vertical, that is, it is the authority of people on their own level, rather than the vertical authority of leaders, parents, and the like.[7] They mold their behavior, and in a way their identity, using implicit or explicit messages from their horizontal peers. They tend, by and large, to conform, to watch, and imitate what people like them are doing. They react to what other people expect from them.

Their behavior seems on the surface very different from the individualism that modern life permits and even fosters. "Other-direction" looks like conformity because in a crucial sense it *is* conformity. All over the developed world people dress alike, listen to the same music, go to the same movies. Even the external world is conformist. People drive the same cars; they work and live in the same kind of buildings. The very shape of cities is global and strikingly conformist. One style of architecture dominates. A skyscraper in Shanghai or Dubai is no different from a skyscraper in New York. People may have eclectic tastes in food, but in one sense this, too, is conformity: sushi, hamburgers, and pizza are everywhere. Clothing is global too. People choose styles and colors, but within a fairly narrow range. Traditional costumes and dress are dying out. A Japanese secretary, sitting at her computer, wears a dress or slacks rather than a kimono. Her boss, the sarariman, wears a suit and tie. Young people in Amsterdam and Rotterdam wear blue jeans or chino pants; nobody wears wooden shoes. Middle-class dress is the same the world over. Arab sheiks dress differently—the man in the street in Cairo does not. Even the concept of fashion, though it implies constant change, also implies conformity—obedience to twists and turns of skirt length or type of shoe or glove. Today, ideas, images, and fashions have the power to sweep over the planet in seconds. This is not what causes conformity and uniformity, but it is a condition, a prerequisite.

The two notions—fluidity of choice on the one hand; sheeplike conformity on the other—seem utterly inconsistent. Yet, in a deeper sense, they are sisters; they reflect the same social forces. In traditional societies, conformity was never an issue, it was simply taken for granted. In modern societies, conformists are people who play follow the leader, but the individual can *choose* what leader to follow, what fashions to adopt—and what fashions to discard for something new; what leaders to select. A person who leaves the Catholic Church and becomes a Buddhist, who becomes an activist for civil rights, or a member of a neo-Nazi party, or a groupie who follows a rock band wherever it goes—these people, indeed, become conformists, but, although they may be like sheep, they chose the flock they belong to. If you follow the zigzags of fashion and buy clothes because "everybody" is wearing that style, you are of course conforming. But dressing in the "latest style" means you are open to change; indeed, change is the rule of your life. Traditional people are "conformists" too, but they wear what their ancestors wore. The old-order Amish dress in the style of the eighteenth century.

Choice and fluidity: these are crucial to modern character and modern personality. But choice has to be understood in context. Choice can cost money. In the developed world, there is a huge middle class; this widens the range of alternatives for millions of people and makes possible a consumer society.[8] For the poorest of the poor, the menu is constricted. It is hunger or the soup kitchen rather than a French restaurant or a sushi bar. Moreover, although people *think* they have free choice (and do, to a degree), they are, or can be, unaware of the powerful constraints on their behavior: psychological, cultural, and social. Choice, in short, may be an illusion. Suddenly, a fashion grips millions. Kids begin to wear baseball caps backward. Young women get tattoos. But why? What makes pizza or sushi so desirable? The reasons are mysterious. Society is a kind of puppet master pulling the strings. The puppets imagine they are in control. And, ironically, free choice does not mean choosing freedom or democracy. Thousands may blindly follow some guru. Millions freely vote for a dictatorial candidate.

Concepts of personal identity change over time. Most people probably find some sort of stable balance in their lives. It may take something of a search. The Pew Research Center found, as we saw, that millions of people in the United States seem to be looking for a spiritual home. Perhaps they eventually find it. Others look to clothing styles, types of cuisine, home decorations, hobbies, music and sports, to find satisfaction. Very often, they end up sharing attitudes and behavior with like-minded people: peers, friends, people they admire. In a curious way, conformity and free choice do not necessarily stand in opposition to each other.

A further point: Yes, the menu of choices has expanded and yet, in many ways, world cultures are converging. Powerful forces push us toward assimilation and a global melting pot. People in Japan, or the Netherlands, or New Zealand, are closer than in the past in their habits, culture, ways of life. Regional differences are flattened out. Minority languages disappear along with the cultures they represent. Majority culture is simply too powerful. TV and universal education tend to homogenize. National cultures replace a jumble of local customs and dialogues. In 1800, most people in France did not speak Parisian French. They spoke a dialect, or a different language altogether (Breton, Provencal, Catalan, Basque). Life centered on one's village and one's region. Today, a single language dominates as well as a sense of nationhood. As Eugen Weber has shown, better roads, national schools, service in the army were forces that promoted a single, national culture. Railroads, radio, TV, movies, the internet, the automobile—each also played a role.[9] This process took place in many nation states. Dialects and minority languages withered away. In the United Kingdom, Manx and Cornish are extinct; Welsh struggles to survive. In Germany people speak "German," not Swabian or Plattdeutsch. More and more people in Italy speak Italian, not the dialect of Venice or Rome, which Grandma spoke. Mexicans speak Spanish, by and large, not indigenous languages. A common patriotism, a common flag, a common *identity*: these are the hallmarks of modern nationalism. There is no international government; and none seems likely. But a global *culture* is very much a reality: the culture of sushi, Beethoven, rock and roll, and blue jeans. And, to an extent, the culture of constitutional government and human rights.

IDENTITY POLITICS

Convergence, and the spread of a global culture, seem to run contrary to another mighty cultural and political force in today's world: so-called identity politics. This is a vast and volcanic tendency that erupts with tremendous strength over the global landscape. Indigenous people demand their rights: rights to speak their language, to hunt and fish, land rights, religious rights, customary rights—above all, the right to be *themselves*, to assert their identity, to resist absorption into the general cultural, political, and social mass. Women, racial minorities, ethnic minorities, religious minorities, sexual minorities, the elderly, the handicapped, prisoners and aliens: each has developed a powerful movement, demanding a place at the table in contemporary society, all of them asserting a right to claim their specific and special identity.

These movements feed off each other, but they are, of course, each distinct, and different from the others. Also, they express themselves in different ways in different countries. Sometimes they join forces, sometimes they contend with each other. But they represent a single broad trend: a demand for the right to express, acknowledge, even to glory in, a "true" identity for group members. Indeed, some members insist that this element, this "true" identity, is, or can be (or should be), stronger and more meaningful than other elements of identity. This "true" identity, which trumps all the others, could be race, religion, or some form of gender. It could be old age, or deafness or blindness, or the fact that one speaks Quechua or Navajo or Breton at home, or a combination of these various possibilities.

In the United States, the civil rights movement was the most dramatic example of this trend. It brought about massive changes in society and set in motion a powerful political force. The feminist movement has been perhaps even more spectacular; it, too, has made a permanent mark on society. There is something of a feminist movement in perhaps every single country. The aggregate impact of all of the movements listed has been enormous, immeasurable, and global. Gender equality, racial equality, fundamental rights: the constitutions of most modern nations (at least those that have at least some semblance of democracy) embody these principles together with international and regional charters of human rights. Legal texts are, on the whole, effects of social movements rather than causes. Nonetheless, they are meaningful. Each society, as we said, has its own story to tell. But there are common elements. Feminists have a harder time in Japan, say, than in Sweden. But there is definitely a feminist movement in Japan. Gender rights are on the agenda everywhere, even in Saudi Arabia where women were not allowed to drive cars until 2021. Women protest against rape and domestic violence in India as well as in Spain or France. Indigenous rights are an issue in Canada, Australia, and New Zealand, as well as in Bolivia, Ecuador, and Peru. There are gay pride parades in Tel Aviv. Gay marriage is now legal in Ireland. One can speak, indeed, of a general and global *culture* of human rights, which is found in different countries in various dialects, but with a common core.[10]

People talk, loosely, of the rights of *groups*, that is, the rights of the elderly, or women, or people who speak Basque, or illegitimate children, or Australian natives. It might be more accurate to talk about group *claims*: reparations, hunting and fishing rights, respect for minority languages, restoration of lost tribal lands or, more broadly, the rights of women to enter professions that were historically only for men, or the rights of social untouchables. In the nineteenth century, nationalism developed dramatically. Minorities demanded recognition for their cultures and languages within national frameworks. In the late twentieth century, other minority claims became salient: prisoners, the elderly, the handicapped, indeed, almost everybody. Yet, at their core, what is at stake in all of these are *individual* rights, not group rights. What is at stake is the right to choose. The right to join the mainstream—or not. Women's rights mean the rights of women to stay home and darn socks, but only if they want to; or, on the other hand, to join the fire department, or start a business, or run for Parliament. Group rights simply means empowering members to follow their own sense of who they are, what they are, and what they want to be, despite membership in what was, and is, socially defined as a class or category of people.

Of course, this means dismantling obstacles to choice. It means rejecting castes and ghettos. But the essential point is choice. The choice of an identity. Discrimination, after all, means denying the right to assert an identity. Just as a Spanish woman from Madrid can decide to go to a Hungarian restaurant, or become a Buddhist, she can also decide to do things that only men could do in earlier times. An African can decide to leave his village for Nairobi or Mombasa or stay behind and lead a more traditional life, or he can even try to go as far as Europe or the United States.

This is, after all, an age of individualism. Of course, so was the nineteenth century—particularly in economic life. Markets were, for many people, empowering. The story of choice, which is crucial to this narrative, is also a story of societies getting richer, a story of rampant consumerism and the triumph of advertising. It is also the age of what has been called *expressive* individualism, as we have mentioned.[11] Expressive individualism goes beyond jobs and markets and free labor: it is an individualism of choice and personal identity. The central idea is this: Each person is a unique being, with unique talents and desires (and unique flaws, no doubt). Each has, or should have, the ability to aim for one's personal goals. Setting goals involves the "construction of a 'possible self' in which one is different from the now self and in which one realizes the goal."[12] In short, it is the right and the power to imagine a different future, to choose a personal identity, or some aspect of personal identity.

As we have said, this is not what real life is like. I have made this point before, but it is worth repeating, and even emphasizing. Changes are relative, not absolute. Choice has expanded, but the choices for a truck driver, or a salesclerk at Walmart, or a single mother with three children in Italy, or a Somali refugee in Sweden, whatever their hopes and dreams, is limited by poverty, discrimination, background, and education. Poverty, in particular, is a kind of prison cell. And social inequality, the distance between classes and strata, between rich and poor, is immense—and seems, in fact, to be growing.

THE MELTING POT

Identity politics seems to stand in sharp contrast to the politics of assimilation. In the American context, identity politics seems to contradict the classic metaphor of the "melting pot." The idea was that all cultures, races, and creeds go into the pot and somehow fuse into a single identity, presumably one that is distinctively American. "Cooking" transforms the raw ingredients; the finished dish is not simply the sum of its parts. "Assimilation" and the "melting pot" also implied that immigrants would get rid of get rid of most of the trappings of their old identities, old loyalties and customs; the new, fused American culture would swallow them up; if not them, then their children and grandchildren.

But today, assimilation has become an issue in countries where it never was before. Sweden is one example. Once Sweden was basically homogeneous. Most everyone was born there, spoke Swedish, and belonged to (or ignored) the same religion. Many Swedes left for America in the nineteenth century. Nobody left Africa for Sweden. Today, there are refugees and asylum-seekers in Sweden who come from Africa and the Middle East. How much they, and their children, will "assimilate" is hard to predict. Many Swedes resent the newcomers, especially those that are dark-skinned or Muslim, or both. Tension and discrimination make absorption and assimilation more difficult.

Even in the classic immigration countries, it has not always been easy to absorb new arrivals. In the United States, some dialect of White Protestant culture was dominant, politically and culturally. There were nativist movements throughout American history. Race was, of course, a sharp dividing line. It was also a dividing line in Canada and Australia. Race and religion separated welcome from unwelcome immigrants. The Protestant majority in the United States was never comfortable with Catholic immigrants—especially the Irish who came in droves in the late 1840s. The Ku Klux Klan of the 1920s was virulent anti-Catholic.[13] Chinese exclusion laws assumed that the Chinese were so different, racially and culturally, that they could never be assimilated. The "White Australia" policy rested on something of the same assumption.

As we mentioned, when large numbers of Italian, Greek, Jewish, and Slavic immigrants landed in New York Harbor in the late nineteenth century, they touched off a cultural panic among old-line Americans. The result was to tighten immigration law.[14] These blatantly discriminatory immigration laws are gone. But the issue remains. Muslim and Hispanic immigrants have inherited the role of immigrant scapegoats.

In many European countries, immigration has created a political crisis. Sweden is one example; but nativist groups are in every European country. They resent immigrants who are Black, or Muslim; people from Africa and the Middle East. They resent the desperate people in rickety boats on the Mediterranean; the Africans trying to scale the fence in Ceuta; the Syrians fleeing their wrecked and war-torn country. Refugees look for safe haven and a new life in a Europe which does not want them. They evoke fears and resentment. People say they steal jobs. They cause crime. They will never be true Finns or true Italians. The fears, of course, are overblown. The main debate, however, is how best to shut the door on these unwelcome visitors. Perhaps many people want to welcome then; and believe in assimilation. Just give them time. But others are skeptical.

In the United States, the Trump administration had massively xenophobic impulses. The government called the immigrants—Muslim and Hispanic—a danger, a pestilence, an invasive species, or worse, a Trojan horse hiding criminals and terrorists. Ironically, the immigration crisis was, in a way, a tribute to globalization, to the culture of choice, to modernity, and, yes, to convergence and assimilation. Truly traditional people did not, and do not, migrate. A Brazilian tribe, in the depths of the Amazon jungle, surrounded by a strange green world of anacondas and piranhas, cut off from "civilization," contributes nothing to the immigration crisis. Members of the tribe would not, and could not, move to the slums of Rio de Janeiro let alone the streets of New York City or Tokyo or London. For them, the move would be as alien (and as impossible) as a trip to the moon.

Actual immigrants fleeing gang violence in Honduras, or the grinding poverty of their homes in Africa, or the bombed-out rubble of their Syrian town, are all, to a degree, at least half-way ready (culturally speaking) for a new life in Europe or Australia or North America. They wear T-shirts and blue jeans; they use cell phones. They have seen the promised land on television. They know some English or French. They may have a cousin in Stockholm or Minneapolis. They may be only half-way to the promised land, culturally speaking; or even less. But that portion is critical. Cultural convergence means that they can at least *imagine* the journey, and the endpoint of the journey as well. Fewer societies and social groups find it impossible to make cultural and geographical changes: few are too cut off from the rest of the world to live outside their villages. In a world of television, movies, the internet, cell phones, and social media, personal identity has become more fluid than ever. Vivid images show other ways of life; ways that seem different, and in many cases, better. It becomes more and more possible to change cultures and countries and to shift, in a sense, a person's identity.

Of course, "modernity" (however one defines it) is not a monolith. The issues mentioned here—immigration, assimilation, convergence, the politics of diversity—are each maddeningly complex. In addition, every aspect of modernity has generated some sort of counter aspect, some sort of resistance or backlash—for example, the rise of religious fundamentalism. To the ultra-devout, religion still dominates every aspect of life. Some deeply religious people reject majority cultures. They may also reject democracy. They do not accept the human rights culture. Many countries in the Middle East, for example, see no place for women in public life. The ultra-devout may live among infidels, may see them on the street every day, may work alongside them, yet at some level they cannot accept them as equals. Free choice is not an option. You cannot choose sin. You cannot choose what God has forbidden. In extreme cases, you *may* choose outright war against nonbelievers.

This is extreme. Today, even the ultra-devout accept, as they must, bits and pieces of modernity. A Muslim woman may appear in public only when wrapped like a mummy and invisible except for eye-slits in her niqab. Yet, at home, she may step into another world altogether, a kind of looking-glass world. There, behind closed doors, she may watch television, use a computer, and (yes) eat pizza and sushi. Terrorists fight the West with Western implements—cell phones, social media, video recordings, GPS systems—not to mention drones, bombs, and automatic weapons. These terrorists, for the most part, were not born into the role. This choice, in the last analysis, is as much a matter of expressive individualism, as much a matter of fluid identity, as the decision to eat Chinese food instead of traditional cuisine or to shift from one church on Sunday to another. Or to align oneself with the right or the left, to choose socialism or to choose a charismatic leader; or to forgo politics altogether. You can choose to be Jekyll or Hyde. In many ways, the choice of identity, in a world of strangers, lies open.

Chapter 9

Brave New World

Much of the material discussed in earlier chapters of this book have been historical. Though some aspects of contemporary life have already been touched upon, in this chapter I will discuss topics that deal with identity and related matters in the twenty-first-century world. To do this properly would take many pages, perhaps many books. But I do want to expand—briefly—on a number of these themes.

Today, problems of blurred and counterfeit identity have not disappeared. Their form may be different. There is no shortage of confidence men, for example. There are still gullible people, and con men to cheat them. In fact, modern technology, especially the internet, has given clever crooks a battery of new tools. Blackmail will survive as long as there are people who have things to hide. Bigamy, too, is not extinct. In 2009, it was reported that Douglas Ulysses Johnson, described as a "Don Juan bigamist," had left behind a trail of cheated women.[1] In Savannah, Georgia, Johnson married a woman and stole a car and cash. In Jacksonville, Florida, he dated a woman he met on the internet, proposed to her, and began plans for yet another wedding. He stole $12,000 worth of jewelry while she was at work, then packed up and left in a red four-door Nissan. Johnson, of course, is essentially a thief: a Mr. Hyde posing as Dr. Jekyll, and "passing" for honest. Yet, on the whole, old-fashioned bigamy is probably not taken as seriously today as it was. Living in sin is not what it used to be. A woman tricked into marrying a married man has a right to be outraged, but is not likely to be considered "ruined goods" in the Victorian sense.[2]

In the civil rights era, light-skinned men and women in the United States, who have Black ancestry, no longer feel the same need to "pass." They are more likely simply to take pride in their heritage; and take an active role in Black cultural and political life. In 1945, as we mentioned in chapter 4, Harry Murphy, who passed for White, enrolled in the University of Mississippi, which would have rejected him in a flash had the school known of his background. Today, "Ole Miss" is more likely to welcome his children and grandchildren; indeed, they might qualify for affirmative action.

Sexual "passing" still exists, but it is more a matter of choice. Openly gay people march in pride parades, appear on TV, run for office, and are prominent in the arts and in business. Homophobia, like racism, is of course far from dead. A lot depends on circumstances—and on geography. In a small, deeply religious town in the Deep South, it might still be wise to "pass" for straight. The situation in San Francisco is entirely different. The mayor of Chicago, Lori Lightfoot, is a gay woman. Pete Buttigieg, a gay man married to another gay man, was appointed to the cabinet by President Biden.

The world is an uncertain and perilous place. Uncertainties have an impact on the way people live, and what they think and do. Some older risks have been eliminated, or have become less deadly. Multitudes are alive today who might have died from smallpox, cholera, yellow fever, or plague. Antibiotics and surgical miracles save lives. The polio virus is virtually extinct. Diabetics, thanks to insulin, can live close to normal lives. Chemotherapy, radiation, and other medical procedures save or extend life for victims of cancer. In developed countries, women rarely die in childbirth. Their babies, too, survive. Life expectancy has increased. People live longer and healthier lives. Yet, at the time of this writing (summer 2022), the COVID-19 virus still wreaks havoc throughout the world.

The pandemic of 2020–2021 harmed the economy in many countries. Its long-run impact is still uncertain. Still, in developed countries, economic uncertainty is less of an existential threat to the population. Banks still fail, but deposit insurance protects the customers' money. Currency is sound; and nobody worries about fake bank notes anymore. In wealthier countries, a vigorous welfare state, and strong economic growth, have smoothed out many wrinkles in the lives of millions of people and reduced the amount of sheer, grinding poverty. There are pensions for the elderly, and for the disabled. There is unemployment compensation, free education through high school; and, in most countries, there is a national medical insurance plan (the United States is something of a laggard here). Many people have life insurance policies. Governments step in when disasters strike: floods, earthquakes, hurricanes. There are still homeless people, many of them mentally ill. Some people still go hungry, but there are fewer famines. Nobody in the Netherlands or Malta or New Zealand starves to death.

In the welfare state, people talk about the "social safety net." It is an apt metaphor. The phrase calls to mind a circus performer, walking a tightrope high above the crowd. If performers fall, they will not be killed or badly injured. More people will walk tightropes (including metaphorical ones) if there is in fact a net. The social safety net provides protection for those who plunge from the tightrope, economically or otherwise. In an age where people may choose (to a degree) their way of life, social safety nets permit them to take chances. A lost job, a natural disaster: these will not necessarily mean utter ruin. Even bankruptcy laws are safety nets, in a way. A family puts all of their money into a new restaurant. This is a precarious business. Most new restaurants fail. Bankruptcy laws permit second chances for businesses and wage-earners who are swamped with debt. In general, contemporary societies are more generous with second chances than those of the past. Not totally, of course. An ex-convict still has enormous trouble getting a job.

Social guarantees allow people to try out new identities. To be sure, people still suffer, even in rich countries, from job insecurity, low wages, bills that can't be paid, sicknesses that can't be cured or cured quickly. Calamities still occur. Inequality—vast gaps between the haves and have-nots—exist in all societies and (as we said) may even be growing. Superbugs evolve; they are in a deadly arms race with the armory of antibiotics. COVID-19 is testing the capacity of the world. Meanwhile, a nuclear war could wipe out whole civilizations. Population growth and loss of habitat are causing a wave of mass extinctions of plants and animals.[3] The Yangtze river dolphin is gone: What is next? Climate change, we are warned, will have catastrophic consequences; we are already experiencing some of these. Waters are rising. Glaciers are melting. Hurricanes seem more frequent and more deadly. Wildfires consume millions of acres of forest and burn down thousands of houses.

Victorians had many worries, but ordinary people did not lose sleep over the danger from terrorists. There were, to be sure, political assassinations. Gunmen killed four American presidents: Lincoln, Garfield, McKinley, and Kennedy. There were at least eight attempts to kill Queen Victoria.[4] The czar of Russia, Alexander II, was assassinated in 1881. An assassination in Serbia touched off the First World War. Today's terrorist attacks are different: they are on a bigger scale, for one thing. Thousands died in the attack on the World Trade Center on 9/11. In March 2004, 193 people died after an attack on commuter trains in Madrid. A major attack targeted the London underground on July 7, 2005. Consider, too, the horrific toll taken by suicide bombers, mostly but not entirely in the Middle East. Modern terror seems to come out of nowhere. Nobody is safe, there is no haven—not a café, not a theater, not a public building, not an airport, not the Boston marathon. The 9/11 attack was the product of long, careful, and meticulous planning. Attacks of this kind are rare. Still, anybody can rent a van and plow down pedestrians.

Worse, victims are not kings and prime ministers, but ordinary people, going about their business, working, eating dinner, strolling down a boulevard, riding on a bus or in the subway. Random, unpredictable attacks give terrorists enormous psychological power. People feel helpless and vulnerable; they become afraid of strangers, especially those who "belong to unfamiliar, hostile, and potentially harmful groups."[5] This kind of fear builds up powerful political momentum. It justifies the "war on terror," a war of staggering cost. Consider how much is spent on airport security; think also of the price tag for surveillance cameras. Add to all this the costs in lost time and opportunity, the sheer inconvenience, imposed on millions of travelers—and on ordinary people trying to enter a bank or a courthouse.

Fear of crime is another form of uncertainty. Millions of people stay home behind locked and bolted doors, afraid of crime. Serial killers, like terrorists, kill at random. Burglars and armed robbers are more rational, but no less dangerous or harmful. Jack the Ripper was, perhaps, an isolated case, and unlike modern terrorists, he had only a handful of victims. At that time, the well-off could take comfort in the fact that Jack's victims were women from the bottom layers of society. But a terrorist's bombs on a bus, train, or a subway can kill across lines of class, gender, and race. Terrorists, like spies or Jack the Ripper, might be persons we see every day on the street: people with secret identities, whose plans are invisible to us. In this sense, too, the issue of blurred identity still survives.

THE NEW SEXUAL FREEDOM

As we mentioned, beginning in the late nineteenth century, a strong social movement attacked the Victorian compromise. War was declared against prostitution and vice. In the United States, the high point of this movement was Prohibition, the struggle (ultimately hopeless) against liquor and the culture of saloons.

Prohibition had a short and bitter life. It was a political failure. The repeal of Prohibition was a straw in the wind: vice would go on to win its war in many ways in the late twentieth century. Social practices and social norms changed dramatically. The legal rules relating to sex and vice were rewritten. An active sex life, even outside of marriage, was no longer a vice, a disgrace, and it was not considered particularly dangerous. It became, in some circles, the new normal. In many states and countries, sodomy laws were wiped off the books. Adultery and fornication, in most American states, are no longer crimes. In a few states, these laws survive as living fossils, but are almost completely unenforced.

Today, on the whole, sexual behavior of any type is legal, so long as the partners are competent adults and all parties consent. Moreover, all over the developed world, millions of couples (straight and gay) cohabit, that is, they live together as sexual partners, without bothering with a marriage ceremony. This was once called "living in sin." The phrase, except as a joke, is totally obsolete. The so-called sexual revolution is the new reality. Sexual identity, and indeed, sexuality itself, came more and more out of the closet.

One sign of the times was the astonishing career of Hugh Hefner, who founded *Playboy* magazine in 1953. The genius of *Playboy* was its attempt to make sexuality respectable. The magazine was printed on glossy paper; it ran pictures of beautiful naked women. But the magazine also printed works of respectable, even prize-winning writers. Hip young men would not be ashamed to put it on their coffee tables.

Playboy was a sign, too, that the old rules about pornography were gone. To be sure, laws against pornography are still on the books, but they are feebly enforced, if at all. The very definition of pornography has changed. Legally, any work with even a scintilla of scientific or literary merit, is protected speech, and can appear openly in print. The Supreme Court of the United States still allows, in theory, some degree of control over hard-core pornography,[6] But this seems to have little effect. Books and movies deal openly with subjects that were once completely taboo. They describe sex in graphic terms. Images shown on movie screens and television would have utterly horrified Victorians. The new edition of the Oxford Dictionary gives ample space to the four-letter words the first edition left out. Pornographic sites flood the internet. The law takes child pornography seriously, but largely leaves adult pornography alone. Basketball stars brag about how many women they have bedded. Women's magazines, along with recipes, print articles about ways to achieve better orgasms.

At one time, so-called experts told people that sexual repression was good for you. Sex was dangerous, except in small doses. Modern opinion has turned these ideas upside-down. Now it is repression that is considered problematic. Gorging on cheeseburgers may be dangerous; frequent sex is not. On one website, supposedly dedicated to health concerns, we are told (for example) that sexual intercourse can lower blood pressure and burn up calories. People who had "frequent sex" gained benefits to their health. Sex could increase the amount of immunoglobulin A in their saliva. Those who had "infrequent sex" had less of this valuable "antibody." Sexual activity could also help a woman "strengthen" her "pelvic floor" it could "improve bladder control." Men who had "frequent orgasms" lowered their mortality risk. Masturbation, that Victorian bugaboo, was pronounced "entirely safe." It "increases mental well-being" and "can offer many of the same benefits as sex."[7] Conservatives wring their hands about the sexual revolution. They demand (and get) campaigns, backed by tax money, to teach young people abstinence before marriage. This, they tell teenagers, is the only safe sexual option. Not every teenager seems to be listening.

The sexual revolution, like other important forms of social change, does not lend itself to simple explanations; but that attitudes about sexuality have changed, and behavior most likely also, seems undeniable. This "revolution" has had a powerful impact also on the way people self-identify. The success of the gay rights movement encouraged gays and lesbians to come out of the closet if they chose to do so. More recently, the same has been true for transgender people. The movement was, of course, connected with the more general civil rights movement. At any rate, in the United States, and in most developed countries, same-sex behavior is no longer a crime. In 2020, the United States Supreme Court held that an employer could not discriminate against gay or transgender employees.[8]

The gay rights movement met with furious opposition at first. Then a few countries began to allow gays to marry. So did some American states. In 2015, the United States Supreme Court held, 5–4, that there was a constitutional right to gay marriage—a decision that applied to the whole country. Even the recalcitrant states of the Bible Belt had to grit their teeth and accept the decision.[9] At this writing (2022), the court has veered sharply to the Right, after Trump appointed three new conservative justices. The gay rights case could conceivably be overruled. But the Victorian Humpty Dumpty cannot be put together again. Heather can have two mommies, and the children of Adam and Steve can have two daddies. Or, if Adam and Steve so wish, they can stay unmarried, like many straight couples in their towns. The world has changed. Children of unmarried couples are no longer "bastards"; they have no reason to be ashamed of their birth identity. Like the children of married couples, they have rights.

The sex act is still extremely private: it takes place behind closed doors, for the most part. And the naked body is still covered up. Clothes have many functions: to keep people warm, to give off messages about your style, your habits, and even who you are, or at least who you claim to be.[10] Another function is to hide the naked body. The taboo against nudity is quite ancient. In the book of Genesis, Noah, who is drunk, lies naked. Two of his sons cover their father's body, careful to avoid seeing his genitals. Taboos against nudity are and have been culturally variable. Male nudity was the norm for sports in ancient Greece. Japanese baths and Finnish saunas are expressions of local culture. The taboo against nudity was strong in the nineteenth century. Victorians kept the physical body under wraps, just as they kept the cultural and psychological body.

A nudist movement did arise, particularly in Germany, in the late nineteenth century.[11] These nudists were, on the whole, a rather conservative group. They insisted that the naked body was pure, natural, and healthy. Sexuality had nothing to do with nudism (outside of bed, of course). In a way, classical nudism turned conservative religious attitudes toward the body (especially the female body) inside out. Conservative Muslim countries swaddle women from head to toe in the interests of modesty; nudism, at the other extreme, removes *all* clothing, as if to say, "See, the body [including a woman's body] is not evil, is not inherently seductive." Nudist propaganda loved to picture families cavorting in the nude playing volleyball or having a picnic, for example, with the children of course included. (Photographs usually used a discreet bush or tree branch to hide the sexual organs.) Today, the nude men in San Francisco neighborhoods make quite a different statement. The same is true of young people in naked bike races or who patronize nude beaches. The Palais de Tokyo, an art museum in Paris, sponsored a “nudist tour”; hundreds of people signed up for this thrilling artistic event. Indeed, the “most uncomfortable thing” about the tour was not the nudity (according to a report), it was the temperature. The “cold air circulating through the cavernous galleries” was proof that the museum was not really the place for “people wearing only sneakers.”[12]

Victorian prudery is gone, probably, forever. Technically, in the United States, and in other countries, pornography is still subject, as we have seen, to legal limits. It can be banned in some localities, or at least controlled. But in most parts of the country, it is hard to see evidence of limits, especially on the internet. Society allows far more openness with regard to sexual identity and sexual behavior. You are allowed to peel off layer after layer of secrecy and repression. Of course, prudery—and modesty—have not been abolished. True, there are nude beaches, naked bike races, naked department store sales—none of it (as it were) in plain brown wrappers. Still, most people stay away from nude beaches (except to gawk), and would never dream of going into a department store or museum without clothing on. And whether or not it is officially illegal—in many places it is not—you would be well advised not to roam the streets or enter a restaurant stark naked. Or even (if you are a woman) to go naked from the waist up. When Gwen Jacob, a Canadian student, decided on a “hot summer day” to go topless in public, she created a “veritable orgy of public disorder. . . . Dozens of people came out to see [her] . . . traffic ground to a halt; a city bus stopped temporarily; men drinking beer on front porches ogled and whistled, and various police officers, beginning with a beat constable . . . attempted to persuade her to put her shirt back on.” She was convicted of indecent exposure, but an appeals court reversed her conviction.[13]

Ms. Jacob’s story illustrates both the triumph and the limits of free choice in contemporary life. A full exploration of the subject would take another book (or a whole library). Choice is not a one-way street. How choices affect other people matters greatly. Sex has been released from some of its chains—but sexual partners have to be adults, and they have to give consent. At the time when (say) all pornography was totally banned, when it simply circulated underground, there were no special rules to protect the young. But today, society is awash in pornography or near-pornography. This brings on strict rules about child pornography; it can be forbidden, and violators can be severely punished.[14] Sexual abuse of children has become a major social issue. For adults, there is vigorous debate about what "consent" actually means. Women insist that no must mean no and that even more subtle forms of male coercion are intolerable. Men in power positions who have abused, or assaulted, women have been driven from office, or driven all the way into prison. Rape law has been reformed and modernized.[15] Women in the United States, in India, in many countries, fight back against male dominance and male sexual predation. The sexual offenses of Catholic priests, mostly against boys, have made headlines in recent years. In France alone, according to a report by an "independent commission" in 2021, Catholic clergy "sexually abused more than 200,000 minors" over a period of seventy years.[16] The cover up by the Catholic hierarchy has been almost as great a scandal as the sexual conduct itself.

Moreover, it is still wrong to live the way Captain Alving lived. It is still shameful and wrong to hide diseases that can infect other people. Modern medicine has helped tame the scourge that haunted *Ghosts.* But when AIDS burst on the scene, Captain Alving's problem roared back to life in an acute and frightening form. At the time, AIDS was a death sentence. Today, it is still a chronic and dangerous condition. If you are HIV positive, passing for healthy is a crime. Sex partners have to be told about your condition. In Illinois, if you share drug paraphernalia with another person and in Florida, if you donate blood or other tissue, you have a duty to disclose your status.[17] A federal law of 1990 provided money for AIDS research, but with conditions. States had to make it a crime to hide HIV status from a partner. Today, Captain Alving, secretly harboring his disease, could be prosecuted in many countries. In the modern world, Dr. Jekyll no longer has to suppress all aspects of Mr. Hyde, but there are definite and significant limits—morally, culturally, and (in many ways) legally as well.

THE IMAGE

In the modern world, people are, or can be, acutely conscious of who they are in a new and important sense: they can explore their ancestry, physically and culturally. They can (for a small price) examine their genomes and trace themselves back into time. Technology has given the world memory that it never had before. Cavemen (we assume) had memories. Perhaps they also had clan or tribal traditions that went back into the dim, uncharted past. But these were shared, communal, rather than individual memories. In later periods, kings, queens, nobles, and the very rich had portraits painted. We know, more or less, what some of the pharaohs looked like, as well as Henry VIII, various popes, or the rich Dutch merchants of the seventeenth century. But almost nobody else. Thus, only elites had a certain kind of historical or deep family memory. For the great mass of humanity, the past was gone with the wind. What great-grandparents looked like was simply lost, or even what people themselves looked like as children. And when the body died, so did the image.

The invention of the camera brought about a dramatic change. In 1839, the *Gazette de France* announced something new: Louis Daguerre had developed a way to fix images in a permanent way. These images, like paintings or engravings, could be moved about; they were not dependent on "the presence of the objects."[18] Thus began the camera's amazing career. Very quickly, photography shops sprang up on city streets like mushrooms. Photographs became cheap and accessible. The camera acted as a social equalizer; personal and family images were now available to ordinary people. Photography influenced the very concept of personal identity. By the end of the nineteenth century, dead ancestors were preserved in family albums. Historical and psychological continuity was within universal grasp. We have seen how, in the nineteenth century, certain aspects of personal identity had become problematic. But other aspects, thanks to the camera, got new meaning and depth.

Photography, in fact, was perhaps one factor that fed the growth of a more democratic society. Society, in the nineteenth century, still distinguished sharply between rich and poor, between nobles and commoners (in England), and between men and women of good "breeding" and the rest of the population. High taxes and expanded voting rights, together with major social and economic change, brought down the status of many members of the English nobility. The middle class gained power in all developed countries. The camera gave this middle class its own claim to history, to ancestry, even (in a sense) to "breeding." The camera played at least a minor role in the restructuring of society. Ultimately, it democratized culture and entertainment through its powerful descendants: movies and television. The notorious "fifteen minutes of fame," the goal of so many people in more recent times, would be impossible to achieve without the camera and its progeny.

WHERE DO I COME FROM? WHO MADE ME?

Personal identity, as we mentioned, has both a subjective and an objective meaning. Objectively, it is the label that society pins on you. Key aspects of identity—even race and gender—are "objective" in the sense that these labels come on the whole from outside; but they are not aspects of the real world, they are socially constructed. That "race" rather than hair color or body weight matters so much in society, is not something given by human biology, whatever people might think. Identity is also deeply subjective: it is who we *think* we are. Our own self-image. This includes what we think of as our race (and how others define it as well). Today, race in the United States and elsewhere is much less "binary." You were once either White or non-White. "Mixed" or "other" were not legal or social categories, but now, to a degree, they are.

In the modern world, the issue of identity is, as we have argued, deeply problematic in many ways. People can and do make dramatic changes—in place, in ways of life. Immigrants who move to a new country abandon an old way of life; they are molting their old skin—at least in part. Yet, as we pointed out, two almost contradictory processes take place: on the one hand, assimilation (and cultural convergence); on the other hand, a process that is (or seems to be) almost the reverse. People whose grandparents were only too eager to discard everything about the old country now try to explore their roots. They are even interested in their remote ancestors. They pay money to companies like 23andMe to unlock secrets locked inside DNA. Ancestry.com promises to help you dig into the archaeology of your past: millions of people have, in the process, "uncovered something new" about their ethnic heritage. In some ways, this is the opposite of "passing." Many people find it exciting to discover a few drops of Asian or African blood. The process can also reveal medical secrets. There is no time machine, of course. You cannot go back and change your ancestry. But, like the camera, the search for the past provides a sense of who we are; it gives people more choices, more identities to accept or reject.

Basically, genetic inheritance is fixed. There is no way to change it. Our identity includes, for all of us, a physical element: our body, our shape, what our hair, feet, ears, and fingernails look like. Physical identity, however, is malleable to a degree: consider hair dyes and various forms of plastic surgery. More radically, transgender people can sometimes switch from male to female or female to male. That was once totally impossible in the physical sense; and the idea of transgender *rights* was almost unthinkable. But now subjective identity can be converted into an identity that is objectively different; and which corresponds to what transgender people consider their "true" identity, their "real" gender. Sexual identity, like race, is no longer "binary." Few people go the whole distance and make the most radical changes. But for others, there is a whole new spectrum of decisions and choices.

Technology is key here: but in the service of wishes and demands and desires that are, are, in origin, social or cultural. And of course, choices of patterns of sexual behavior and gender identity are not only for transgender people. Millions of people make choices about sex and reproduction, that were once difficult or disfavored, because they want to, and because they *can.* Modern medicine has ways to help childless couples. Surrogacy allows the childless to buy, or borrow, another woman's womb. This is controversial, and, in some places, downright illegal. In the well-known case of Baby

M (1988), the highest court in New Jersey refused to enforce a surrogacy contract.[19] Yet surrogacy persists, even where it is supposed to be illegal. For infertile couples, and single women, there is always the sperm bank. In vitro fertilization is also possible. Modern science can soon make "designer babies" possible. For those who choose not to have babies, designer or otherwise, contraception is easier, more reliable, and more widespread than ever. And when contraception fails, there is abortion. This, to be sure, is still wildly controversial. The Catholic Church and many Protestant denominations are bitterly opposed.[20] The Supreme Court in 2022 held that there is no constitutional right to an abortion in the United States. Abortions will continue, however, one way or another. Thanks to modern medicine, couples can learn about potential birth defects; they can learn if the unborn baby would suffer from Down's syndrome or some other serious problem. Most such couples can, and do, choose to abort.[21]

ADOPTION

The law in England and the United States, historically, never recognized such a thing as the (formal) adoption of children. You were a child of the blood, a genetic child, or not a legal child at all with none of the rights of a child. Civil law countries—like France and Germany—that traced many of their institutions back to the Roman Empire did recognize adoption fully. The adoption process transformed *legal* identity. It cut the umbilical cord, as it were. Legally, birth parents vanished completely from the life of the child. The adoptive parents replaced them.

In the United States, the law changed in the middle of the nineteenth century. Mississippi passed a general adoption law in 1846; Massachusetts enacted an influential statute in 1851. In England, adoption did not enter the law until 1926.[22]

Of course, a family does not need formal adoption to take a child in, to care for it, love it, and nurture it. Death in childbirth, and rampant disease, guaranteed a large supply of orphans in the nineteenth century. Some children went to orphanages, some found homes with relatives or with neighbors or friends. But before states enacted adoption laws, these children lacked inheritance rights, if their parents failed to execute a will. In a country with a growing middle class, in which millions of families at least owned a farm, or a city lot, and a bit of money, family inheritance was a crucial issue.

Over time, the function of adoption has changed greatly. As modern medicine and better public health measures kept more and more parents alive, the supply of orphans shrank. Illegitimacy became a major motive for adoption. Women, particularly middle-class women, faced stigma and shame if they gave birth out of wedlock. Better to give these babies up for adoption. At this point, adoptive parents were less likely to be aunts, uncles, grandparents, neighbors, more likely to be childless couples looking for the child they could not make for themselves. Law and custom wrapped adoptions of this type in bands of tight secrecy. Birth mothers (and fathers) wanted to move past their scandal; adoptive parents also wanted the facts of birth hidden and inaccessible. In Illinois, for example, in the 1930s, adoptive parents had the right to a "clean" birth certificate—a kind of legal fiction, listing them as parents and never mentioning adoption at all.[23] In Nebraska, when a child was adopted, the decree of adoption was not allowed to state that the child "was born out of wedlock." A judge could allow "inspection" of any papers "relating to the adoption" only "on good cause shown."[24] Adopted children had, in general, no way to break through this wall of secrecy—no way to explore their past, no way to find their "real" parents.

Today, adoption has changed radically. Adopted children themselves led the way. They formed organizations like the Adoptees' Liberty Movement Association or the flamboyantly named Bastard Nation, dating from 1996. The "Nation" demanded "recognition of the full human and civil rights of adult adoptees." They wanted absolute, unconditional access to their "historical, genetic, and legal identity, including the original birth certificate and adoption decree." There was, they insisted, "nothing shameful" in birth out of wedlock, or in adoption.[25] Today, adopted children can often find their "real" parents—that is, if they choose to. The birth parents, of course, may also have something to say about this.

Adopted children are thus in a rare social and legal position. Most people are stuck with the parents they were born with. Adopted children often have a choice between two different sets. Law and practice reflect, of course, the permissive society and the sexual revolution. A bastard was once a social pariah: filius nullius, that is, nobody's child.[26] Today, in the age of cohabitation, thousands of children are what one might call "soft-core bastards"; they live in solid bourgeois households, conventional in all ways except one: their parents are not actually married. Many more live in single parent households, usually headed by a mother. Many of these households are poor; but even the prudish middle class no longer considers this situation scandalous. The new social norms permit the "bastard nation" to stick up proudly for its rights. Moreover, adopted children claim—quite rationally—that they have a right to know their genetic background, for medical reasons if nothing else. Still, at the core, is a notion of choice: citizens of the "bastard nation" must have the right to elect which family identity they prefer—which are the "real" parents; and which ones are not.

PRIVACY AND IDENTITY

The "bastard nation" is at war with a tradition of secrecy. Yet, in our times, personal privacy—the right to be alone, the right to keep secrets—stands high on the social agenda. The word "privacy" has many meanings. To discuss privacy in modern society, the politics of privacy, the threats to privacy, and related issues, would take another book, indeed a big book, and very likely a whole library of books.[27] There is, for example, the so-called constitutional "right to privacy," a line of Supreme Court cases including, very notably, *Roe v. Wade*, the famous (and controversial) abortion case struck down in 2022.[28] This line of cases seems to have little to do with "privacy" in the sense of an individual's personal space or the right to be left alone. It does concern, of course, the right to make certain personal (that is, private) choices free from government regulation.

At its core, the right of privacy is tied up closely with identity. Or, more precisely, it is tied up with control over aspects of identity. Most people feel, particularly in our times, living in what I have called the republic of choice, that they should decide on their own, without interference, how to live; and that includes deciding when and where to be private and when and where to be public, when to be open and when to be closed. In US law, an explicit right to privacy, discussed as such, did not emerge until the late nineteenth century. Something akin to the right of privacy was implicit in the law much earlier. The Fourth Amendment to the federal Constitution, part of the Bill of Rights, outlawed unreasonable searches and seizures—warrants were to be issued only "upon probable cause," supported by "oath or affirmation," which described the "place to be searched" and who or what was to be seized. A man's home, according to an old saying, is his castle, meaning that the home is sacred for most purposes, walled off from the outside world, safe from the long arm of the government. The home is private property, in the most fundamental sense: a haven for the family that lives in it.

Yet a person's home was a castle for people who actually lived in castles, not for most other people. "Private" life in the modern sense, as a practical matter, hardly existed for the poor, who shared crowded spaces in huts and shacks with family members, and perhaps chickens and hogs as well. And in small, face-to-face communities, everybody knew everybody else, and more or less knew everybody's business. "Privacy" in the most primitive and obvious sense belongs to the middle class in the developed world. Middle-class people, on the whole, have small families. Ideally, each child has its own room. The parents, too, have their private space. The outside world is not allowed to intrude into the home. Certainly not into the bedroom. A hidden camera would be an extreme invasion of privacy, whether installed by the government, a private business, or a nosy neighbor.

Formal recognition of a right of privacy in American law is usually traced to an article by Samuel D. Warren and Louis D. Brandeis (the future Supreme Court justice) published in 1890 in the *Harvard Law Review*.[29] Warren and Brandeis were upset by the mass media; the raw, pushy, and vulgar "yellow press" which often invaded the privacy of prominent and respectable people. The earliest cameras had not been able to handle motion—anything moving, human or animal, turned into a meaningless blur. By 1890, cameras were adroit enough to handle motion. This meant that, for the first time, someone could take your picture, without your permission, perhaps even without your knowledge. (Warren and Brandeis explicitly referred to this fact.) Since that time, the law of privacy has developed in complex and convoluted ways. In our day, the law in many countries recognizes some kind of general right to privacy. But what this right means, and what situations it covers, and who it applies to, is difficult to reduce to a formula. "Public figures," for example, have less of a right to privacy than ordinary citizens.

The centrality of privacy, as a social and legal concept, is closely related to the centrality of *choice* in modern society. This is the age of expressive individualism. It is an age that insists on the right to craft an identity. This includes, or implies, at least some sort of right, under some circumstances, to control presentation of self to the outside world; to decide what to keep secret and what to reveal. Technology has devised many fiendish ways to pierce the veil of privacy, ways to unmask the inner person. The war on terror provides governments with many excuses for invading privacy, in all sorts of ways. The right, then, has become all the more precious—and all the more brittle and precarious.

Two concepts, which we can call *anonymity* and *evanescence* are closely related to privacy. When you walk on the street, drink coffee in a café, or shop in a department store, you are, quite literally, "in public." But only as part of a large and anonymous crowd. In a way, you are both visible and invisible. Normally, nobody will pay much attention to you, and to the people around you, so long as you and they obey the (unwritten) rules of public behavior. But if you scream, or go naked, for example, anonymity collapses like a burst balloon. Anonymity, then, is fragile; still, it is real, and for most people, important. And if you stare at someone, for example, or follow that person down the street, you are violating norms of good behavior. In extreme cases (stalking is one instance), your behavior might even constitute a crime.

Evanescence is the idea that much of what we say or do today, should (for the most part) disappear tomorrow. Or, to put it another way, we should be able to choose what is recorded, what lasts, and what should be gone with the wind. Most of life is evanescent. It would horrify us to find out that our friend, a person we were chatting to, was actually "wired." Or that a camera was recording our behavior. Evanescence and anonymity are closely related. If we march in a parade, or join in a public rally or demonstration, everybody nearby can see and hear us. Still, it would make many people uncomfortable if video cameras were capturing our every move.

Privacy is, among other things, the right to protect our identity or, perhaps more accurately, to control the image we project to other people. In the city, we are surrounded with strangers. People pass us by on the street, ride with us in elevators at the office, sit at the next table in a restaurant—people we do not know, and who have no idea who we are. Nor do we know who *they* are. By and large, we want it that way. Most of us want anonymity, we want evanescence. But these things cannot be taken for granted. There are cameras everywhere today. There are cameras that look at distant galaxies and cameras that can look inside your intestinal tract. More to the point, there are cameras that can look at you as you go about your daily life. Millions of people carry a smartphone wherever they go, and each of these phones is also a camera. Street cameras record your license plate as you drive by a toll gate. Surveillance cameras monitor banks, airports, and public buildings. Tiny house cameras can be hidden in a clock or under the bed.

The camera, as we mentioned, freezes time. It preserves images that once disappeared forever. It can capture and perpetuate memory. Cameras record images of happy moments: a child's birthday party, the magic of a wedding, precious images of the dear departed, memories of a wonderful vacation. The camera can also capture and expose police brutality. It can fight and prevent crime. It has also many dark uses. It is a weapon in the hands of modern Peeping Toms. It is a sinister weapon in the hands of governments and big institutions. In our times, there is a kind of arms race between rights of privacy and the technology of intrusion. At stake is the right to safeguard both our inner and outer identities.

THE SCIENCE OF IDENTITY

A critical concept in the law of privacy is the concept of the "reasonable expectation of privacy." This refers to what people expect, and demand, by way of privacy. Privacy rights, and privacy norms, are socially determined. They change over time. People accept surveillance measures today, and even bodily intrusions, which would have outraged them in the past: x-rays at the airport, for example.

Over the years, the sheer capacity to invade privacy has gone from very little to something massively great. This includes the government's capacity to know basic facts about members of a population. The kings and queens of the Middle Ages knew virtually nothing statistical about their subjects. In the past, people lived, for the most part, anonymous lives. Queen Elizabeth I and Louis XIV had only vague ideas about what their subjects thought, or what they did, or even how many there were. The lord of the manor knew how many tenants he had and what rents they paid. There was, of course, tax collection, and some rudimentary information, but on the whole, for the central government—if you can speak of a central government at all—individuals hardly mattered, except in the aggregate. And even in the aggregate, knowledge about the population was crude and indefinite.

Today, governments know more and more about all of us. Governments gather statistics by the carload. Governments can and do measure how many people are under eighteen or over sixty-five; how many have college educations, where they live, what they do for a living, how many are employed, how many have children, who was born and who died during any particular year. Countries also have censuses, surveying and counting the whole population. In the United States, the census is as old as the federal Constitution. Article I, section 2 of the Constitution calls for an "enumeration" of the public to be taken every ten years. The census comes around like clockwork. There are, to be sure, disputes about what is asked, and how. Whether, for example, census-takers in 2020 could ask residents if they were citizens or not. In Germany, the census has been an object of controversy. One version was struck down by the courts in 1983.[30] Later versions avoided constitutional issues. In the United Kingdom, the census is taken every ten years and in Canada and Japan every five years.

Governments aggregate data and make it into giant data bases. On the individual level, people fill out forms, file tax returns, apply for driver's licenses, dog licenses, hunting licenses. They give personal information to companies when they buy online. What happens to this data is unclear. So far, governments and big institutions cannot actually read people's minds. Thoughts are still private. We can still hide who we "really" are; or what we are really thinking.

A mobile society made it easy for people to escape their pasts; this was one of the themes of this book. A convict, thief, bigamist, even a murderer, could change places, move to a new location, start a new life, adopt a new identity. This was true for people in general, even more so for people with a guilty past. Change a name, shave off a beard, slip into the general population. Police departments and detective squads struggled to find ways to counteract this: photographs, then the Bertillon method, and later on, fingerprinting. More recently, there is DNA, forensic science, and other new tricks of the trade.

In many countries, people carry identity cards wherever they go. This is true, for example, in Chile and in Spain. In some countries, identity cards are optional. The Indian government introduced Aadhaar, a biometric scheme using fingerprints, personal details, and iris patterns. The plan was for Aadhaar to cover some 90 percent of the population. The Indian Supreme Court sustained the plan, for the most part, but refused to let private companies make use of Aadhaar.[31] A few countries, including the United States and Canada, refuse to issue national identity cards. But driver's licenses, issued by individual states and provinces, are local equivalents. For those who can't or won't drive, states and provinces provide a nondriver's license, which looks like a driver's license and works as a kind of identity card. A passport is another kind of identity card. Security personnel at the airport ask for picture IDs. In some states, voting depends on some type of personal identification.

Billions are spent gathering statistical data. Identities are measured, counted, stored, and analyzed. Businesses, too, in addition to governments, heap up data about their customers, their wants and their likes. When I buy a book from Amazon, I get messages suggesting other books I might like. Amazon feels it knows me because of my past behavior. Other companies also feel they know me. Many people find this aspect of modern life spooky, and vaguely unsettling, either because the companies get it wrong or equally likely because they might be getting it right. Nobody wants to be reduced to a cluster of statistics—a consuming and buying machine, whose behavior is predictable. A kind of robot. A walking form of artificial intelligence.

Social networks help people communicate, and stay in touch. They help people conquer barriers of space and of time. They make it possible to reach out to other people with similar interests, to find soul mates: people who think the earth is flat, or who collect old bottles or Nigerian postage stamps, or whose children suffer from a rare disease. Or people looking for a new life partner. Or, unfortunately, white supremacists looking for other white supremacists.

In this brave new world, people still feel the need to hide their "true" identity, for all sorts of reasons. Or at least to try. There are new dangers, but also new ways to hide. The internet is a way to display yourself, but it can also foster anonymity: good and bad. Anonymous entities spread fake news, spew out hatred, and foster conspiracy theories. Anonymous entities hack into databases or prowl the internet looking for gullible victims. The internet permits rogue countries to distort the politics of nations. It allows messages from the best of humanity and also the worst. In Rotenburg, Germany, Armin Meiwes, a warped soul if there ever was one, had a single burning desire: to kill and eat another man, preferably a young one. With the miraculous aid of the internet, he was able to find such a person: a man who was willing to be killed and eaten. The story only came to light when Meiwes started searching for a next victim. Meiwes ended up in prison.[32]

The internet has a kind of schizophrenic character. You can expose your naked self to a vast audience. Or you can hide your identity completely. In a well-known cartoon in the *New Yorker* magazine, two dogs are seen talking in front of a computer screen. The caption is simply this: "On the internet, nobody knows you're a dog."[33] Nobody knows, if you are in fact Armin Meiwes. Or a terrorist. Or Dr. Jekyll. Or Mr. Hyde.

Conclusion

As this book has made clear, identity is a quicksilver concept. It changes from culture to culture and from period to period. Cultures themselves shift prismatically. Waves of social change mold and influence concepts of identity—who we think we are, who we really are (whatever that might mean), and what images and messages about identity we project to the outside world.

The world of the industrial revolution was a world of great social and spatial mobility. In this world, identity became blurred, fluid, and changeable. In a traditional village, or in any face-to-face community, people knew, or thought they knew, who the people around them really were. It was a world of familiar faces, familiar behavior, familiar roles. Big city life, or life in a raw new town, a settlers' town, was profoundly different. This had deep and significant consequences. We have explored some of these in these pages: the so-called crimes of mobility—for example, like bigamy and the confidence game—and the crimes of a man like Jack the Ripper or the (fictional) Mr. Hyde. Out of this new situation rose new literary genres about spies and detectives—literature that reflected the ambiguity of identity. Conditions of life made it possible for people to "pass" in various ways, allowed them to hide some aspects of their identity.

Societies, through their leaders and elites, reacted in many ways to this new situation. The rise of the confidence man led to the creation of detective squads. A mobile society was a society of opportunity; but also a society that felt it needed strong measures to restrain social energy let loose in this world. Sexual identity and behavior, in particular, had to be restrained and repressed in ways that may seem absurd today, but which leaders, tastemakers, rule-makers, and others, considered absolutely necessary at the time. Otherwise (they thought), the very pillars of society might crumble.

Still, for the Victorians, personal identity had become a matter of choice to a degree. Lines between classes and strata were more porous. New opportunities emerged. Opportunities to rise in society and opportunities to fall. Society was, as always, changing. Gradually, and certainly by the late twentieth century, a social revolution overturned many forms of Victorian repressions. Personal identity became even more a matter of choice. This was an age of expressive individualism; more people felt free to chart their own course and craft their own way of life, to choose their own identity. Of course, no such freedom was ever absolute, or even close to absolute. We spelled out a few ways in which choice manifested itself; on such questions as what to eat for dinner, or, more importantly, what religion to belong to, what ways of life to pursue, how to deal with sex, reproduction, and parenthood. Even (in special situations) who to consider as one's "real" Mom and Dad. We touched briefly, too, on some problems that emerged in what I have called the republic of choice.[1] New risks arose along with new opportunities. New uncertainties replaced old uncertainties. New ways to live private lives and new threats to that privacy.

This book has been largely an exploration of the period since the Industrial Revolution. It was meant to explain, or try to explain, and not to pass judgment. Above all, it was not meant to act as a guide to the future, or to make predictions. The world never stands still. History has no ending. We live in a world that mobility helped make. Mobility, as I argue, has been a powerful force, bulldozing the past, making it possible for people to construct new identities, new habits, and new ways of life. But is this still true? And, even if true, can it continue? Today, wiping out a past and starting over is not as easy as it was. Yes, you can move from Scranton to Yuma, or from Leeds to London, or from Lima to Buenos Aires, but your digital history follows you wherever you go. In a sense, it is harder to escape one's past. Are we, in a way, slowly cycling back to conditions that were true of village life? This is, after all, a global village, for better or for worse.

We have more and more choices, but what the choices *mean* is always in flux. Once it was daring for a Swede or a Brazilian to eat sushi—it was new, different, perhaps somewhat exotic. Now sushi is everywhere. Eating it is no longer daring. Nothing about a croissant is foreign except its name. What choices say about personal identity is itself in flux. Meanings of personal identity have changed, do change, and will continue to change. I began this book with the saying, "You cannot get into the same river twice." I will end with it as well.

Notes

INTRODUCTION

1. Dror Wahrman, *The Making of the Modern Self: Identity and Culture in Eighteenth-Century England* (New Haven, CT: Yale University Press, 2004), preface, xii.

2. Eugen Weber, *Peasants into Frenchmen: The Modernization of Rural France, 1870–1914* (Stanford, CA: Stanford University Press, 1976).

3. Wahrman, *The Making of the Modern Self*, 202.

4. Natalie Zemon Davis, *The Return of Martin Guerre* (Cambridge, MA: Harvard University Press,1983).

5. Valentin Groebner, *Who Are You? Identification, Deception, and Surveillance in Early Modern Europe* (Princeton, NJ: Princeton University Press, 2007), 212–18.

CHAPTER 1

1. Larry Long, *Migration and Residential Mobility in the United States* (New York: Russell Sage Foundation, 1988), 29.

2. Patricia Kelly Hall and Steven Ruggles, "Restless in the Midst of Their Prosperity: New Evidence on the Internal Migration of Americans, 1850–2000," *Journal of American History* 91 (2004): 829.

3. Frederick J. Turner, "The Significance of the Frontier in American History," in *Annual Report of the American Historical Association for the Year 1893* (Washington, DC: 1894), 199.

4. Lawrence M. Friedman and Paul Davies, "California Death Trip," *Indiana Law Review* 36 (2003): 17.

5. Andrew Miles, *Social Mobility in Nineteenth and Early Twentieth-Century England* (London: Macmillan, 1999), 177–78.

6. See in general, Alexander Keyssar, *The Right to Vote: The Contested History of Democracy in the United States* (New York: Basic Books, 2000).

7. Frances Trollope, in *Domestic Manners of the Americans* (New York: Alfred A. Knopf, 1949, published originally in 1832), noted that in the United States "it is more than petty treason to the Republic, to call a free citizen a *servant.*" She felt that, for a young woman, even "abject poverty" was "preferable to domestic service," which was probably an exaggeration (Trollope, 1949 edition, p. 52).

8. Trollope, *Domestic Manners*, 234. Chewing tobacco was a "vile and universal habit."

9. Anthony Trollope, *North America* (New York: Penguin, 1951, published originally in 1862), 266–67.

10. See, in general, J. R. Pole, *The Pursuit of Equality in American History*, 2nd ed. (Berkeley: University of California Press, 1993).

11. Trollope, *Domestic Manners*, 121.

CHAPTER 2

1. Simon A. Cole, *Suspect Identities: A History of Fingerprinting and Criminal Identification* (Cambridge, MA: Harvard University Press, 2001), 3. As Judith Flanders put it in *The Invention of Murder: How the Victorians Revelled in Death and Detection and Created Modern Crime* (New York: Basic Books, 2011), 295, urbanization "had created a world where large numbers of strangers lived side by side in ignorance of others' real natures."

2. Flanders, *The Invention of Murder*,112n.

3. The most famous of those who pursued this rather dubious art was Mary Elizabeth Braddon. Her most famous book was *Lady Audley's Secret* (New York: Broadview Press, 2003, originally published in 1862).

4. Flanders, *The Invention of Murder*, 108–9.

5. The nickname came from a letter received by the Central News Agency in London. It claimed to come from the killer and was signed "Jack the Ripper." The letter was "in all probability penned by a deceitful journalist with one eye on newspaper sales," but the name stuck and has gone down in history. John Bennett, *Mob Town: A History of Crime and Disorder in the East End* (New Haven, CT: Yale University Press, 2017), 146.

6. On this, see L. Perry Curtis Jr., *Jack the Ripper and the London Press* (New Haven, CT: Yale University Press, 2001).

7. On the early history of plea bargaining, see George Fisher, *Plea Bargaining's Triumph: A History of Plea Bargaining in America* (Stanford, CA: Stanford University Press, 2003).

8. On the significance and typology of headline cases, see Lawrence M. Friedman, *The Big Trial: Law as Public Spectacle* (Lawrence: University Press of Kansas, 2015).

9. The literature on the Lizzie Borden case is extremely extensive. Of particular interest is the analysis of the meaning of the case in Cara W. Robertson, "Representing 'Miss Lizzie': Cultural Convictions in the Trial of Lizzie Borden," *Yale Journal of Law and the Humanities* 8 (1996): 350. Robertson has now exhaustively treated the

trial in *The Trial of Lizzie Borden: A True Story* (New York: Simon & Schuster, 2019); see also Joseph A. Conforti, *Lizzie Border on Trial: Murder, Ethnicity, and Gender* (Lawrence: University Press of Kansas, 2015); A. Cheree Carlson, *The Crimes of Womanhood: Defining Femininity in a Court of Law* (Urbana: University of Illinois Press, 2009), 85–110; Sarah Miller, *The Borden Murders: Lizzie Borden and the Trial of the Century* (New York: Schwartz & Wade, 2016).

10. Edwin H. Porter, *The Fall River Tragedy: A History of the Borden Murders* (Fall River, MA: King Philip Publishing Company, 1985; facsimile of the 1893 edition), 268.

11. Conforti, *Lizzie Borden on Trial*, 194.

12. Robertson, *The Trial of Lizzie Borden*. 283–84.

13. The stepmother was the first to die. Had Andrew Borden been murdered before his wife, she would have had a share in the estate. As it was, the two daughters gained the full inheritance. At least this state of affairs suggests a more or less plausible motive. Andrew Borden apparently died intestate. Emma Borden administered the estate and reported that she and Lizzie were the "only children and heirs at law" of Andrew Borden (*New Bedford Journal,* February 9, 1894, 4). When Lizzie died in 1927, she left an estate of nearly $1 million, a very considerable sum for the time (*New York Times,* June 8, 1927, 20).

14. Paul Collins, *Blood and Ivy: The 1849 Murder That Scandalized Harvard* (New York: W. W. Norton & Company, 2018), 201.

15. The case was *Sheppard v. Maxwell*, 384 U.S. 333 (1966).

16. See Cynthia L. Cooper and Sam Reese Sheppard, *Mockery of Justice: The True Story of the Sheppard Murder Case* (Boston, MA: Northeastern University Press, 1995). The coauthor was the son of Dr. Sheppard.

17. Or part of the family of a celebrity. In 1932, the infant child of Charles Lindbergh, perhaps the most famous American hero, was kidnapped and killed. Two years later, Richard Hauptman, a German immigrant, was arrested, tried, convicted, and executed for this crime.

18. This kind of issue could be raised, at times, in civil trials as well. In 1875, Theodore Tilton accused Henry Ward Beecher, the most famous and respected clergyman in the country, of committing adultery with Tilton's wife. The case ended with a hung jury. See Richard Wightman Fox, *Trials of Intimacy: Love and Loss in the Beecher-Tilton Scandal* (Chicago: University of Chicago Press, 1999). The nation "ultimately did not—could not—accept the thought that Beecher . . . could have betrayed his home and family." See Richard White, *The Republic for Which it Stands: The United States During Reconstruction and the Gilded Age, 1865–1896* (Oxford: Oxford University Press, 2017), 163–64.

19. Kate Summerscale, *The Suspicions of Mr. Whicher* (London: Bloomsbury, 2008) is a full discussion of this case. The quote is from page 155.

20. On this see Tom Cullen, *The Mild Murderer: The True Story of the Dr. Crippen Case* (Boston, MA: Houghton Mifflin, 1989).

21. Crippen insisted throughout that he was innocent. Some doubts persist to this day. A team of American researchers has argued that the body in the cellar was not Crippen's wife. They based their conclusion on DNA taken from grandnieces of Cora

Crippen, which, they claimed, did not match the DNA of the torso under Crippen's basement. "Crippen Mystery Remains Despite DNA Claim," BBC News, http://news .bbc.co.uk/2/hi/uk_news/7050714.stm, October 18, 2007.

22. Hal Higdon, *The Crime of the Century: The Leopold and Loeb Case* (Urbana: University of Illinois Press, 1975).

23. Peter Graham, *So Brilliantly Clever: Parker, Hulme, and the Murder that Shocked the World* (Wellington: Awa Press, 2011), 173.

24. On this theme, see Lawrence M. Friedman, *The Horizontal Society* (New Haven, CT: Yale University Press, 1999).

25. See Debbie Nathan and Michael Snedeker, *Satan's Silence: Ritual Abuse and the Making of a Modern American Witch Hunt* (New York: Macmillan, 1995); Paul and Shirley Eberle, *The Abuse of Innocence: The McMartin Preschool Trial* (Buffalo, NY: Prometheus, 1993).

26. John Johnson, "Conviction Tossed after 19 Years," *Los Angeles Times*, May 1, 2004.

27. Nathan and Snedeker, *Satan's Silence*, 3. Here, too, one might mention the case of the "Boston nanny," a young English au pair accused of causing the death of a child. The trial of the au pair, Louise Woodward, was sensational—and controversial. It is hard to know what actually happened. She was convicted, but the conviction was set aside. See Carey Goldberg, "Massachusetts High Court Backs Freeing Au Pair in Baby's Death," *New York Times,* June 17, 1998. Widespread parental anxieties, like those in the McMartin trial, no doubt were at least partly responsible for the notoriety of this case.

28. On the history of witchcraft see, for example, Sigrid Brauner, *Fearless Wives and Frightened Shrews: The Construction of the Witch in Early Modern Germany* (Amherst: University of Massachusetts Press, 1995).

29. Cotton Mather, *The Wonders of the Invisible World* (1692), subtitled "Being an Account of the Tryals of Several Witches Lately Executed in New-England."

30. Owen Davies, *America Bewitched: The Story of Witchcraft after Salem* (Oxford: Oxford University Press, 2013), 100.

31. John W. Fountain, "Exorcists and Exorcisms Proliferate Across U.S.," *New York Times*, November 28, 2000. A disputed incident in the 1940s gave rise to a novel and also to a popular movie, *The Exorcist* (1973). The movie "spurred an onslaught of movies dealing with demon possession and Satanism" (Fountain, 2000).

32. See Jim Steinmeyer, *Who Was Dracula? Bram Stoker's Trail of Blood* (New York: Penguin, 2013).

33. For example, Sheridan Le Fanu wrote a vampire tale, "Carmilla," which appeared in 1872. This was, moreover, a female vampire. See William Veeder, "Carmilla: The Arts of Repression," *Texas Studies in Literature and Language* (1980) 22: 197.

34. Indeed, *good* vampires have a place in modern popular culture. The Twilight series of novels, written by Stephanie Meyers in the early twenty-first century, feature a vampire family that drinks animal, not human blood.

CHAPTER 3

1. There were to be sure exceptions, as we noted. See Natalie Zemon Davis, *The Return of Martin Guerre* (Cambridge, MA: Harvard University Press, 1983).

2. Jeanne Fahnestock, "Bigamy: The Rise and Fall of a Convention," *Nineteenth-Century Fiction* 36 (1981): 47.

3. See Lawrence M. Friedman, *Crime and Punishment in American History* (New York: Basic Books, 1993), 198–99.

4. Ginger S. Frost, *Living in Sin: Cohabiting as Husband and Wife in Nineteenth-Century England* (Manchester: University Press, 2008), 72.

5. Beverly Schwartzberg, "'Lots of Them Did That': Desertion, Bigamy, and Marital Fluidity in Late-Nineteenth-Century America," *Journal of Social History* 37 (2004): 573, 576.

6. Schwartzberg, "'Lots of Them Did That,'" 577.

7. Ginger S. Frost, *Living in Sin*, 74. Most of the defendants were convicted: 81 percent in fact (Frost).

8. David J. Cox, "'Trying to Get a Good One': Bigamy Offenses in England and Wales, 1850–1950," *Plymouth Law & Justice Review* (2012): 27.

9. Patricia D. Maida, *Mother of Detective Fiction: The Life and Works of Anna Katharine Green* (Madison, WI: Popular Press, 1989), 98. Green was the first major mystery novelist in the United States. In her novels, bigamy was a frequent plot device.

10. Schwartzberg, "'Lots of Them Did That,'" 578–79.

11. However, under an English law of 1828, if the defendant had not heard from the spouse for seven years or more, the defendant could not be convicted of the *crime* of bigamy. Frost, *Living in Sin*, 73.

12. "Charged with Bigamy," *New York Times*, August 23, 1885.

13. "Alleged Bigamy," *New York Times*, March 11, 1876.

14. Frost, *Living in Sin*, 75.

15. Isaac Metzger, ed., *A Bintel Brief: Sixty Years of Letters from the Lower East Side to the Jewish Daily Forward* (New York: Schocken, 1971), 56–58. The letter writer felt sorry for her husband "behind bars in his dark cell" and pity for his second wife, who "certainly loves him." The two families, both with children, are suffering, because their "their bread-winner" is in jail.

16. See Lawrence M. Friedman, *Guarding Life's Dark Secrets: Legal and Social Controls over Reputation, Propriety, and Privacy* (Stanford, CA: Stanford University Press: 2007), 81–100.

17. Walter Block, "Trading Money for Silence," *University of Hawaii Law Review* 8 (1986): 73.

18. See Friedman, *Guarding Life's Dark Secrets* 81–100 and Angus McLaren, *Sexual Blackmail: A Modern History* (Cambridge, MA: Harvard University Press, 2002).

19. Friedman, *Guarding Life's Dark Secrets*, 85.

20. McLaren, *Sexual Blackmail*, 14–16.

21. Matthew Hale Smith, *Sunshine and Shadow in New York* (Hartford, CT: B. Burr and Company, 1880), 132–33.

22. "Fake Dry Agents Got $2,000 Weekly," *New York Times*, January 23, 1923.

23. *Collins v. State*, 14 Ala. 68 (1848).

24. See Maia McAleavey, *The Bigamy Plot: Sensation and Convention in the Victorian Novel* (Cambridge: Cambridge University Press, 2015).

25. See, in general, Winifred Hughes, *The Maniac in the Cellar: Sensation Novels of the 1860s* (Princeton, NJ: Princeton University Press, 1980).

26. On this see, Robert E. Mensel, "'A Diddle at Brobdingnag': Confidence and Caveat Emptor during the Market Revolution," *University of Memphis Law Review* 38 (2007): 97, 112; Michael Pettit, *The Science of Deception: Psychology and Commerce in America* (Chicago: Chicago University Press, 2013), 25.

27. Robert Douglas-Fairhurst, ed., abridged edition of Henry Mayhew, *London Labour and the London Poor* (Oxford: Oxford University Press, 2010), 388.

28. Herbert Asbury, *The Gangs of New York: An Informal History of the Underworld* (New York: Capricorn Books, 1927), 193–95.

29. Helen Campbell, *Darkness and Daylight: Lights and Shadows of New York Life* (Hartford, CT: The Hartford Publishing Company, 1891), 729. Confidence men, as Thomas Byrnes put it in *Professional Criminals of America* (New York: Chelsea House Publishers, 1886), 40, were "men of education, possessed of plenty of assurance, gifted with a good knowledge of human nature, and a fair amount of ingenuity." They have no trouble helping themselves to "other people's money."

30. David W. Maurer, *The Big Con: The Story of the Confidence Man and the Confidence Game* (Indianapolis, IN: Bobbs Merrill Company: 1940), 15.

31. "The Man-Traps of New York: What They Are and Who Work Them," *National Police Gazette*, October 1, 1881, 10. The article is attributed to "a celebrated detective."

32. "Spoiled the Colonel's Game," *New York Times,* March 21, 1894.

33. Campbell, *Darkness and Daylight*, 597–98.

34. Bluford Adams, *E Pluribus Barnum: The Great Showman and the Making of U.S. Popular Culture* (Minneapolis: University of Minnesota Press, 1997), 2–3.

35. James W. Cook, *The Arts of Deception: Playing with Fraud in the Age of Barnum* (Cambridge, MA: Harvard University Press, 2001), 78–85.

36. Her tale is told (as much as possible about a woman who lied about absolutely everything) in William C. Davis, *Inventing Loreta Velasquez: Confederate Soldier Impersonator, Media Celebrity, and Con Artist* (Carbondale: Southern Illinois University Press, 2016).

37. Kathleen De Grave, *Swindler, Spy, Rebel: The Confidence Woman in Nineteenth-Century America* (Columbia: University of Missouri Press: 1995), 39.

38. James D. McCabe Jr., *New York by Sunlight and Gaslight* (Philadelphia: Douglas Brothers Publishers, 1882), 525–26.

39. This is the title of a 1939 movie starring W. C. Fields, but the sentiment, if not the exact phrase, is much older.

40. "Lost $40,000 in Fake Bets," *New York Times*, February 23, 1929.

41. Edward H. Smith, *Confessions of a Confidence Man: A Handbook for Suckers* (New York: Scientific American Publishing Company, Munn and Co., 1923), 151–52.

42. See, for a rather colorful instance, Angela Pulley Hudson, *Real Native Genius: How an Ex-Slave and a White Mormon Became Famous Indians* (Chapel Hill: University of North Carolina Press, 2015).

43. Rohan McWilliam, *The Tichborne Claimant: A Victorian Sensation* (London: Hambledon Continuum, 2007).

44. Peter Kurth, *Anastasia: The Riddle of Anna Anderson* (Boston: Little, Brown & Co., 1983).

45. For much of this section, see Friedman, *Crime and Punishment*, especially pages 31–42. As is true today, only a few women were condemned to death.

46. Ann. Stats. Wisc. 1889, Vol. I, sections 1543, 1546, 1547d; pp. 937, 939.

47. Gen. Stats. R. I, 1872, ch. 232, sec. 24, p. 555.

48. Robert D. Putnam and David E. Campbell, *American Grace: How Religion Divides and Unites Us* (New York: Simon & Schuster, 2010).

49. Americans today are still amazingly prone to change religions; see below, chapter 8, 112–13.

50. Alex Beam, *American Crucifixion: The Murder of Joseph Smith and the Fate of the Mormon Church* (New York: Public Affairs, 2014).

51. See in general, Sarah Barrington Gordon, *The Mormon Question: Polygamy and Constitutional Crisis in Nineteenth Century America* (Chapel Hill: The University of North Carolina Press, 2004); Edwin B. Firmage and Richard C. Mangrum, *Zion in the Courts: A Legal History of the Church of Jesus Christ of Latter-Day Saints* (Urbana: University of Illinois Press, 1988).

CHAPTER 4

1. On the subject in this chapter in general, see Lawrence M. Friedman and Joanna L. Grossman, "Double Take: The Law of Embezzled Lives," *University of Cincinnati Law Review* 83 (2014): 117; see also Lawrence M. Friedman and Joanna L. Grossman, *The Walled Garden: Law and Privacy in Modern Society* (Lanham, MD: Rowman & Littlefield, 2022), 205–10.

2. In re Estate of Torregano, 54 Cal. 2d 234, 352 P. 2d 505 (1960).

3. Henry Wiencek, *Master of the Mountain: Thomas Jefferson and His Slaves* (New York: Farrar, Straus and Giroux, 2012), 32; see, for a full account of the family, Annette Gordon-Reed, *The Hemingses of Monticello: An American Family* (New York: Norton & Company, Incorporated, 2008).

4. Wiencek, *Master of the Mountain*, 227.

5. In a sense, this novel's theme can be compared to Shaw's *Pygmalion* since it expresses or implies that the lines between classes (and even races) is fluid, and can be learned, at least to a degree.

6. James O'Toole, *Passing for White: Race, Religion, and the Healy Family* (Amherst: University of Massachusetts Press, 2002).

7. Allyson Hobbs, *A Chosen Exile: A History of Racial Passing in American Life* (Cambridge, MA: Harvard University Press, 2014).

8. "To Colored People," an address by a prominent African-American clergyman, *Atlanta Constitution*, January 13, 1895.

9. Hobbs, *A Chosen Exile*, 164–65.

10. Hobbs, *A Chosen Exile*, 11.

11. For the story of these families, see Daniel J. Sharfstein, *The Invisible Line: Three American Families and the Secret Journey from Black to White* (London: Penguin Books, 2011); the quote is from page 322.

12. Martha A. Sandweiss, *Passing Strange: A Gilded Age Tale of Love and Deception Across the Color Line* (London: Penguin Books, 2009). A modern instance was the case of Rachel Dolezal, a White woman who passed for Black; see Allyson Hobbs, "Rachel Dolezal's Unintended Gift to America," *New York Times*, June 17, 2015.

13. The subject is dealt with in Ariela Gross, *What Blood Won't Tell: A History of Race on Trial in America* (Cambridge, MA: Harvard University Press, 2008).

14. Gross, *What Blood Won't Tell*, 60.

15. Quoted in Peggy Pascoe, *What Comes Naturally: Miscegenation Law and the Making of Race in America* (Oxford: Oxford University Press, 2009), 77. "Kanaka" refers to Hawaiians or other Polynesians.

16. Pascoe, *What Comes Naturally*, 127–28.

17. On this trial see, for example, Earl Lewis and Heidi Ardizzone, *Love on Trial: An American Scandal in Black and White* (New York: W. W. Norton & Company, 2001); A. Cheree Carlson, *The Crimes of Womanhood: Defining Femininity in a Court of Law* (Champaign: University of Illinois Press, 2009), 136–55.

18. George Watt, *The Fallen Woman in the Nineteenth Century English Novel* (London, Routledge: 1984), 59–64. In *Lady Audley's Secret* (1862), Mary Elizabeth Braddon's sensational novel—a runaway bestseller—Lady Audley, a woman from a lower class background, married (or purported to marry) into the aristocracy with ultimately evil results.

19. Ginger S. Frost, *Living in Sin: Cohabiting as Husband and Wife in Nineteenth-Century England* (Manchester: Manchester University Press, 2008).

20. 32 Cal. 2d 711, 196 P. 2d 17 (1948); Andrea Perez was a Mexican American woman and was classified for marital purposes as White; Sylvester Davis was African American. On this case, see Pascoe, *What Comes Naturally*, 205–23; and R. A. Lenhardt, "Beyond Analogy: Perez v. Sharp, Antimiscegenation Law, and the Fight for Same-Sex Marriage," *Cal. L. Rev.* 96 (2008): 839.

21. *Loving v. Virginia*, 318 U.S. 1 (1967).

22. Janet Liebman Jacobs, *Hidden Heritage: The Legacy of the Crypto-Jews* (Berkeley: University of California Press, 2002), 6. Ironically, this kind of list became a kind of guide for conversos. They "defined Jewish practice for both the Christian public and the crypto-Jewish practitioners." David M. Gitlitz, *Secrecy and Deceit: The Religion of the Crypto-Jews* (Lincoln: University of Nebraska Press, 1996), 40.

23. Liebman, *Hidden Heritage*, 89.

24. In *U.S. v. Wong Kim Ark*, 169 U.S. 649 (1898).

25. Estelle T. Lau, *Paper Families: Identity, Immigration Administration, and Chinese Exclusion* (Durham, NC: Duke University Press Books, 2006).

26. On Billy Tipton, and Boursicot, see Friedman and Grossman, "Double Take," 159–60. The weird story of Boursicot was turned into a successful play, *M Butterfly*, by David Henry Hwang, which later became a movie (1993).

27. On the development of British intelligence, see Stephen Twigge, Edward Hampshire, and Graham MacKim, *British Intelligence: Secrets, Spies, and Sources* (London: Bloomsbury Academic, 2009).

28. Ben Macintyre, *The Spy and the Traitor: The Greatest Espionage Story of the Cold War* (New York: Crown, 2018). Gordievsky was ultimately exposed, but the British, in a daring move, were able to smuggle him out of the Soviet Union to a safe haven in the West.

29. Bob Drogin and Geraldine Baum, "A Spy Story Set in Suburbia," *Los Angeles Times*, June 30, 2010.

30. Jerry Markon and Philip Rucker, "The Spies Next Door," *Washington Post*, June 30, 2010.

31. Markon and Rucker, "The Spies Next Door."

32. Peter Baker and Benjamin Weiser, "10 Plead Guilty in Spy Ring Case as Swap Unfolds," *New York Times*, July 9, 2010.

33. This is the theme of the movie *Invasion of the Body Snatchers*, discussed below.

34. Toby Harnden, "Richard and Cynthia Murphy: Suburbia's Spies Next Door," a story in the *Telegraph,* at https://www.telegraph.co.uk/news/worldnews/northamerica/usa/7871348/Richard-and-Cynthia-Murphy-suburbias-Spies-Next-Door.html, accessed January 24, 2019.

35. Ervin Goffman, *The Presentation of Self in Everyday Life* (New York: Anchor, 1959), 61.

36. David L. Rosenhan, "On Being Sane in Insane Places," *Science*, New Series, 179 (1973): 250.

37. Susannah Cahalan, *The Great Pretender* (New York: Grand Central Publishing, 2019). The quote is from page 295.

38. Cahalan, *The Great Pretender*.

39. *New York Times,* April 15, 2018.

CHAPTER 5

1. An earlier version of this chapter, "Mysterious Ways," appeared in FIU Law Review 16:235 (2022). I want to thank my colleague, Robert W. Gordon, for helpful comments on a prior draft.

2. There is a considerable literature on the history of the genre. See, for example, A. E. Murch, *The Development of the Detective Novel* (London: Peter Owen Publishers, 1968); Julian Symons, *Bloody Murder: From the Detective Story to the Crime Novel* (New York: Mysterious Press, 1972); T. J. Binyon, *Murder Will Out: The Detective in Fiction* (London: Faber, 1989); see also Judith Flanders, *The Invention of Murder: How the Victorians Revelled in Death and Detection and Created Modern Crime* (New York: St. Martin's Griffin, 2011); Ian Ousby, *Bloodhounds of Heaven: The Detective in British Fiction from Godwin to Doyle* (Cambridge, MA: Harvard University Press,

1976); Lucy Worsley, *The Art of the British Murder* (New York: Pegasus Books, 2014). Full disclosure: I myself have succumbed to the temptation to write mysteries. More than ten of them have been published and are in print as of 2022, all featuring a (fictional) lawyer, Frank May, whose practice, in San Mateo, California, is mostly about wills, trusts, and estate matters, but who somehow gets entangled in one mysterious death after another.

3. A novel by William Godwin, *Caleb Williams* (1794), is sometimes claimed to be the first mystery novel. See P. D. James, *Talking about Detective Fiction* (New York: Knopf Doubleday, 2009), 19–20; Charles J. Rzepka, *Detective Fiction* (New York: Vintage Books, 2005), 54–56; A. E. Murch, *The Development of the Detective Novel* (Westport, CT: Greenwood Press, 1968), 29–33. But most experts on the history of the genre give the credit to Poe.

4. On the case, and Poe's story, see Daniel Stashower, *The Beautiful Cigar Girl: Mary Rogers, Edgar Allan Poe, and the Invention of Murder* (New York: Berkley, 2006).

5. Dupin also figures in "The Purloined Letter" (1844). The mystery in this story is the location of the letter, which was of great political importance. Authorities knew who stole the letter and that it was somewhere in his house. They searched every nook and cranny to no success. Dupin's great powers of deduction solved the mystery. The letter, somewhat altered in appearance, was right under the noses of the investigators.

6. A modern edition was published by the Poisoned Pen Press in 2015. The book originally appeared as a serial in a magazine, written under the name of Charles Felix.

7. A new edition of this novel was published in 2010 with an introduction by Anne-Marie Beller.

8. An English translation was recently (2015) published by First Rate Publishers. The book still repays reading; it has a cleverly convoluted plot that twists and turns in various ways. The identity of the killer struck me as fairly obvious, but it is, as I said, not officially revealed until the end.

9. A reprint edition appeared in 2018 by Neo Books.

10. On her life and career, see Patricia D. Maida, *Mother of Detective Fiction: The Life and Works of Anna Katharine Green* (Bowling Green: Popular Press, 1989).

11. See Judith Flanders, *The Invention of Murder* (New York: St. Martin's Griffin, 2011). For the United States, see Andie Tucher, *Froth and Scum: Truth, Beauty, and the Ax Murder in America's First Mass Medium* (Chapel Hill, NC: The University of North Carolina Press, 1994). Lucy Worsley, in *The Art of the English Murder*, argues that the rise of "sensational journalism . . . and the whole body of detective fiction" can be linked to the rise of civilization itself. "Civilisation" made people feel safe: "Barricaded behind locked doors, sitting by the fire," people almost felt nostalgia for the days of violence, death, and rampant crime, which had "once been all too much part of daily life," but were now "recast" in the form of "entertainment" (New York: Pegasus Books, 2014), 17. But it seems more likely that, if anything, it was the anonymity and insecurity of city life that fed the appetite for this kind of "entertainment."

12. See Flanders, *The Invention of Murder*, 17; see also Amnon Kabatchnik, *Blood on the Stage 1800 to 1900: Milestone Plays of Murder, Mystery, and Mayhem*

(Lanham, MD: Rowman & Littlefield Publishers, 2017), 153–62. The playwright was Edward Fitzball (1792–1873).

13. See Flanders, *The Invention of Murder*, 57.

14. There is a sizable literature on the history of the police. See, for example, Wilbur R. Miller, *Cops and Bobbies: Police Authority in New York and London, 1830–1870* (Chicago: University of Chicago Press, 1977). Boston authorized a police force in 1838, but the department was not formally recognized until the 1850s.

15. P. D. James, *Talking About Detective Fiction* (New York: Vintage Books, 2009), 13.

16. See, on Whicher, Kate Summerscale, *The Suspicions of Mr. Whicher* (London: Bloomsbury, 2008).

17. Ronald R. Thomas, *Detective Fiction and the Rise of Forensic Science* (Cambridge: Cambridge University Press, 1999), 121.

18. Simon A. Cole, *Suspect Identities* (Cambridge: Harvard University Press, 2002), 63–67.

19. Cole, *Suspect Identities*, 203.

20. For England, see Haia Shpayer-Makov, "Explaining the Rise and Success of Detective Memoirs in Britain," in *Police Detectives in History 1750–1950*, eds. Clive Emsley and Haia Shpayer-Makov (London: Routledge, 2017), 103; for an American example, see George S. McWatters, *Knots Untied, or Ways and By-Ways of American Detectives* (Hertford: J. B. Burr and Hyde, 1872).

21. Edmund Wilson, in a well-known essay (1945), called the habit of reading mysteries "a kind of vice . . . somewhere between crossword puzzles and smoking." Edmund Wilson, "Who Cares Who Killed Roger Ackroyd: A Second Report on Detective Fiction," *New Yorker*, January 20, 1945. The reference in the title is to a novel by Agatha Christie, *The Murder of Roger Ackroyd* (New York: William Morrow Paperbacks, 1926). Willard Huntington Wright, in "The Detective Novel," *Scribner's* (London: Charles Scribner's Sons: 1926), 532, called the detective novel "a complicated and extended puzzle cast in fictional form," and he, too, compared its popularity to crossword puzzles. Wright himself was a very successful writer of detective fiction, under the pseudonym of S. S. Van Dine.

22. W. H. Auden, "The Guilty Vicarage," in *Detective Fiction: A Collection of Critical Essays*, ed. Robin W. Winks (Woodstock, VT: Foul Play Press, 1988), 15.

23. See John Walton, *The Legendary Detective: The Private Eye in Fact and Fiction* (Chicago: University of Chicago Press, 1915); on Pinkerton, see Frank Morn, *"The Eye That Never Sleeps": A History of the Pinkerton National Detective Agency* (Bloomington: Indiana University Press, 1982); James MacKay, *Allan Pinkerton: The First Private Eye* (Collingdale: Diane Publishing Company, 1996).

24. In one of her novels, *The Unpleasantness at the Bellona Club* (New York: Harper, 1928), the setting is an exclusive London club and the victim is an old ex-general who dies of an apparent heart attack.

25. Ian Patterson, "The Body in the Library Is Never Our Own," *London Review of Books* 42, no. 37 (November 5, 2020). Patterson's essay is chiefly about Ngaio Marsh, a famous mystery writer from New Zealand. Patterson argues that the "golden age" of the British mystery (the period between the two World Wars) reflected the

"unprecedented" social changes of the period; detective fiction "was a symptom of the need to reassert . . . conventional social order," nonetheless, the unmasking of the "murderer's identity may conceal a more troubling and less detectable subtext."

26. As Robert W. Gordon (private communication) has pointed out, one could even invoke the Freudian idea of the unconscious: the notion that strange and non-Victorian motives and tendencies lie deep inside people who otherwise seem, on the surface, to be the very personification of respectability.

27. See Edward J. Larson, *Summer for the Gods: The Scopes Trial and America's Continuing Debate over Science and Religion* (New York: Basic Books, 1997).

28. Drew Gilpin Faust, *This Republic of Suffering: Death and the American Civil War* (New York: Knopf Doubleday, 2008), 180–83.

29. On Mumler, see Peter Manseau, *The Apparitionists: A Tale of Phantoms, Fraud, Photography, and the Man who Captured Lincoln's Ghost* (Boston: Houghton Mifflin Harcourt, 2017).

30. See, for example, Sheridan Le Fanu, *In a Glass Darkly* (first published 1872; reprinted, 2008); M. R. James, *Collected Ghost Stories* (London: Longmans, Green, & Company, 1931).

31. Flanders, in *The Invention of Murder*, 295, sees a distinction between "sensation-fiction," and "crime fiction" (i.e., the mystery story): "Sensation-fiction implied a world in which every respectable person had a potentially unrespectable secret life, while crime fiction reassured the reader that only one person did" and that person would be revealed at the end. But in a great many mysteries, *many* characters are shown to have a secret life though only one of them turns out to be the culprit. And the idea that, even if only one person in some group had a secret life, it is hardly "reassuring" to realize that, without the skill of Miss Marple or Sherlock Holmes, it is impossible to know who that person really is.

32. There are elements of the locked door mystery in Poe's *Murders in the Rue Morgue* as well.

33. Quoted in Martin Edwards, *The Golden Age of Murder: The Mystery of the Writers Who Invented the Modern Detective Story* (New York: HarperCollins, 2015), 316–17. For a good example of a locked door mystery, with a clever solution (I find it unconvincing), see Rupert Penny, *Sealed Room Murder* (Shreveport, LA: 2007, originally published 1941). Gaston Leroux, the French author best known for *The Phantom of the Opera*, published a locked room mystery, *The Mystery of the Yellow Room* (Paris: Lafitte, 1907); an English version was published in 2021 (Berkeley, CA: West Margin Press); Leroux's solution to this kind of puzzle is one of the best.

34. In *Crime Fiction* (Milton, UK: Routledge, 2005), John Scaggs claims that in golden age fiction the "threat of social disruption comes from within," arguably, then, when Miss Marple unmasks the killer who has disturbed the peace of her village, she is in fact restoring a kind of order. But in a wider sense, order can never be restored because society has changed too much, personal identity will remain ambiguous and uncertain, and thousands of closets will contain their hidden skeletons.

35. James, *Talking About Detective Fiction*, 193–94.

36. See, for an example of a Japanese mystery which is quintessentially Japanese and yet deeply reflects the influence of Western mysteries, Seishi Yokomizo, *The*

Honjin Murders (London: Pushkin Press, 2019) (originally published in 1973), which is, in fact, a classic "locked room" mystery.

37. Wendy Lesser, *Scandinavian Noir: In Pursuit of a Mystery* (New York: Farrar, Strauss and Giroux, 2020).

38. "Ice-cold Cases," *The Economist,* May 23, 2020, 72.

39. See, for example, Patricia Cornwell, *Postmortem* (New York: Charles Scribner's Sons, 1990). Her protagonist is Dr. Kay Scarpetta, a medical examiner.

40. *Postmortem*, cited above, concerns the search for a serial killer in Virginia who has killed (at the beginning of the book) four women in a brutal and torturous way. Dr. Scarpetta (the narrator) says of the (unknown) killer: "He could be anybody. . . . He is ordinary by most standards. . . . He could be anybody and he was nobody. Mr. Nobody. The kind of guy you don't remember" (3).

41. Eric Brach, *Double Lives: True Tales of the Criminals Next Door* (Coral Gables: Mango, 2018), 11.

42. See, on his career, Erik Larson, *Devil in the White City* (New York: Crown Publishers, 2003). Roseanne Montillo, *The Wilderness of Ruin* (New York: William Morrow Paperbacks, 2015), recounts the career of Jesse Pomeroy, "America's youngest serial killer," in the middle of the nineteenth century.

43. See Dean Jobb, *The Case of the Murderous Dr. Cream: The Hunt for a Victorian Era Serial Killer* (Chapel Hill: Algonquin Books, 2021).

44. Thomas Fuller and Christine Hauser, "Ex-Cop Arrested in Golden State Killer Case: 'We Found the Needle in the Haystack,'" *New York Times,* April 25, 2018.

45. Scaggs, *Crime Fiction*, 91.

46. On the Korean War in general, see for example, Stanley Weintraub, *MacArthur's War: Korea and the Undoing of an American Hero* (New York: Free Press, 2000).

47. The three movies discussed were all adaptations of books.

CHAPTER 6

1. John Samuel Ezell, *Fortune's Merry Wheel: The Lottery in America* (Cambridge: Harvard University Press, 1960), 55–60, 78.

2. Nathaniel H. Carter and William L. Stone, reporters, *Proceedings and Debates of the Convention of 1821, assembled for the purpose of amending the Constitution of the State of New York* (1821), 569–70.

3. 81 How. 163, 99 U.S. 168 (1850).

4. "An Act for the Suppression of Lottery Traffic through National and Interstate Commerce and the Postal Service," 28 Stat. 963, Act of March 2, 1895, ch. 191.

5. Lottery Case (Champion v. Ames), 188 U.S. 321 (1903).

6. Lottery Case, at 357–58. This was a 5 to 4 decision. The dissent focused on whether forbidding lottery tickets across state lines was a valid exercise by Congress of its power to regulate interstate commerce.

7. Edward J. Balleisen, *Fraud: An American History from Barnum to Madoff* (Princeton, NJ: Princeton University Press, 2017), 18.

8. See Charles E. Rosenberg, *The Cholera Years: The United States in 1832, 1849, and 1866* (Chicago: Chicago University Press, 1962).

9. Stephen Mihm, *A Nation of Counterfeiters: Capitalists, Con Men, and the Making of the United States* (Cambridge, MA: Harvard University Press, 2007), 181. Mihm's book is the source of much of the material discussed on the currency problem.

10. On these, in general, see Michelle Landis Dauber, *The Sympathetic State: Disaster Relief and the Origins of the American Welfare State* (Chicago: Chicago University Press, 2013) and see the table on page 46 in Dauber, *Sympathetic State.*

CHAPTER 7

1. Ronald Pearsall, *The Worm in the Bud: The World of Victorian Sexuality* (London: Weidenfeld & Nicolson, 1969). For this chapter, I am particularly indebted to Joanna L. Grossman and our book, *The Walled Garden: Law and Privacy in Modern Society* (Lanham, MD: Rowman & Littlefield, 2022), dealing with some aspects of the history and social meaning of privacy.

2. R. L. Dugdale, *"The Jukes": A Study in Crime, Pauperism, Disease and Heredity*, 6th ed. (New York: G.P. Putnam's Sons, 2012), 8, originally published in 1877.

3. Oscar C. McCulloch, *The Tribe of Ishmael: A Study in Social Degradation*, 4th ed. (Indianapolis, IN: Charity Organization Society, 1891), 8.

4. McCulloch, *The Tribe of Ishmael*, 2, 3.

5. Henry H. Goddard, *The Kallikak Family: A Study in the Heredity of Feeble-Mindedness* (New York: Macmillan, 1912).

6. This study, along with others, can be found in Nicole Hahn Rafter, ed., *White Trash: The Eugenic Family Studies, 1877–1919* (Boston: Northeastern University Press, 1988). The quote about Sam Sixty's abilities is at page 187. The study of this family was published in 1916.

7. For a study of Goddard's work, the reaction to it, and its utterly unscientific nature, see J. David Smith and Michael L. Wehmeyer, *Good Blood, Bad Blood: Science, Nature, and the Myth of the Kallikaks* (Washington, DC: American Association on Intellectual and Developmental Disabilities, 2012).

8. Ettie A. Rout, *Safe Marriage: A Return to Sanity* (London: William Heinemann, 1922).

9. There was a movement, in the first part of the twentieth century, to improve childcare and child rearing, including (weirdly) the device of "better baby contests." This was a genuine public health movement, but it did have some kinship with eugenics. See Alexandra M. Stern, "Making Better Babies: Public Health and Race Betterment in Indiana, 1920–1935," *American Journal of Public Health* 92 (2002): 742.

10. Laws Indiana 1907, ch. 215; see Philip R. Reilly, *The Surgical Solution: A History of Involuntary Sterilization in the United States* (Baltimore, MD: The Johns Hopkins University Press, 1991).

11. Laws Cal. 1909, ch. 710, p 1093.

12. Ethan Blue, "The Strange Career of Leo Stanley: Remaking Manhood and Medicine at San Quentin State Penitentiary, 1913–1951," *Pacific Historical Review* 78 (2009): 210, 225, 228.

13. 274 U.S. 200 (1927). There is quite a literature on this case; see Paul A. Lombardo, *Three Generations, No Imbeciles: Eugenics, the Supreme Court, and* Buck v. Bell (Baltimore, MD: Paul A. Lombardo, 2010); Henry T. Greely, *The End of Sex and the Future of Human Reproduction* (Cambridge, MA: Harvard University Press, 2016), 254–58.

14. James Q. Whitman, *Hitler's American Model: The United States and the Making of Nazi Race Law* (Princeton: Princeton University Press, 2017).

15. Japanese eugenics laws were uncommonly persistent: they were abolished only in 1996. On some of the ideas lying behind the Japanese eugenics movement, see Jennifer Robertson, "Blood Talks: Eugenic Modernity and the Creation of New Japanese," *History and Anthropology* 13 (2002): 191.

16. Dan Balz, "Sweden Sterilized Thousands of 'Useless' Citizens for Decades," *Washington Post*, August 29, 1997.

17. 316 U.S. 535 (1942); the case is dealt with in detail in Victoria F. Nourse, *In Reckless Hands:* Skinner v. Oklahoma *and the Near Triumph of American Eugenics* (New York: W. W. Norton & Company, 2008).

18. Probably this was a crime in every state; see, for example, Texas Penal Code, Art. 524 (sodomy), 2 Vernon's Texas Stats. 1948; McKinney's Consolidated Laws of NY (1967), Penal Law, §§130.40, 130.45, 130.50.

19. Colin Simpson, Lewis Chester, and David Leitch, *The Cleveland Street Affair* (Boston: Little, Brown and Company, 1976) is a full account of the scandal; see also Jim Steinmeyer, *Who Was Dracula?: Bram Stoker's Trail of Blood* (New York: Jeremy P. Tarcher/Penguin, 2013), 217–18.

20. See Margot Canaday, *The Straight State: Sexuality and Citizenship in 20th Century America* (Princeton, NJ: Princeton University Press, 2009).

21. The crackdown on gay bars in its own way embodied the Victorian compromise, in a kind of mid-twentieth century version. Many members of vice squads insisted that "they cared little about private homosexual activity" but opposed "overt displays that might cause a public nuisance." Anna Lvovsky, *Vice Patrol: Cops, Courts, and the Struggle over Urban Gay Life before Stonewall* (Chicago: University of Chicago Press, 2021), 103.

22. Patricia J. Campbell, *Sex Education Books for Young Adults, 1892–1979* (Chatham: R. R. Bowker Company, 1979), 6.

23. Alfred C. Kinsey et al., *Sexual Behavior in the Human Male* (Bloomington: Indiana University Press, 1948), 513.

24. J. Richardson Parke, *Human Sexuality: A Medico-Literary Treatise*, 4th rev. ed. (Philadelphia: Professional Publishing Company, 1909), 379–80.

25. Parke, *Human Sexuality*, 100, 101. Sylvester Graham suggested solutions to the problem of self-abuse: the "patient" might go "to the gymnasium . . . let him swing upon and climb the poles, and ropes," he might also go in for some horseback riding (though this should be avoided if it "causes involuntary emissions"). Sleeping on a "hard bed" was also a help, followed by a "shower-bath of cold water" and a vigorous

scrubbing with "a good, stiff flesh-brush" (Sylvester Graham, *A Lecture to Young Men on Chastity* [Boston, Light & Stearns]).

26. Harry Hascall Moore, *Keeping in Condition: Handbook on Training for Older Boys* (New York: Macmillan, 1916), quoted in Patricia J. Campbell, *Sex Education Books for Young Adults, 1892–1979* (Chatham: R. R. Bowker Company, 1979), 38.

27. Quoted in Walter Kendrick, *The Secret Museum: Pornography in Modern Culture* (Berkeley: University of California Press, 1987), 140.

28. F. S. Brockman, "A Study of the Moral and Religious Life of 251 Preparatory School Students in the United States," *Pedagogical Seminary* 9 (1902): 266, 268.

29. Alfred C. Kinsey et al., *Sexual Behavior in the Human Female* (Bloomington: Indiana University Press, 1953), 142, 158.

30. See, for a general assessment, Julia A. Ericksen, "With Enough Cases, Why Do You Need Statistics? Revisiting Kinsey's Methodology," *Journal of Sex Research* 35 (1998): 132. Her conclusion: "His methodology has been superseded, but his influence appropriately continues" (139).

31. Sylvester Graham, *A Lecture to Young Men, on Chastity* (Boston: Light & Stearns, 1837), 42. The book was not just for young men. The cover page recommended it also "for the serious consideration of Parents and Guardians." Graham also warned about the dangers of "high-seasoned food, and richly prepared dishes" and such stimulants as tea, coffee, and wine, not to mention things like a "feather bed and enervating dress." A "stimulating and depraving diet," he felt, tended to increase "animal propensities" and a "preternatural excitability of the nerves or organic life" (51–52). On Graham's career and influence, see Stephen Nissenbaum, *Sex, Diet, and Debility in Jacksonian America: Sylvester Graham and Health Reform* (Westport: Praeger, 1980).

32. Graham, *Lecture to Young Men*, 73.

33. Graham, *Lecture to Young Men*, 74.

34. B. G. Jefferis and J. L. Nichols, *Searchlights on Health: Light on Dark Corners* (Naperville: J. L. Nichols, 1920), subtitled "A Complete Sexual Science and a Guide to Purity and Physical Manhood, Advice to Maiden, Wife, and Mother, Love, Courtship, and Marriage," 208.

35. Lydston, *Diseases of Society* (Philadelphia: J. B. Lippincott Company, 1904) 354; G. Frank Lydston, *Sex Hygiene for the Male* (Chicago: The Riverton Press, 1912), 133.

36. Graham, *Lecture to Young Men*, 64.

37. The advertisement for these books can be found in Helen Lefkowitz Horowitz, *Attitudes toward Sex in Antebellum America: A Brief History with Documents* (Boston: Bedford/St. Martin's, 2006), 104.

38. Dominic Shellard and Steve Nicholson, *The Lord Chamberlain Regrets: A History of British Theatre Censorship* (London: British Library, 2004), 9–10.

39. H. L. Mencken, *The American Language: Supplement I* (New York: Alfred A. Knopf, 1945), 646.

40. Donna Dennis, *Licentious Gotham: Erotic Publishing and its Prosecution in Nineteenth-Century New York* (Cambridge, MA: Harvard University Press, 2009); the quote is from p. 174.

41. Tariff Act of 1842, ch. 270, sec. 28, 5 Stat. 566. The law was repealed in 1846.

42. The Comstock Act, "An Act for the Suppression of Trade in, and Circulation of, Obscene Literature and Articles of Immoral Use," was 17 Stat. 598, ch. 261 (act of March 3, 1873).

43. Andrea Tone, *Devices and Desire: A History of Contraceptives in America* (New York: Hill and Wang, 2001), 38.

44. Tone, *Devices and Desire*, 30.

45. Similarly, the text (in English) of the *Satyricon of Petronius Arbiter*, a late Latin work, might suddenly lapse into Latin—here, too, sending the message that the original dealt with objectionable matters.

46. Whitney Strub, *Obscenity Rules: Roth v. United States and the Long Struggle over Sexual Expression* (Lawrence: University Press of Kansas, 2013), 40; see, in general, Jeremy Geltzer, *Dirty Words & Filthy Pictures: Film and the First Amendment* (Chicago: University of Chicago Press, 2015).

47. For the text of the Ohio law on the board of censors, see, for example, Gen'l Code of Ohio, 1926, §871.49.

48. *Mutual Film Corp. v. Industrial Commission of Ohio*, 236 U.S. 230 (1915).

49. *Matter of American Committee on Maternal Welfare, Inc.v. Mangan*, 257 App. Div. 570, 14 N. Y. Supp. 2d 39 (N. Y. App. Div. 1939).

50. H. L. Mencken, *The American Language: Supplement I* (New York: Alfred A. Knopf, 1945), 645.

51. See Laura Wittern-Keller, *Freedom of the Screen: Legal Challenges to State Film Censorship, 1915–1981* (Lexington: University Press of Kentucky, 2008).

52. *Damaged Goods* was reprinted in 2018; the text is also available online through Project Gutenberg. See also Alexandra M. Lord, *Condom Nation: The U.S. Government's Sex Education Campaign from World War I to the Internet* (Baltimore: Johns Hopkins University Press, 2010), 27.

53. *Report of the Hartford Vice Commission* (July 1913), 21.

54. Many US states also raised the "age of consent." Sex with a female below the age of consent was considered rape. Consent—or even eagerness—was irrelevant, nor did it matter if the male himself was underage. The law, in short, made teenage sex a crime—at least for him. The common law "age of consent" had been ten (absurdly low). Some states now opted for an age that was absurdly high: eighteen or even twenty-one. See Lawrence M. Friedman, *Crime and Punishment in American History* (New York: Basic Books, 1993), 332–34.

55. *Report of the Vice Commission of Minneapolis to His Honor, James C. Haynes, Mayor* (1911), 95.

56. See, in general, David J. Langum, *Crossing over the Line: Legislating Morality and the Mann Act* (Chicago: University of Chicago Press, 1994).

57. There is, of course, a huge literature on Prohibition and the Prohibition era. On the background, see Richard F. Hamm, *Shaping the 18th Amendment: Temperance Reform, Legal Culture, and the Polity, 1880–1920* (Chapel Hill: University of North Carolina Press, 1995).

58. *Vice Commission of Minneapolis*, 55.

CHAPTER 8

1. Oliver Strand, "Japanese Chefs Make their Mark in Paris," *New York Times*, March 29, 2016.

2. The Executive Summary begins with the following statement: "Americans change religious affiliation early and often. In total, about half of American adults have changed religious affiliation at least once during their lives." The actual figure (shown in a chart on the same page) is 44 percent (Pew Forum on Religion and Public Life, *Faith in Flux: Changes in Religious Affiliation in the U.S.* [April 2009], 1).

3. For an exhaustive survey of American religious practices, see Robert D. Putnam and David E. Campbell, *American Grace: How Religion Divides and Unites Us* (New York: Simon & Schuster, 2010).

4. John T. McQuiston, "Christine Jorgensen, 62, Is Dead; Was First to Have a Sex Change," *New York Times*, May 4, 1989.

5. David Riesman, with Nathan Glazer and Reuel Denny, *The Lonely Crowd: A Study of the Changing American Character* (New Haven, CT: Yale University Press, 1955), 37.

6. Riesman, *The Lonely Crowd*, 38, 41.

7. See Lawrence M. Friedman, *The Horizontal Society* (New Haven, CT: Yale University Press, 1999).

8. See, for the United States, Lizabeth Cohen, *A Consumer's Republic: The Politics of Mass Consumption in Postwar America* (New York: Vintage Books, 2003).

9. On the development of National Identity in France, see Eugen Weber, *Peasants into Frenchman: The Modernization of Rural France, 1870–1914* (Stanford, CA: Stanford University Press), 1976. On the United Kingdom, see Linda Colley, *Britons: Forging the Nation 1707–1837* (New Haven, CT: Yale University Press), 1992. She stresses, among other factors, a common religious heritage.

10. Lawrence M. Friedman, *The Human Rights Culture: A Study in History and Context* (New Orleans, LA: Quid Pro, LLC, 2011).

11. On this form of individualism, see Robert N. Bellah et al., *Habits of the Heart: Individualism and Commitment in American Life* (Berkeley: University of California Press, 1985).

12. Hazel Markus and Ann Ruvolo, "Possible Selves: Personalized Representations of Goals," in *Personality and Social Psychology*, Lawrence A. Pervin, ed. (Hillsdale, NJ: Lawrence Erlbaum Associates, 1989), 211.

13. On the movement, see Thomas R. Pegram, *One Hundred Percent American: The Rebirth and the Decline of the Ku Klux Klan in the 1920s* (Chicago: Ivan R. Dee, 2011).

14. See, for example, Elliott Robert Barkan, *And Still They Come: Immigrants and American Society, 1920 to the 1990s* (Wheeling: Wiley-Blackwell, 1996).

CHAPTER 9

1. "Don Juan Bigamist Duping Women Across the Country of Love and Finances," *Jacksonville Free Press*, March 9, 2009.

2. On bigamy prosecutions in modern England, which are few, and do not in general lead to severe punishment, see Keith Soothill et al., "The Place of Bigamy in the Pantheon of Crime," *Medical Science and Law* 38 (1999): 65.

3. See Elizabeth Kolbert, *The Sixth Extinction: An Unnatural History* (New York: Henry Holt and Co., 2014).

4. Paul Thomas Murphy, *Shooting Victoria: Madness, Mayhem, and the Rebirth of the British Monarchy* (New York: Pegasus Books, 2012).

5. Sally Engle Merry, *Urban Danger: Life in a Neighborhood of Strangers* (Philadelphia: Temple University Press, 1981), 160.

6. Jeremy Geltzer, *Dirty Words and Filthy Pictures* (Chicago: University of Chicago Press, 2016), 249–50.

7. Health Line, https://www.healthline.com/health/healthy-sex-health-benefits, visited September 15, 2018.

8. *Bostock v. Clayton County*, 140 S. Ct. 1731 (2020). This was a 6 to 3 decision.

9. *Obergefell v. Hodges*, 576 U.S. 644, 135 S. Ct. 2071 (2015).

10. See Richard Ford, *Dress Codes: How the Laws of Fashion Made History* (New York: Simon & Schuster, 2021).

11. Nudism "strove to make Germans into a healthy, beautiful people"; a "central tenet of the ideology" was the "promise of good health and a life free of both disease and doctors," Chad Ross, *Naked Germany: Health, Race and the Nation* (Oxford: Berg Publishers, 2005), 83. See also Maren Möhring, *Marmorleiber: Kõrperbildung in der deutschen Nacktkultur (1890–1930)* (Cologne: Böhlau Verlag, 2004).

12. Thomas Rogers, "Exposed to Art, From Head To . . . Ankles," *New York Times*, May 8, 2018.

13. Mariana Valverde, "The Harms of Sex and the Risks of Breasts: Obscenity and Indecency in Canadian Law," *Social and Legal Studies* 8 (1999): 181–91.

14. Federal Law: 18 U.S. C. A. sections 2251 and 2252; see also Cal. Penal Code section 311.

15. There is a large literature: see, for example, Cassia C. Spohn, "The Rape Reform Movement: The Traditional Common Law and Rape Law Reform," *Jurimetrics* 39 (1999): 119.

16. Aurelien Breeden, "Report Describes Abuse of Minors Permeating Catholic Church in France," *New York Times*, October 6, 2021.

17. N. J. Stat. Ann. Sec. 2C:34–5 (2016); 720 Ill. Comp. Stat. sec. 5/12.5.01 (a) (3) (2016); Fla. Stat. Ann, sec. 381.004 (11) (b) (2016).

18. Quoted in Beaumont Newhall, *The History of Photography*, revised ed. (New York: Museum of Modern Art, 2006), 19.

19. In re Baby M, 537 A. 2d 1227 (N. J., 1988); see Elizabeth S. Scott, "Surrogacy and the Politics of Commodification," *Law & Contemporary Problems* 72 (2009): 109.

20. In the famous case of *Roe v. Wade*, 410 U.S. 112 (1973), the United States Supreme Court declared that early-pregnancy abortion was constitutionally protected, but millions never came to terms with this decision, and the case has been overturned (see n. 28).

21. More than two-thirds of prospective parents choose to abort such fetuses in the United Sates, and even higher percentages elsewhere. In Denmark, for example, this occurs for 98 percent of all Down syndrome babies. But eliminating these babies remains controversial. See, for example, Brittany Raymer, "A World with No Down Syndrome Babies," https://www.focusonthefamily.com/socialissues/down-syndrom /a-world-with-no-down-syndrome-babies, Focus on the Family, visited January 21, 2019.

22. Joanna L. Grossman and Lawrence M. Friedman, *Inside the Castle* (Princeton: Princeton University Press, 2014), 305.

23. Grossman and Friedman, *Inside the Castle*, 315.

24. Rev. Stats. Neb. 1943, section 43–109 (2), 43–113.

25. These statements are from the Mission Statement of Bastard Nation (1996), found at https://pages.uoregon.edu/adoption/archive/BNMS.htm, visited August 24, 2018.

26. Lawrence M. Friedman, "No Name," *SMU Law Review.* 74 (2021): 235.

27. A recent treatment is Sarah E. Igo, *The Known Citizen: A History of Privacy in America* (Cambridge, MA: Harvard University Press, 2018). Many aspects of the law of privacy and norms of privacy are also dealt with in Lawrence M. Friedman and Joanna L. Grossman, *The Walled Garden: Privacy in Modern Society* (Lanham, MD: Rowman & Littlefield, 2022); and much of the material in this chapter is indebted to that work.

28. 410 U.S. 113 (1973); see David J. Garrow, *Liberty and Sexuality: The Right to Privacy and the Making of* Roe v. Wade (Berkeley: University of California Press, 1994). Roe was overruled in Dobbs v. Jackson Women's Health Organization, 597 U.S._(2022).

29. Samuel D. Warren and Louis D. Brandeis, "The Right to Privacy," *Harvard Law Review* 4 (1890): 193.

30. BverfG, 1BvR 209/83.

31. N.a., "Identification in India: Court Gestures," *Economist*, September 29, 2018, 43.

32. On this see Lawrence M. Friedman and Nina-Louisa Arold, "Cannibal Rights: A Note on the Modern Law of Privacy," *Northwestern Interdisciplinary Law Review* 4 (2011): 235.

33. The cartoon appeared in the magazine on July 5, 1993; the cartoonist was Peter Steiner.

CONCLUSION

1. Lawrence M. Friedman, *The Republic of Choice: Law, Authority, and Culture* (Cambridge, MA: Harvard University Press 1990).

Bibliography

Adams, Bluford. *E Pluribus Barnum: The Great Showman and the Making of U.S. Popular Culture*. Minneapolis: University of Minnesota Press, 1997.

Asbury, Herbert. *The Gangs of New York: An Informal History of the Underworld*. New York: Vintage Books, 2008.

Balleisen, Edward J. *Fraud: An American History from Barnum to Madoff*. Princeton, NJ: Princeton University Press, 2017.

Barkan, Elliott Robert. *And Still They Come: Immigrants and American Society 1920 to the 1990s*, first ed. Wheeling, IL: Wiley-Blackwell, 1996.

Beam, Alex. *American Crucifixion: The Murder of Joseph Smith and the Fate of the Mormon Church*. New York: Public Affairs, 2014.

Bellah, Robert Neelly, Richard Madsen, William M. Sullivan, Ann Swidler, and Steven M. Tipton. *Habits of the Heart: Individualism and Commitment in American Life*. Berkeley: University of California Press, 1985.

Bennett, John. *Mob Town: A History of Crime and Disorder in the East End*. New Haven and London: Yale University Press, 2017.

Binyon, Timothy J. *Murder Will Out: The Detective in Fiction*. New York: Oxford University Press, 1989.

Block, Walter. "Trading Money for Silence." *University of Hawaii Law Review* 8 (1986): 57.

Blue, Ethan. "The Strange Career of Leo Stanley: Remaking Manhood and Medicine at San Quentin State Penitentiary, 1913—1951." *Pacific Historical Review* 78, no. 2 (2009): 210–41.

Brach, Eric. *Double Lives: True Tales of the Criminals Next Door*. Coral Gables, FL: Mango Media Inc., 2018.

Brauner, Sigrid. *Fearless Wives and Frightened Shrews: The Construction of the Witch in Early Modern Germany*. Amherst: University of Massachusetts Press, 1995.

Brockman, F. S. "A Study of the Moral and Religious Life of 251 Preparatory School Students in the United States." *The Pedagogical Seminary* 9, no. 3 (September 1, 1902): 255–73.

Byrnes, Thomas. *Professional Criminals of America*. New York: Cassell, 1886.

Cahalan, Susannah. *The Great Pretender: The Undercover Mission That Changed Our Understanding of Madness*. New York: Grand Central Publishing, 2019.

Campbell, Helen. *Darkness and Daylight; Or, Lights and Shadows of New York Life.* Hartford, CT: A. D. Worthington & Company, 1892.

Campbell, Patricia J. *Sex Education Books for Young Adults, 1892–1979*. New Providence, NJ: Rr Bowker Llc, 1979.

Canaday, Margot. *The Straight State*. Princeton, NJ: Princeton University Press, 2009.

Carlson, A. Cheree. *The Crimes of Womanhood: Defining Femininity in a Court of Law*. Champaign: University of Illinois Press, 2010.

Cohen, Lizabeth. *A Consumer's Republic: The Politics of Mass Consumption in Postwar America*. New York: Knopf, 2003.

Cole, Simon A. *Suspect Identities: A History of Fingerprinting and Criminal Identification*. Cambridge, MA: Harvard University Press, 2009.

Colley, Linda. *Britons: Forging the Nation, 1707–1837*. New Haven, CT: Yale University Press, 1992.

Collins, Paul. *Blood & Ivy: The 1849 Murder That Scandalized Harvard*. New York: WW Norton & Company, 2018.

Conforti, Joseph. *Lizzie Borden on Trial: Murder, Ethnicity, and Gender*. Lawrence: University Press of Kansas, 2015.

Cook, James W. *The Arts of Deception: Playing with Fraud in the Age of Barnum*. Cambridge, MA: Harvard University Press, 2001.

Cooper, Cynthia L., and Sam Reese Sheppard. *Mockery of Justice: The True Story of the Sheppard Murder Case*. Boston, MA: Northeastern University Press, 1995.

Cornwell, Patricia Daniels. *Postmortem*. New York: Charles Scribner's Sons, 1990.

Cox, David. "Trying To Get A Good One' Bigamy Offences in England and Wales, 1850–1950." *The Plymouth Law & Criminal Justice Review* 4 (2012): 1–32.

Cullen, Tom A. *The Mild Murderer: The True Story of the Dr. Crippen Case*. New York: Houghton Mifflin, 1977.

Curtis Jr., L. Perry. *Jack the Ripper and the London Press*. New Haven & London: Yale University Press, 2001.

Dauber, Michele Landis. *The Sympathetic State: Disaster Relief and the Origins of the American Welfare State*. Chicago: University of Chicago Press, 2013.

Davies, Owen. *America Bewitched: The Story of Witchcraft After Salem*. Oxford: Oxford University Press, 2013.

Davis, William C. *Inventing Loreta Velasquez: Confederate Soldier Impersonator, Media Celebrity, and Con Artist*. Carbondale: Southern Illinois University Press, 2016.

De Grave, Kathleen R. *Swindler, Spy, Rebel: The Confidence Woman in Nineteenth Century America*. Columbia: University of Missouri Press, 1995.

Dugdale, R. L. *"The Jukes": A Study in Crime, Pauperism, Disease and Heredity*. New York: G.P. Putnam's Sons, 1877.

Eberle, Paul. *The Abuse of Innocence: The McMartin Preschool Trial*. Buffalo, NY: Prometheus Books, 2010.

Edwards, Martin. *The Golden Age of Murder*. New York: HarperCollins, 2016.

Edwards, P. D. *The Maniac in the Cellar: Sensation Novels of the 1860s*. Princeton, NJ: Princeton University Press, 1981.

Ericksen, Julia A. "With Enough Cases, Why Do You Need Statistics? Revisiting Kinsey's Methodology." *Journal of Sex Research* 35, no. 2 (1998): 132–40.

Ezell, John Samuel. *Fortune's Merry Wheel: The Lottery in America*. Cambridge, MA: Harvard University Press, 1960.

Fahnestock, Jeanne. "Bigamy: The Rise and Fall of a Convention." *Nineteenth-Century Fiction* 36, no. 1 (1981): 47–71.

Faust, Drew Gilpin. *This Republic of Suffering*. New York: Knopf Doubleday Publishing Group, 2008.

Firmage, Edwin Brown, and Richard Collin Mangrum. *Zion in the Courts: A Legal History of the Church of Jesus Christ of Latter-Day Saints, 1830–1900*. Champaign: University of Illinois Press, 2001.

Fisher, George. *Plea Bargaining's Triumph: A History of Plea Bargaining in America*. Stanford, CA: Stanford University Press, 2003.

Flanders, Judith. *The Invention of Murder: How the Victorians Revelled in Death and Detection and Created Modern Crime*. New York: St. Martin's, 2013.

Ford, Richard Thompson. *Dress Codes: How the Laws of Fashion Made History*. New York: Simon & Schuster, 2021.

Fox, Richard Wightman. *Trials of Intimacy: Love and Loss in the Beecher-Tilton Scandal*. Chicago: University of Chicago Press, 1999.

Friedman, Lawrence M. *Crime and Punishment In American History*. New York: Basic Books, 1994.

———. *Guarding Life's Dark Secrets: Legal and Social Controls over Reputation, Propriety, and Privacy*. Stanford, CA: Stanford University Press, 2007.

———. "No Name." *SMU Law Review* 74 (2021): 235.

———. *Río Torrentoso: La Identidad Personal En Tiempos Modernos*. Vol. 18. Lima: Palestra Editores, 2020.

———. *The Big Trial: Law as Public Spectacle*. Lawrence: University Press of Kansas, 2015.

———. *The Horizontal Society*. New Haven, CT: Yale University Press, 2008.

———. *The Human Rights Culture: A Study in History and Context*. New Orleans, LA: Quid Pro Books, 2011.

———. *The Republic of Choice: Law, Authority, and Culture*. Cambridge, MA: Harvard University Press, 1990.

Friedman, Lawrence M., and Paul W. Davies. "California Death Trip." *Indiana Law Review* 36 (2003): 17.

Friedman, Lawrence M., and Joanna L. Grossman. "Double Take: The Law of Embezzled Lives." *University of Cincinnati Law Review* 83 (2014): 117.

Friedman, Lawrence M., and Joanna L. Grossman. *The Walled Garden: Law and Privacy in Modern Society*. Lanham, MD: Rowman & Littlefield, 2022.

Frost, Ginger S. *Living in Sin: Cohabiting as Husband and Wife in Nineteenth-Century England*. Manchester, UK: Manchester University Press, 2008.

Garrow, David J. *Liberty and Sexuality: The Right to Privacy and the Making of* Roe v. Wade. New York: Macmillan Publishing Company, 1994.

Geltzer, Jeremy. *Dirty Words and Filthy Pictures: Film and the First Amendment*. Austin: University of Texas Press, 2016.

Gitlitz, David Martin. *Secrecy and Deceit: The Religion of the Crypto-Jews*. Philadelphia: Jewish Publication Society, 1996.

Goddard, Henry Herbert. *The Kallikak Family: A Study in the Heredity of Feeble-Mindedness*. New York: Macmillan, 1912.

Goffman, Erving. *The Presentation of Self in Everyday Life*. New York: Doubleday, 1959.

Gordon, Sarah Barringer. *The Mormon Question: Polygamy and Constitutional Crisis in Nineteenth Century America*. Chapel Hill: The University of North Carolina Press, 2002.

Gordon-Reed, Annette. *The Hemingses of Monticello: An American Family*. New York: WW Norton & Company, 2009.

Graham, Peter. *So Brilliantly Clever*. Wellington, NZ: Awa Press, 2011.

Graham, Sylvester. *A Lecture to Young Men, on Chastity*. Boston, MA: Light & Stearns, 1837.

Greely, Henry T. *The End of Sex and the Future of Human Reproduction*. Cambridge, MA: Harvard University Press, 2016.

Groebner, Valentin. *Who Are You?: Identification, Deception, and Surveillance in Early Modern Europe*. Translated by Mark Kyburz and John Peck. New York: Zone Books, 2007.

Gross, Ariela J. *What Blood Won't Tell: A History of Race on Trial in America*. Cambridge, MA: Harvard University Press, 2010.

Grossman, Joanna L., and Lawrence M. Friedman. *Inside the Castle*. Princeton, NJ: Princeton University Press, 2011.

Hall, Patricia Kelly, and Steven Ruggles. "'Restless in the Midst of Their Prosperity': New Evidence on the Internal Migration of Americans, 1850–2000." *The Journal of American History* 91, no. 3 (2004): 829–46.

Hamm, Richard F. *Shaping the Eighteenth Amendment: Temperance Reform, Legal Culture, and the Polity, 1880–1920*. Chapel Hill: University of North Carolina Press, 1995.

Higdon, Hal. *Leopold and Loeb: The Crime of the Century*. Champaign, IL: University of Illinois Press, 1975.

Hobbs, Allyson. *A Chosen Exile: A History of Racial Passing in American Life*. Cambridge, MA: Harvard University Press, 2014.

Horowitz, Helen Lefkowitz. *Attitudes toward Sex in Antebellum America: A Brief History with Documents*. New York: Macmillan Higher Education, 2006.

Hudson, Angela Pulley. *Real Native Genius: How an Ex-Slave and a White Mormon Became Famous Indians*. Chapel Hill: University of North Carolina Press, 2015.

Igo, Sarah E. *The Known Citizen: A History of Privacy in Modern America*. Cambridge, MA: Harvard University Press, 2018.

Jacobs, Janet Liebman. *Hidden Heritage: The Legacy of the Crypto-Jews*. Berkeley: University of California Press, 2002.

James, M. R. *Collected Ghost Stories—A Collection of 22 M. R. James Stories*. Oxford: Benediction Classics, 2011.

James, P. D. *Talking About Detective Fiction*. New York: Knopf Doubleday, 2009.

Jefferis, B. G., and J. L. (James Lawrence) Nichols. *Searchlights on Health: Light on Dark Corners. A Complete Sexual Science and a Guide to Purity and Physical Manhood, Advice to Maiden, Wife, and Mother, Love, Courtship, and Marriage.* Naperville: J. L. Nichols, 1920.

Jobb, Dean. *The Case of the Murderous Dr. Cream: The Hunt for a Victorian Era Serial Killer*. New York: Algonquin Books, 2021.

Kabatchnik, Amnon. *Blood on the Stage, 1600 to 1800: Milestone Plays of Murder, Mystery, and Mayhem*. Lanham, MD: Rowman & Littlefield, 2017.

Kendrick, Walter. *The Secret Museum: Pornography in Modern Culture*. Berkeley: University of California Press, 1996.

Keyssar, Alexander. *The Right to Vote: The Contested History of Democracy in the United States*. New York: Basic Books, 2009.

Kinsey, Alfred C., Wardell Baxter Pomeroy, and Clyde Eugene Martin. *Sexual Behavior in the Human Male*. Bloomington: Indiana University Press, 1948.

Kinsey, Alfred C., Wardell B. Pomeroy, Clyde E. Martin, and Paul H. Gebhard. *Sexual Behavior in the Human Female*. Bloomington: Indiana University Press, 1998.

Kolbert, Elizabeth. *The Sixth Extinction: An Unnatural History*. London: A&C Black, 2014.

Kurth, Peter. *Anastasia: The Riddle of Anna Anderson*. New York: Little, Brown, 1983.

Langum, David J. *Crossing Over the Line: Legislating Morality and the Mann Act*. Chicago: University of Chicago Press, 2006.

Larson, Edward J. *Summer for The Gods: The Scopes Trial and America's Continuing Debate Over Science And Religion*. New York: Basic Books, 1997.

Larson, Erik. *The Devil in the White City: Murder, Magic, and Madness at the Fair That Changed America.* New York: Vintage Books, 2003.

Lau, Estelle T. *Paper Families: Identity, Immigration Administration, and Chinese Exclusion*. Durham, NC: Duke University Press, 2007.

Le Fanu, J. Sheridan. *In a Glass Darkly*. Peterborough, Canada: Broadview Press, 2018.

Lenhardt, Robin A. "Beyond Analogy: Perez v. Sharp, Antimiscegenation Law, and the Fight for Same-Sex Marriage." *California Law Review* 96 (2008): 839.

Lesser, Wendy. *Scandinavian Noir: In Pursuit of a Mystery*. New York: Farrar, Straus and Giroux, 2020.

Lewis, Earl, and Heidi Ardizzone. *Love on Trial: An American Scandal in Black and White*. New York: W.W. Norton & Company, 2002.

Lombardo, Paul A. *Three Generations, No Imbeciles: Eugenics, the Supreme Court, and Buck v. Bell*. Baltimore, MD: Johns Hopkins University Press, 2010.

Long, Larry. *Migration and Residential Mobility in the United States*. New York: Russell Sage Foundation, 1988.

Lord, Alexandra M. *Condom Nation: The U.S. Government's Sex Education Campaign from World War I to the Internet*. Baltimore, MD: Johns Hopkins University Press, 2010.

Lvovsky, Anna. *Vice Patrol: Cops, Courts, and the Struggle over Urban Gay Life before Stonewall*. Chicago: University of Chicago Press, 2021.

Lydston, George Frank. *Sex Hygiene for the Male and What to Say to the Boy*. Chicago: Riverton Press, 1912.

———. *The Diseases of Society*. Philadelphia, PA: J.B. Lippincott, 1906.

Macintyre, Ben. *The Spy and the Traitor: The Greatest Espionage Story of the Cold War*. New York: Crown, 2018.

Mackay, James. *Allan Pinkerton: The First Private Eye*. New York: Wiley, 1997.

Maida, Patricia D. *Mother of Detective Fiction: The Life and Works of Anna Katharine Green*. Madison: Popular Press, 1989.

Manseau, Peter. *The Apparitionists: A Tale of Phantoms, Fraud, Photography, and the Man Who Captured Lincoln's Ghost*. New York: Houghton Mifflin Harcourt, 2017.

Markus, Hazel, and Ann Ruvolo. "Possible Selves: Personalized Representations of Goals." In *Goal Concepts in Personality and Social Psychology*, 211–41. Hillsdale, NJ: Lawrence Erlbaum Associates, Inc., 1989.

Mather, Cotton. *The Wonders of the Invisible World: Being an Account of the Tryals of Several Witches Lately Executed in New England*. Boston, MA: John Russell Smith, 1862 (originally published 1693).

Maurer, David. *The Big Con: The Story of the Confidence Man*. New York: Knopf Doubleday Publishing Group, 2010.

Mayhew, Henry. *London Labour and the London Poor*. Oxford, UK: Oxford University Press, 2010 (originally published in 1850s and 1860s).

McAleavey, Maia. *The Bigamy Plot: Sensation and Convention in the Victorian Novel*. New York: Cambridge University Press, 2015.

McCabe, James D. *New York by Sunlight and Gaslight: A Work Descriptive of the Great American Metropolis.* Philadelphia: Douglass Brothers, 1882.

McCulloch, Oscar Carleton. *The Tribe of Ishmael: A Study in Social Degradation*. Indianapolis: Charity Organization Society, 1891.

McLaren, Angus. *Sexual Blackmail: A Modern History*. Cambridge, MA: Harvard University Press, 2002.

McWatters, George S. *Knots Untied: Or, Ways and By-Ways in the Hidden Life of American Detectives*. Hartford: JB Burr and Hyde, 1871.

McWilliam, Rohan. *The Tichborne Claimant*. New York: Bloomsbury Academic, 2007.

Mencken, Henry Louis. *The American Language: Supplement 1*. New York: Alfred A. Knopf, 1945.

Mensel, Robert E. "A Diddle at Brobdingnag: Confidence and Caveat Emptor during the Market Revolution." *University of Memphis Law Review* 38 (2007): 97.

Merry, Sally Engle. *Urban Danger: Life in a Neighborhood of Strangers*. Philadelphia, PA: Temple University Press, 1981.

Metzker, Isaac. *A Bintel Brief: Sixty Years of Letters from the Lower East Side to the Jewish Daily Forward*. New York: Knopf Doubleday, 2011.

Mihm, Stephen. *A Nation of Counterfeiters: Capitalists, Con Men, and the Making of the United States*. Cambridge, MA: Harvard University Press, 2009.

Miles, Andrew. *Social Mobility in Nineteenth- and Early Twentieth-Century England.* London: Springer, 1999.

Miller, Sarah. *The Borden Murders: Lizzie Borden and the Trial of the Century*. New York: Schwartz & Wade, 2016.

Miller, Wilbur R. *Cops and Bobbies: Police Authority in New York and London, 1830–1870*. Chicago: University of Chicago Press, 1977.

Möhring, Maren. *Marmorleiber: Körperbildung in Der Deutschen Nacktkultur (1890–1930)*. Cologne: Böhlau Verlag, 2004.

Montillo, Roseanne. *The Wilderness of Ruin: A Tale of Madness, Fire, and the Hunt for America's Youngest Serial Killer*. New York: HarperCollins, 2015.

Moore, Harry Hascall. *Keeping in Condition: A Handbook on Training for Older Boys*. New York: Macmillan, 1915.

Morn, Frank. *"The Eye That Never Sleeps": A History of the Pinkerton National Detective Agency*. Bloomington: Indiana University Press, 1982.

Murch, Alma Elizabeth. *The Development of the Detective Novel*. London: Peter Owen Limited, 1968.

Murphy, Paul Thomas. *Shooting Victoria: Madness, Mayhem, and the Rebirth of the British Monarchy*. Berkeley: Pegasus Books, 2012.

Nathan, Debbie, and Michael R. Snedeker. *Satan's Silence: Ritual Abuse and the Making of a Modern American Witch Hunt*. New York: Basic Books, 1995.

Newhall, Beaumont. *The History of Photography*. New York: Museum of Modern Art, 1982.

Nissenbaum, Stephen. *Sex, Diet, and Debility in Jacksonian America: Sylvester Graham and Health Reform*. Westport, CT: Greenwood Press, 1980.

O'Toole, James M. *Passing for White: Race, Religion, and the Healy Family, 1820–1920*. Amherst: University of Massachusetts Press, 2002.

Ousby, Ian. *Bloodhounds of Heaven: The Detective in English Fiction from Godwin to Doyle*. Cambridge, MA: Harvard University Press, 2013.

Parke, Joseph Richardson. *Human Sexuality: A Medico-Literary Treatise on the History and Pathology of the Sex Instinct.* Philadelphia: Professional Publishing Company, 1906.

Pascoe, Peggy. *What Comes Naturally: Miscegenation Law and the Making of Race in America*. Oxford, UK: Oxford University Press, 2009.

Patterson, Ian. "The Body in the Library Is Never Our Own." *London Review of Books* 42, no. 21 (2020): 37–40.

Pegram, Thomas R. *One Hundred Percent American: The Rebirth and Decline of the Ku Klux Klan in the 1920s*. Chicago, IL: Ivan R. Dee, 2011.

Penny, Rupert. *Sealed Room Murder*, Denver: Ramble House, 2007.

Pettit, Michael. *The Science of Deception: Psychology and Commerce in America*. Chicago: University of Chicago Press, 2013.

Pole, J. R. *The Pursuit of Equality in American History*, second ed. Berkeley: University of California Press, 1993.

Porter, Edwin H. *The Fall River Tragedy: A History of the Borden Murders*. Fall River: Geo. R.H. Buffinton, 1893.

Putnam, Robert D., and David E. Campbell. *American Grace: How Religion Divides and Unites Us*. New York: Simon and Schuster, 2010.

Rafter, Nicole Hahn. *White Trash: The Eugenic Family Studies, 1877–1919*. Boston, MA: Northeastern University Press, 1988.

Reilly, Philip R. "Involuntary Sterilization in the United States: A Surgical Solution." *The Quarterly Review of Biology* 62, no. 2 (1987): 153–70.

Riesman, David, Nathan Glazer, and Reuel Denney. *The Lonely Crowd: A Study of the Changing American Character*. New Haven, CT: Yale University Press, 1961.

Robertson, Cara. *The Trial of Lizzie Borden*. New York: Simon and Schuster, 2020.

Robertson, Cara W. "Representing Miss Lizzie: Cultural Convictions in the Trial of Lizzie Borden." *Yale Journal of Law & Humanities* 8 (1996): 351.

Robertson, Jennifer. "Blood Talks: Eugenic Modernity and the Creation of New Japanese." *History and Anthropology* 13, no. 3 (2002): 191–216.

Rosenberg, Charles E. *The Cholera Years: The United States in 1832, 1849, and 1866*. Chicago: University of Chicago Press, 1962.

Rosenhan, David L. "On Being Sane in Insane Places." *Science* 179, no. 4070 (1973): 250–58.

Ross, Chad. *Naked Germany: Health, Race and the Nation*. Oxford: Berg, 2005.

Rout, Ettie Annie. *Safe Marriage: A Return to Sanity*. London: William Heinemann, 1922.

Rzepka, Charles J. *Detective Fiction*. Cambridge, UK: Polity, 2005.

Sandweiss, Martha A. *Passing Strange: A Gilded Age Tale of Love and Deception Across the Color Line*. New York: Penguin, 2009.

Scaggs, John. *Crime Fiction*. Milton Park, U.K.: Routledge, 2005.

Schwartzberg, Beverly. "'Lots of Them Did That': Desertion, Bigamy, and Marital Fluidity in Late-Nineteenth-Century America." *Journal of Social History* 37, no. 3 (2004): 573–600.

Scott, Elizabeth S. "Surrogacy and the Politics of Commodification." *Law & Contemporary Problems* 72 (2009): 109.

Sharfstein, Daniel J. *The Invisible Line: A Secret History of Race in America*. New York: Penguin Books, 2012.

Shellard, Dominic, Steve Nicholson, and Miriam Handley. *The Lord Chamberlain Regrets . . . : A History of British Theatre Censorship*. London: British Library, 2004.

Shpayer-Makov, Haia. "Explaining the Rise and Success of Detective Memoirs in Britain 1." In Clive Emsley and Haia Shpayer-Makov (eds)., *Police Detectives in History, 1750–1950*, 103–33. New York: Routledge, 2017.

Simpson, Colin, Lewis Chester, and David Leitch. *The Cleveland Street Affair*. London: George Weidenfeld & Nicholson, 1977.

Smith, Edward Henry. *Confessions of a Confidence Man: A Handbook for Suckers*. New York: Scientific American Publishing Company, 1922.

Smith, J. David, and Michael L. Wehmeyer. *Good Blood, Bad Blood: Science, Nature, and the Myth of the Kallikaks*. Silver Springs, MD: American Association on Intellectual and Developmental Disabilities, 2012.

Smith, Matthew Hale. *Sunshine and Shadow in New York*. New York: J.B. Burr Publishing Company, 1879.

Soothill, Keith, Elizabeth Ackerley, Barry Sanderson, and Moira Peelo. "The Place of Bigamy in the Pantheon of Crime?" *Medicine, Science and the Law* 39, no. 1 (1999): 65–71.

Stashower, Daniel. *The Beautiful Cigar Girl: Mary Rogers, Edgar Allan Poe, and the Invention of Murder*. New York: Penguin, 2007.

Steinmeyer, Jim. *Who Was Dracula?: Bram Stoker's Trail of Blood*. New York: Jeremy P. Tarcher/Penguin, 2013.

Stern, Alexandra Minna. "Making Better Babies: Public Health and Race Betterment in Indiana, 1920–1935." *American Journal of Public Health* 92, no. 5 (2002): 742–52.

Strub, Whitney. *Obscenity Rules: Roth v. United States and the Long Struggle Over Sexual Expression*. Lawrence: University Press of Kansas, 2013.

Summerscale, Kate. *The Suspicions of Mr. Whicher: A Shocking Murder and the Undoing of a Great Victorian Detective*. New York: Bloomsbury, 2009.

Symons, Julian. *Bloody Murder—From the Detective Story to the Crime Novel: A History*. London: Faber and Faber, 1972.

Thomas, Ronald R. *Detective Fiction and the Rise of Forensic Science*. Vol. 26. Cambridge, UK: Cambridge University Press, 2003.

Tone, Andrea. *Devices and Desires: A History of Contraceptives in America*. New York: Macmillan, 2002.

Trollope, Anthony, and Donald Smalley. *North America: With an Introduction, Notes and New Materials*. New York: Knopf, 1951.

Trollope, Frances. *Domestic Manners of the Americans, 1800–1830*. New Hork: Penguin, 1997.

Tucher, Andie. *Froth & Scum: Truth, Beauty, Goodness, and the Ax Murder in America's First Mass Medium*. Chapel Hill: University of North Carolina Press, 1994.

Twigge, Stephen, Edward Hampshire, and Graham Macklin. *British Intelligence: Secrets, Spies and Sources*. Bloomsbury, UK: Bloomsbury, 2008.

Valverde, Mariana. "The Harms of Sex and the Risks of Breasts: Obscenity and Indecency in Canadian Law." *Social & Legal Studies* 8, no. 2 (1999): 181–97.

Veeder, William. "Carmilla: The Arts of Repression." *Texas Studies in Literature and Language* 22, no. 2 (1980): 197–223.

Wahrman, Dror. *The Making of The Modern Self: Identity and Culture in Eighteenth-Century England*. New Haven, CT: Yale University Press, 2008.

Walton, John. *The Legendary Detective: The Private Eye in Fact and Fiction*. Chicago: University of Chicago Press, 2015.

Warren, Samuel D., and Louis D. Brandeis. "The Right to Privacy." *Harvard Law Review* 4 (1890): 153.

Watt, George. *The Fallen Woman in the Nineteenth-Century English Novel*. Kent, UK: Croom Helm, 1984.

Weber, Eugen. *Peasants into Frenchmen: The Modernization of Rural France, 1870–1914*. Stanford, CA: Stanford University Press, 1976.

Weintraub, Stanley. *MacArthur's War: Korea and the Undoing of an American Hero*. New York: Free Press, 2000.

White, Richard. *The Republic for Which It Stands: The United States during Reconstruction and the Gilded Age, 1865–1896*. New York: Oxford University Press, 2017.

Whitman, James Q. *Hitler's American Model: The United States and the Making of Nazi Race Law*. Princeton, NJ: Princeton University Press, 2017.

Wiencek, Henry. *Master of the Mountain: Thomas Jefferson and His Slaves*. New York: Macmillan, 2012.

Winks, Robin W., ed. *Detective Fiction: A Collection of Critical Essays*. Woodstock, VT: Foul Play Press, 1980.

Wittern-Keller, Laura. *Freedom of the Screen: Legal Challenges to State Film Censorship, 1915–1981*. Lawrence: University Press of Kansas, 2008.

Worsley, Lucy. *The Art of the English Murder*. New York: Simon and Schuster, 2014.

Wright, Willard Huntington. "The Detective Novel." *Scribners Magazine* (1926): 532–38.

Yokomizo, Seishi. *The Honjin Murders*. Hanover, NH: Steerforth Press, 2020.

Zemon Davis, Natalie. *The Return of Martin Guerre*. Cambdrige, MA: Harvard University Press, 1983.

Index

About the Author

Lawrence M. Friedman is the Marion Rice Kirkwood Professor of Law at Stanford University. He is a leading historian of American law and a leading scholar associated with the law and society movement. He is the author or editor of more than thirty books on these subjects.

www.ingramcontent.com/pod-product-compliance
Lightning Source LLC
Chambersburg PA
CBHW022315280326
41932CB00010B/1115
9781538166864